Sporting News BOOKS PRESENTS

The Ballpark Book

REVISED EDITION   By Ron Smith ◆ Illustrations by Kevin Belford

Photo Credits

T = Top B = Bottom L = Left R = Right M = Middle

Page 9: Vincent Laforet/Allsport; 10: The Sporting News Archives; 11: Library of Congress; 12: Library of Congress; 13: B—Library of Congress; 14: TSN Archives; 15: TSN Archives (both); 16: TSN Archives (all); 17: TSN Archives (all); 18: AP/Wide World Photos; 19: AP/Wide World Photos; 24: Paul Tepley; 25: TL—TSN Archives, TR—John Dunn for The Sporting News, B—TSN Archives; 26: Albert Dickson/The Sporting News; 27: T—John Dunn for The Sporting News, B—Albert Dickson/The Sporting News; 28: Albert Dickson/The Sporting News (both); 29: Bob Leverone/The Sporting News; 32: T—TSN Archives, BL—Pete Newcomb for The Sporting News, BL—TSN Archives; 33: Dilip Vishwanat/The Sporting News; 34: Jay Crihfield; 35: TSN Archives; 36: TSN Archives; 37: Robert Seale/The Sporting News; 40: TSN Archives; 41: TSN Archives (both); 42: TSN Archives; 43: TSN Archives; 44: TL—TSN Archives, TR—Albert Dickson/The Sporting News, B—TSN Archives; 45: T—TSN Archives, B—Albert Dickson; 50: TSN Archives; 51: TSN Archives; 52: John Cordes; 53: John Cordes; 56: Bettmann/CORBIS; 57: Bettmann/CORBIS; 58: T—Elsa Hasch/Allsport, B—AP/Wide World Photos; 59: Mike Powell/Allsport; 62: T—AP/Wide World Photos, B—Bob Leverone/The Sporting News; 63: Bettmann/CORBIS; 64: Bob Leverone/The Sporting News (both); 65: Esra Shaw/Allsport; 68: Otto Greule Jr./Allsport; 69: T—TSN Archives, M—AP/Wide World Photos, B—TSN Archives; 70: Otto Greule Jr./Allsport; 71: Otto Greule Jr./Allsport; 75: Vincent Laforet/Allsport; 76: TL—Jeb Jacobsohn/Allsport, TR—John Ferry/Allsport, B—John Ferry/Allsport; 77: Jason Wise; 82: Albert Dickson/The Sporting News (both); 83: TSN Archives; 84: TSN Archives; 85: T—Albert Dickson/The Sporting News, B—TSN Archives; 88: TSN Archives (both); 89: TSN Archives (both); 90: T—TSN Archives, BL—Robert Seale/The Sporting News, BR—Frank Bryan; 91: Robert Seale/The Sporting News; 94: T—TSN Archives, B—Albert Dickson/The Sporting News; 95: Albert Dickson/The Sporting News; 97: TSN Archives; 102: TSN Archives; 103: TSN Archives; 104: TSN Archives; 105: Bettmann/CORBIS; 108: Scott Rovak; 109: Phillip Norton/Montreal Gazette; 110: Phillip Norton/Montreal Gazette; 111: T—Andre Pichette/Montreal Gazette, B—Dave Sidaway/Montreal Gazette; 114: Bettmann/CORBIS; 115: Fred Vulch; 116: Bettmann/CORBIS; 117: Bettmann/

CORBIS; 122: Robert Seale/The Sporting News; 123: Robert Seale/The Sporting News; 124: Robert Seale/The Sporting News (both); 125: Robert Seale/The Sporting News (both); 128: Bob Leverone/The Sporting News; 129: Bob Leverone/The Sporting News; 132: TSN Archives; 133: Robert Seale/The Sporting News; 134: Robert Seale/The Sporting News; 135: Albert Dickson/The Sporting News; 139: TSN Archives; 140: Albert Dickson/The Sporting News (both); 141: Robert Seale/The Sporting News; 144: Bob Leverone/The Sporting News; 145: Bob Leverone/The Sporting News; 146: AP/Wide World Photos; 147: Albert Dickson/The Sporting News (both); 150: Albert Dickson/The Sporting News; 151: Albert Dickson/The Sporting News; 152: Albert Dickson/The Sporting News; 153: Albert Dickson/The Sporting News (all); 156: Albert Dickson/The Sporting News (all); 157: Albert Dickson/The Sporting News; 158: Dilip Vishwanat/The Sporting News; 159: Dilip Vishwanat/The Sporting News; 162: Robert Seale/The Sporting News (all); 163: Robert Seale/The Sporting News (all); 164: Robert Seale/The Sporting News; 168: Zoran Milich/Allsport; 169: Brian Bahr/Allsport; 172: L—Robert Seale/The Sporting News, R—Major League Baseball; 173: L—Dilip Vishwanat/The Sporting News, R—Robert Seale/The Sporting News; 176: Vincent Laforet/Allsport; 177: T—AP/Wide World Photos, B—Vincent Laforet/Allsport; 180: Dilip Vishwanat/The Sporting News; 181: Dilip Vishwanat/The Sporting News; 182: L—Major League Baseball, R—Dilip Vishwanat/The Sporting News; 183: Dilip Vishwanat/The Sporting News; 186: Albert Dickson/The Sporting News (both); 187: Albert Dickson/The Sporting News (all); 188: Albert Dickson/The Sporting News (both); 189: Albert Dickson/The Sporting News (both); 192: Albert Dickson/The Sporting News; 193: Albert Dickson/The Sporting News (both); 194: Albert Dickson/The Sporting News; 195: Bob Leverone/The Sporting News (both); 198: T—Scott Halleran/Allsport, B—Peter Taylor/Allsport; 199: AP/Wide World Photos; 205: TSN Archives (both); 209: T—AP/Wide World Photos, B—Robert Seale/The Sporting News; 210: T and R—Robert Seale/The Sporting News, B—Louis DeLuca; 211: Robert Seale/The Sporting News; 215: TSN Archives; 216: TSN Archives; 217: TSN Archives; 221: TSN Archives (both); 224: TSN Archives; 225: TSN Archives;

226: TSN Archives (all); 228: TSN Archives (all); 229: TSN Archives (both); 232: TSN Archives; 233: TSN Archives (both); 234: TSN Archives (all); 235: TSN Archives; 238: TSN Archives (both); 239: TSN Archives; 240: TSN Archives; 241: TSN Archives (all); 244: L—Bettmann/CORBIS, R—Jonathan Daniel/Allsport; 245: Bettmann/CORBIS; 246: Robert Seale/The Sporting News; 249: Cleveland Press Collection of Cleveland State University; 251: TSN Archives; 254: TSN Archives; 255: TSN Archives; 256: TSN Archives; 257: TSN Archives (both); 260: TSN Archives (both); 261: T—Albert Dickson/The Sporting News, B—TSN Archives (all); 262—Albert Dickson/The Sporting News (all); 263: TSN Archives (both); 264: TSN Archives; 265: Albert Dickson/The Sporting News; 268: TSN Archives (all); 269: Robert Seale/The Sporting News; 270: Robert Seale/The Sporting News; 271: TSN Archives; 274: Bettmann/CORBIS; 275: B—Bettmann/CORBIS, R—TSN Archives; 276: TSN Archives; 277: Bob Leverone/The Sporting News; 280: TSN Archives (both); 284: TSN Archives; 285: TSN Archives (all); 286: TSN Archives (both); 287: TSN Archives; 288: TSN Archives; 289: TSN Archives; 292: TSN Archives; 294: TSN Archives; 295: TSN Archives (all); 297: Library of Congress; 300: TSN Archives; 301: TSN Archives; 302: TSN Archives (both); 303: Bettmann/CORBIS; 306: L—Scott Rovak, R—Fred Vulch; 307: Bettmann/CORBIS; 308: Fred Vulch; 309: Fred Vulch; 312: TSN Archives; 313: TSN Archives; 314: TSN Archives (both); 315: TSN Archives (both); 318: Bob Leverone/The Sporting News; 319: Bob Leverone/The Sporting News (both); 322: TSN Archives (both); 323: TSN Archives; 324: TSN Archives (all); 325: TSN Archives; 328: Ken Kerr/Toronto Sun; 329: Paul Henry/Toronto Sun; 332: Bettmann/CORBIS; 333: AP/Wide World Photos; 334: T—AP/Wide World Photos, B—Bettmann/CORBIS; 335: AP/Wide World Photos.

All photos used on top of ballpark illustrations are TSN Archives except as noted:

Page 54 (Hershiser) and 55 (Gibson): AP/Wide World Photos; 206 (Horner): Janice Rettaliata; 230 (Riot): Bettmann/CORBIS.

All ballpark illustrations by Kevin Belford except pages 154-155, 160-161, 170-171, 178-179, 184-185, 190-191, which are photo illustrations by Pamela Speh.

ISBN: 0-89204-708-8

10 9 8 7 6 5 4 3

Acknowledgements

Any book-creation process is a team effort, filled with important contributions from knowledgeable research sources and those people who plan, edit, proofread, gather, process, design and assist in ways too countless to list. Many dedicated people, both inside and outside the office of THE SPORTING NEWS, participated in preparation of *The Ballpark Book*, often providing valuable insight and assistance in addition to their regular weekly obligations.

The book's direction and concept reflect in large part the vision of books editorial director Steve Meyerhoff, who oversaw the project, assisted with the editing, compiled information boxes and provided much-needed understanding and encouragement. The special photographs that give the book depth and relevance reflect the determination and hard work of TSN chief photographer Albert Dickson and the quality reproduction of those photos reflect the abilities of prepress specialists Steve Romer and Pamela Speh.

The book's design, a collaborative effort by prepress director Bob Parajon and creative director Bill Wilson, was executed by a talented team led by Christen Sager and Becky Carr, and including Michael Behrens, Angie Pillman, Matt Kindt, Beth Carter and Amy Beadle. Romer and Speh received assistance from prepress specialists David Brickey, Jack Kruyne and Vern Kasal.

Many contributions were made to the editorial process, starting with the insights of senior editor Joe Hoppel, a longtime student of ballparks and the games people play there, and the proofreading efforts of associate editor Dave Sloan. The book would have suffered without the knowledge of specific parks offered by staffers Carl Moritz, Bob Hille, Sean Deveney, Steve Gietschier, Mike Nahrstedt and Steve Siegel. Many TSN baseball correspondents also contributed, including Luciana Chavez (Kauffman Stadium), Marc Topkin (Tropicana Field), Mike Berardino (Pro Player Stadium), Stephanie Myles (Olympic Stadium), Henry Schulman (Candlestick Park), Tom Maloney (SkyDome), Susan Slusser (the Oakland Coliseum), Mike DiGiovanna (Anaheim Stadium), Larry LaRue (the Kingdome), John Mehno (Three Rivers Stadium), Chris Edwards (Veterans Stadium) and Tom Krasovic (Jack Murphy Stadium).

A special thanks to TSN executives Kathy Kinkeade and John Rawlings, who provided physical and emotional support for the project, and to everyone at THE SPORTING NEWS, who exemplified the essence of the word "team" by picking up the workload of others to allow this project to move forward. Thanks, also, to Stew Thornley, who shared memories about Minnesota's Metropolitan Stadium and the Metrodome, Rodney Johnson, who helped with Bank One Ballpark in Phoenix, and TSN librarian Jim Meier, who was always ready, willing and able to assist with critical research needs.

◆ ◆ ◆

As you read this book, there no doubt will be questions about the way we refer to particular ballparks, most notably those that in recent years have sold corporate naming rights. Our rule of thumb was simple, albeit subjective: We refer to ballparks by their most commonly known name over the course of their history. So in this book, San Diego's park remains Jack Murphy Stadium, even though it now is officially known as Qualcomm Stadium.

Table of Contents

Ballparks
Now, yesterday and forever

Of course you remember. The crack of the bat and the snap of ball hitting glove are as vivid today as they were 20 years ago when you attended your first major league game. Or 5 years ago. Or 40. Maybe you sat in the bleachers at Fenway Park, the outfield grandstand at old Ebbets Field, next to the center field clubhouse at the Polo Grounds or in the Jury Box at Braves Field. Of course you remember.

You remember the smells, of the hot dogs that always taste better here than anywhere else, roasted peanuts with shells you can throw right on the floor, food-stained concourses, beer, factories and railroad yards beyond the fences, grass—the real, honest-to-goodness natural stuff, like what you have in your front yard. You remember the excited chatter of fans and the sounds of vendors, distinctive public address announcers, umpires making their calls, wild cheers and frustrated, heartfelt boos from people who obviously care.

You remember your heroes, larger than life in victory, painfully human in defeat, and the anticipation you feel before the game and the sadness you feel when it's over. You remember the explosion of green when you spot the field and the comforting sense of camaraderie, pride, fun, excitement and exultation after you sit down. You remember yelling and screaming, as loud as you want, and crying, without fear of ridicule or painful embarrassment.

Of course you remember. A ballpark is personal, it's sensual and it's filled with soul-stirring magic. It's a special place, a special time in your life, a feeling you may never recapture, a bond that can never be broken. A ballpark defines the timeless fascination we have for a game and fills voids in our lives. It's now, it's yesterday and it's forever.

◆ ◆ ◆

Life in late 19th-century America was not about feelings, emotions and soul-stirring magic. It was about an agrarian, working-class society with little leisure time and only a moderate appetite for sporting diversions. Baseball was growing in popularity, but it also was waging a difficult battle against its own reputation as a rowdy, pugilistic sport played by unsavory characters and watched by uncivilized fans who often behaved violently. The gentility that might normally have been attracted to the sport was repulsed.

The baseball venues in this context were little more than open fields with hastily erected wooden stands—maybe dugouts, but seldom a clubhouse and few amenities beyond the joy of watching the local nine in action. Fields, like the teams that played there, were transient and fragile. A team could disappear in the blink of an eye; a field could disappear in a puff of smoke.

Such was the evolution of baseball that the stage upon which it was played

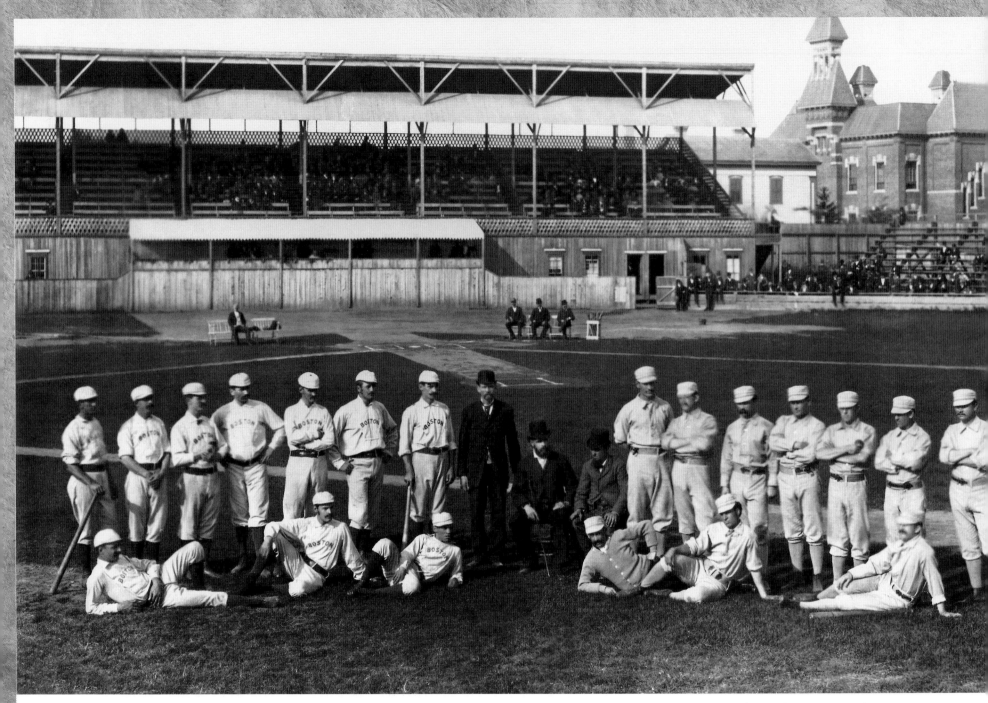

Ballparks like Messer Field in Providence, R.I. (circa 1878) featured wooden grandstands and view-obstructing pillars. In the early 1900s, wood gave way to steel.

seemed inconsequential and fleeting. That would change. As baseball turned the corner on the 20th century and the nation took important steps toward industrialization, the sport began cleaning up its act and became more deeply rooted in neighborhood and community life. So did the ballpark, which became a place to congregate, socialize and get away from the daily grind.

The profile of an early 20th-century major league ballpark focused on the basics: wood based with small grandstands; located on the edge of big-city development; strategically placed on a trolley or subway line, opening up access beyond the immediate neighborhood; usually single-decked; sometimes enclosed, but often an open outfield roped off to viewers; little or no ornamentation; small seating capacities often expanded with temporary bleachers when needed.

Into this profile fit such early parks as Philadelphia's Baker Bowl and Columbia Park, New York's Polo Grounds and Hilltop Park, Pittsburgh's Exposition Park, Brooklyn's Washington Park, Chicago West Side Grounds and South Side Park, Boston's Huntington Avenue Grounds and South End Grounds, Cincinnati's Palace of the Fans, Detroit's Bennett Park, Washington's American League Park and St. Louis' Sportsman's Park.

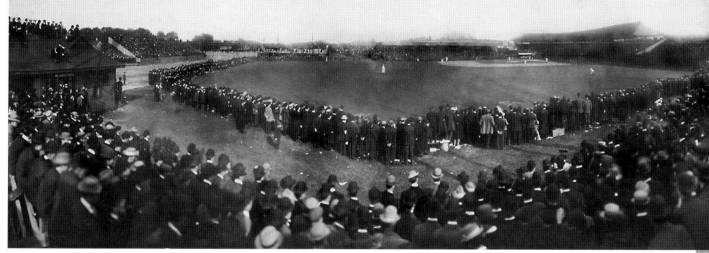

Detroit fans ring the open outfield during Game 5 action between the Tigers and Cubs in the 1907 World Series.

great ballpark building boom that started in 1909 and set the standard by which future facilities would be judged. But there also were other forces at work. A healthier, wealthier society was interested in expanding its sports horizons and wide-eyed major league owners were only too willing to offer their help.

The result was an explosion of large, fireproof, multi-decked ballparks that could help fuel baseball's rising popularity while providing a regional identity for the teams and their fans. Not only were they constructed entirely out of steel and concrete, they were attractive, inviting, amenity-filled arenas that gave new meaning to watching baseball. And new meaning to the profitable way baseball could be packaged.

The Baker Bowl, which served as home for the Phillies from 1887-1938, was an early architectural example of cantilever construction and its home plate grandstand was made of steel and concrete. The early Polo Grounds featured an unusually aggressive double-deck grandstand with prominent Y-shaped support posts spaced about 15 feet apart. The first World Series, with Boston fans ringing the outfield, was decided at Huntington Avenue Grounds in 1903. The entire 1906 fall classic, the Cubs vs. the White Sox, was played in Chicago.

Baseball's formative years were filled with stories of ballparks burning to the ground and being resurrected in short order. That certainly was a factor in the

Philadelphia's Shibe Park, home of the Athletics, was hailed as the crown jewel of baseball when it opened its gates for the first time on April 12, 1909. Its dignified French Renaissance dome, which towered over the intersection of 21st and Lehigh, was flanked by arched windows and entryways that led fans into a marvelously clean ballpark with folding-chair seats, underground garages and restrooms manned by attendants and matrons. This Ben Shibe-Connie Mack production was first class.

So was Forbes Field, which opened 11 weeks later in Pittsburgh and featured baseball's first luxury boxes—a covered row of seats that stretched from one end

of its double-deck grandstand roof to the other. It didn't take long for other owners to take heed. Charles A. Comiskey opened sparkling new Comiskey Park for his Chicago White Sox in 1910, Boston's Fenway Park, Cincinnati's Redland Field (later Crosley) and Detroit's Navin Field (later Tiger Stadium) opened in 1912, Brooklyn's Ebbets Field made its debut in 1913, Boston's Braves Field opened in 1915 and Chicago's Wrigley Field, a former Federal League stronghold built in 1914, played host to its first National League game in 1916.

Joining the parade were the Polo Grounds and Washington's Griffith Stadium, both of which were rebuilt into steel-and-concrete facilities in 1911 after destructive fires. Cleveland's League Park was converted to Shibe-like building standards in 1910.

The profile of these classic-era ballparks is familiar to the 21st-century fan: entirely steel and concrete; baseball-only facilities; often double-decked behind the plate, from first base to third, with single decks down both lines; seats close to the field; some sight-obstructing posts; larger seating capacities with room to expand; large scoreboards, occasionally electric but mostly manual; attractive and fan-friendly—charming.

Charm and charisma were not goals of early century ballpark builders, who were looking for form, function and more fans to stream through their turnstiles. But their idiosyncratic originals would become ballpark masterpieces, wonderful accidents of creation that would transcend time in the hearts and memories of their fans. For many, a Shibe Park or Wrigley Field would be the only ballpark they would know in their lifetime. For most, that would be just fine.

Nothing defined that charm more than the ballpark's relationship with the community, and city, of which it was a part. These were urban centers tucked into a neighborhood like a hand into a glove—in some cases, a very tight one. Invariably, team owners bought their land and drew up ballpark blueprints to correspond to the irregular contours of streets, homes, businesses and railroad yards that might surround it. No two were alike and fans became accustomed to such quirky nuances as angled and concave outfield fences, unexpected inclines, 33-foot screens and fair-territory bullpens.

Because the left field at Fenway Park backed up to Lansdowne Street only 300-plus feet from home plate, a huge wall would be needed to compensate for the short home run distance. Because the Polo Grounds was built between an existing ballpark and a bluff in 1891, it took on an elongated shape that resulted in the biggest center field in baseball. Because the owner of five Washington D.C. duplexes refused to sell, Griffith Stadium was constructed with a center field wall that indented around the obstacles. Oddly shaped Crosley Field was a product of the strangely angled streets that circled its perimeter. And all were subject to the local whims of Mother Nature.

Schoolboy Rowe, an outstanding pitcher who worked in most of the major league parks that existed in the 1930s and '40s, offered this thought in an interview published in 1948.

"Ballparks are individuals to me, not just so much stone, concrete and steel,"

The Miracle Braves, not the Red Sox, were a World Series attraction for Boston fans at Fenway Park in 1914 (above). Note how fans were crammed into temporary bleachers in front of what would become the left field Green Monster. Giants and Phillies players inspect rubble from the Polo Grounds fire of 1911 (left), from which ashes rose the modern-day Polo Grounds.

the former Tigers, Dodgers and Phillies star said. "They are like a lot of old ladies with varying temperaments. You have to study them, go along with their whims on certain days. They are all built differently, dressed differently, react differently to rain, sunshine, fog, wind."

They also were cozy and intimate—and all promoted a special relationship between players and fans.

Players often lived near the ballpark and became family extensions of the community. Fans would see them shopping at the store, eating in a local restaurant. Gil Hodges married a Brooklyn woman and became a fulltime resident of Flatbush, and many of his Dodgers teammates also lived there. Baseball became an intricate part of the Brooklyn fabric, much like it did in other major league cities.

"Brooklyn was a town that lived and died with the Dodgers," said Phil Rizzuto, a Brooklyn native who went on to baseball fame with the New York Yankees. "When the Dodgers were playing, you could walk up and down the streets of Brooklyn and never miss a pitch. Everybody had the game on the radio. It meant so much to them."

Contact also was possible at the ballpark, where a player's path from clubhouse to field often would lead right through the stands—or maybe even the concourse where fans would gather to greet and encourage him. Fans could hear the field chatter of players and coaches during games; players, like it or not, could hear the opinions and ravings of nearby fans. It was a personal experience, equal parts uplifting and humbling.

The 1909 ballpark boom would carry Americans through the deadball era, the Roaring '20s, the Great Depression and two World Wars—a long, memorable period of growth and stability in baseball. For half a century beginning in 1903, the major league franchise alignment remained frozen in time. And for much of that period, those franchises remained committed to the ballparks they called home. Changes, renovations and improvements kept them modern and fan-

Yesterday: Ballparks, like Hilltop Park in New York, weren't the grand edifices of today.

friendly, but nobody was foolish enough to mess with the quirks and personalities that made them special.

After Braves Field opened in 1915, ballpark construction virtually stopped for the next four decades—with two notable exceptions. The first, in 1923, would affect the very essence of the game.

Through the deadball era of Ty Cobb, Walter Johnson, Christy Mathewson, Eddie Collins and Tris Speaker, ballpark dimensions were irrelevant. Most outfields were expansive, set up to encourage gap hitters. That changed with the rise to prominence of a round-faced, pitcher-turned outfielder who demonstrated an amazing ability to hit the ball farther and more frequently than anybody who had played before him. When Babe Ruth, a former Baltimore orphan with a flair for the dramatic, was sold by the Boston Red Sox to New York Yankees in 1920, major league ballparks entered the first stage of what would become a serious identity crisis.

Ruth's arrival helped the game survive the stain of a 1919 World Series scandal and ushered in a new era of prosperity. He pounded 54 home runs in 1920, almost double his previous single-season record, 59 in 1921, 35 in 1922—inconceivable numbers that would draw new waves of fans through the turnstiles. Suddenly, there wasn't a ballpark big enough to hold his towering blasts and opposing teams rushed to find big, powerful hitters who could match his feats. The Yankees, who had been forced to play in the shadow of the Giants at the Polo Grounds since 1913, decided it was time to build their own showcase ballpark, tailored to fit their young star, in the South Bronx, just across the Harlem River from the Polo Grounds. The House That Ruth Built was bigger, grander and more spectacular than anything fans had ever seen.

Yankee Stadium was exactly that—a stadium, massive, imposing and able to seat more than 70,000 fans. New Yorkers marveled at its architecture and atten-

tion to ornamental detail. Early visitors called it a cathedral and, with Ruth and Lou Gehrig leading the charge, it would become the greatest of all baseball shrines and the home of more championship teams than any park before or after.

The only other newcomer to the major league scene in the first half century was another monster—Cleveland's huge, hulking Municipal Stadium, which played host to its first game in 1932. It, too, was large and imposing, able to seat 75,000-plus, but it couldn't match Yankee Stadium's class and charisma. Municipal was barren and hollow, so large that Cleveland officials played their weekday schedules at tiny League Park, which was much less expensive to operate. Municipal was limited to weekend and holiday games for more than 15 years.

It was only three years after the debut of Municipal Stadium, in the shadow of the Great Depression, that ballpark evolution took another giant leap for-

Forever: Ebbets Field, (above) opened to much fanfare in 1913 and remains a special memory for Brooklyn fans; Crosley Field (left) hosted baseball's first night game.

Time was when the ballpark experience was about community, where parks, like Crosley Field, were cut into neighborhoods, and where fans, like those in 1920 Brooklyn (right), dined in the streets and in Boston (below), contributed gifts to players.

ward. When Cincinnati general manager Lee MacPhail installed lights at Crosley Field and staged the first night game in major league history in 1935, he, like Ruth more than a decade earlier, changed the course of history. Night games increased attendance and helped baseball regain its footing after the depression and World War II. Soon it would be expanding its horizons beyond anyone's wildest dreams.

With more efficient automobiles carrying fans to the suburbs, improved air travel triggering a population shift west and the power of television turning the national pastime into a bottom line-oriented

When baseball went West, temporary parks with less-than-ideal playing conditions were used, like the Los Angeles Memorial Coliseum, with its short left field screen.

enterprise, the first chink in baseball's long stability appeared in 1953 when the Boston Braves moved operations to Milwaukee and County Stadium, a longtime minor league facility. The St. Louis Browns became the Baltimore Orioles a year later and moved into Memorial Stadium and the Philadelphia A's took refuge in Kansas City's Municipal Stadium in 1955. Owners suddenly were searching for more fertile markets—fertile as in big. The ballpark business really exploded in 1957 when the Dodgers and Giants, New York staples since the beginning of baseball time, announced their shocking plans to move to Los Angeles and San Francisco.

The Giants spent their first two California seasons at tiny Seals Stadium, another minor league facility, and the Dodgers suffered through four years at the Los Angeles Memorial Coliseum—a 93,000-seat football stadium that had been converted (awkwardly) for baseball. When the Giants moved into new Candlestick Park in 1960, they introduced the first of 20 parks that would become permanent major league home bases over an expansion-filled 18-year period.

One was beautiful Dodger Stadium, a baseball-only gem that opened in 1962 in the hills overlooking Los Angeles. But it was merely a mirage. Most of the newcomers were big, round, sterile, symmetrical, concrete structures that focused on amenities and comfort at the expense of intimacy and atmosphere. With population centers shifting to the suburbs, so did the new ballparks. Most were located in open areas, often surrounded by massive parking lots. Without neighborhood contours to dictate shape, they often were devoid of personality.

By the late 1950s, old favorites Braves Field, League Park and Ebbets Field were gone. By the early 1960s, Griffith Stadium and the Polo Grounds had been cast aside. Sportsman's Park, Shibe Park, Forbes Field and Crosley Field soon would be thrown out like memorabilia from the attic. In their place were the new-wave ballparks, dedicated to technology and comfort and the almighty bottom line. The new buzzword was multi-purpose, as in multiple sports and events that provided year-round revenue streams.

Candlestick Park was a stadium pioneer, the first to be built entirely with reinforced concrete and unobstructed sightlines. It was at first a baseball-only facility located on scenic Candlestick Point overlooking the San Francisco Bay, but it would eventually become a prime example of multi-purpose. Like such followers as the Oakland Coliseum, Anaheim Stadium and Jack Murphy Stadium in San Diego, it would succumb to the lure of the National Football League, substantially increase its seating capacity to accommodate a team and eventually

Seattle's ballpark experience spans the generations, from the departed Kingdome and the Dome Era, to Safeco Field (above) and the New Wave Era.

enclose its once-open outfield, creating a sterile, concrete bowl.

Houston's Astrodome, which was introduced as the Eighth Wonder of the World in 1965, took the multi-purpose concept a step further. Fans marveled at the thought of baseball indoors and they weren't disappointed. They were amazed at its luxury, its size, its state-of-the-art scoreboard and that green carpet it introduced to the world—labeled, appropriately, AstroTurf. They also were shocked at the advanced technology and climate control it introduced to the game. While traditionalists winced, many fans embraced the idea of symmetrical baseball without interference from wind, heat, cold, fog or any other whim of Mother Nature.

The next domed stadium would not appear for another dozen years (Seattle's Kingdome in 1977), but many of the Astrodome's innovations were embraced by outdoor facilities. Technology and luxury were two, but artificial turf was the most important.

When St. Louis' Busch Stadium opened in 1966, nobody entertained any baseball-only illusions—this was absolutely, unequivocally, a multi-purpose stadium. Round, fully enclosed and multiple-decked with retractable seats for foot-

ball, Busch provided the mold for what would eventually be known as the cookie-cutter stadiums—bowl-like, concrete, artificial turf-covered look-alikes that sprang up in Atlanta, Cincinnati, Pittsburgh and Philadelphia.

Because those parks were designed to accommodate both football and baseball, they lacked the intimacy of their predecessors and never allowed a close relationship between players and fans. Seats were free of obstructions, but they often were far away from the action and not angled toward home plate, another football concession. While football might draw 60,000-plus crowds, baseball attendance often averaged only a third of capacity, giving the stadium a hollow, empty feel. Owners relied on technology, gimmicks and promotions to freshen up a sterile atmosphere.

Ambience was not a consideration during this booming expansion, when the major league roster increased from 16 teams (1960) to 26 (1977) and introduced baseball to fans in such cities as Montreal, Toronto, Houston, Dallas-Fort Worth, Minneapolis, San Diego, Anaheim, Oakland, Seattle and Atlanta. Small ballparks like Colt Stadium (Houston), Jarry Park (Montreal) and Wrigley Field (Los Angeles) often served as warmups while bigger, fancier stadiums were being constructed.

When Toronto's SkyDome, a veritable indoor baseball city, opened in 1989, that signaled the end of another era. With player salaries spiraling out of sight and teams searching frantically for new sources of revenue, they began aligning with corporate sponsors and appealing to the nostalgia craze sweeping the nation. Jack Murphy changed its name to Qualcomm Stadium, Anaheim became Edison International Field, Riverfront changed to Cinergy Field and a new retractable-roof facility in Phoenix was introduced as Bank One Ballpark. But change was not limited to names.

New Comiskey Park opened in 1991, right across the street from old Comiskey and with many of the same features and nuances of its venerable predecessor. A year later, Baltimore took the budding "retro park" concept to new levels when it replaced Memorial Stadium with Oriole Park at Camden Yards—a beautiful throwback facility with all the quirks and oddities of old, but all the amenities and comforts fans have come to expect. In short order, Cleveland unveiled Jacobs Field, Texas opened The Ballpark in Arlington, Atlanta introduced Turner Field and the Rockies introduced us to mountain ball in Coors Field.

The ballpark-building craze continued into the new century with every city trying to outquirk and outquaint the other. Several of the parks were nestled into downtown areas, like the parks of old, but others were positioned away from the city, within the walls of self-contained neighborhoods that offered fans every amenity known to man and many never before imagined.

As the building spree continues—Safeco Field replaced the Kingdome, Pacific Bell Park replaced Candlestick, Comerica Park replaced Tiger Stadium, Minute Maid Park replaced the Astrodome, PNC Park replaced Three Rivers and Miller Park replaced County Stadium—and the corporate sponsors line up, it's easy to get a feeling of deja vu. But in reality, the modern appeal to old-time ballparks is nothing more than an illusion.

The old ballpark sounds have been shut off by nonstop recorded music, scoreboards go into pyrotechnic convulsions and tell fans when to "chaaaarge!", lifesize mascots romp around the field and through the stands, cartoon characters and advertisements bombard our senses on huge video boards, giveaways dominate the P.A. system, clam chowder, mountain oysters and tacos compete with hot dogs for fan affection and we fall victim to such corporate gimmicks as dot races and Mexican hat dances.

This is cutting-edge, 21st-century baseball. It's now, it's yesterday and it's forever.

Out with the old, in with the new. Cinergy Field (left) played host to its final major league game in 2002, giving way to Great American Ball Park (right) for the 2003 season. Cinergy has since been demolished, another victim of baseball's retro-ballpark craze.

The Classics

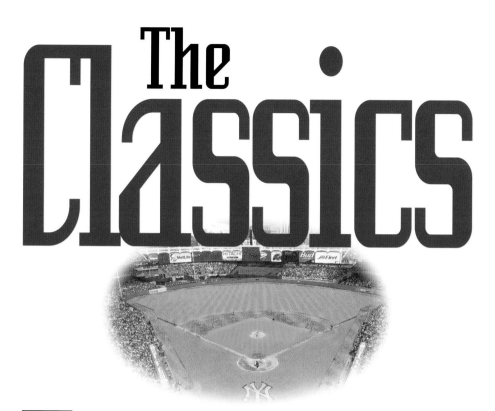

They are the elders of baseball society, ballparks that have endured for more than 80 years; ballparks that have withstood the pressures and urgings to change with the times; ballparks that are comfortable and cozy, charming in their presentation and stories of days gone by.

With the 1999 passing of Tiger Stadium, only three Classics remain—Boston's Fenway Park, Chicago's Wrigley Field and New York's Yankee Stadium.

These, too, will someday pass, but here's hoping the lessons they have learned will be passed to succeeding generations, that their legacies will live long after the wrecking ball has buried them in the earth.

Fenway Park

The former site of Duffy's cliff—an incline at the base of left field wall

Former home of Tris Speaker, one of the great center fielders in baseball history

Where Carlton Fisk hit dramatic 12th-inning homer, winning Game 6 of '75 World Series

Williams and Yaz, both left fielders, had a special rapport with Fenway's Green Monster

Site of Williams' big All-Star show: 4-for-4, 2 home runs in 1946

Former stomping ground of Joe Cronin; current home of Nomar Garciaparra, 1999 and 2000 batting champ

TED WILLIAMS: The Splendid Splinter batted .344, hit 521 homers, won 2 Triple Crowns and earned 2 MVPs

Lou Boudreau's two home runs lift Indians past Red Sox in playoff to decide 1948 N.L. pennant

Roger Clemens strikes out record 20 Mariners en route to 24-4 record and MVP-Cy Young double in 1986

The red-brick facade, which camouflages the entryway to heaven on the corner of Brookline and Yawkey Way, stands frozen in time—like a picture of Dorian Gray. It's no illusion. Fenway Park appears to a first-time visitor much the way it must have looked to Babe Ruth, to Lefty Grove, to Ted Williams and to Carl Yastrzemski during the prime of their long-ended careers. It's a Boston relic and landmark—an artifact etched into a city's psyche like its name was carved into the concrete exterior nine decades ago.

This is a love affair that won't go away. Boston fans have renewed their

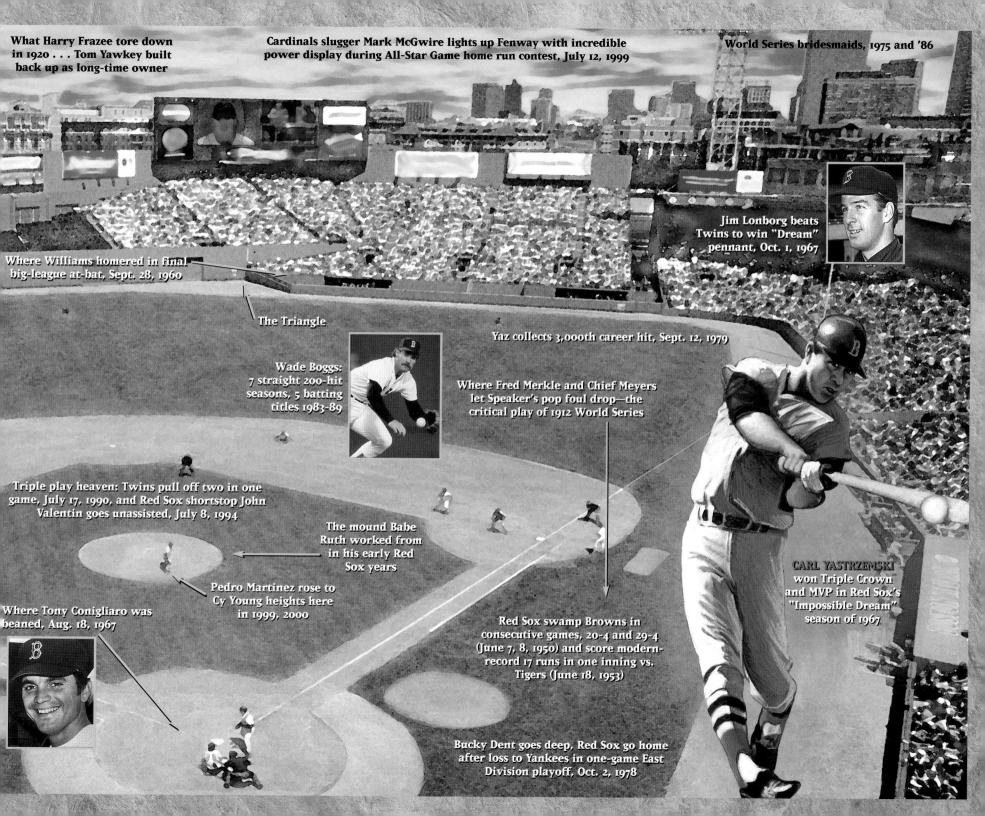

What Harry Frazee tore down in 1920 . . . Tom Yawkey built back up as long-time owner

Cardinals slugger Mark McGwire lights up Fenway with incredible power display during All-Star Game home run contest, July 12, 1999

World Series bridesmaids, 1975 and '86

Jim Lonborg beats Twins to win "Dream" pennant, Oct. 1, 1967

Where Williams homered in final big-league at-bat, Sept. 28, 1960

The Triangle

Yaz collects 3,000th career hit, Sept. 12, 1979

Wade Boggs: 7 straight 200-hit seasons, 5 batting titles 1983-89

Where Fred Merkle and Chief Meyers let Speaker's pop foul drop—the critical play of 1912 World Series

Triple play heaven: Twins pull off two in one game, July 17, 1990, and Red Sox shortstop John Valentin goes unassisted, July 8, 1994

The mound Babe Ruth worked from in his early Red Sox years

Pedro Martinez rose to Cy Young heights here in 1999, 2000

CARL YASTRZEMSKI won Triple Crown and MVP in Red Sox's "Impossible Dream" season of 1967

Where Tony Conigliaro was beaned, Aug. 18, 1967

Red Sox swamp Browns in consecutive games, 20-4 and 29-4 (June 7, 8, 1950) and score modern-record 17 runs in one inning vs. Tigers (June 18, 1953)

Bucky Dent goes deep, Red Sox go home after loss to Yankees in one-game East Division playoff, Oct. 2, 1978

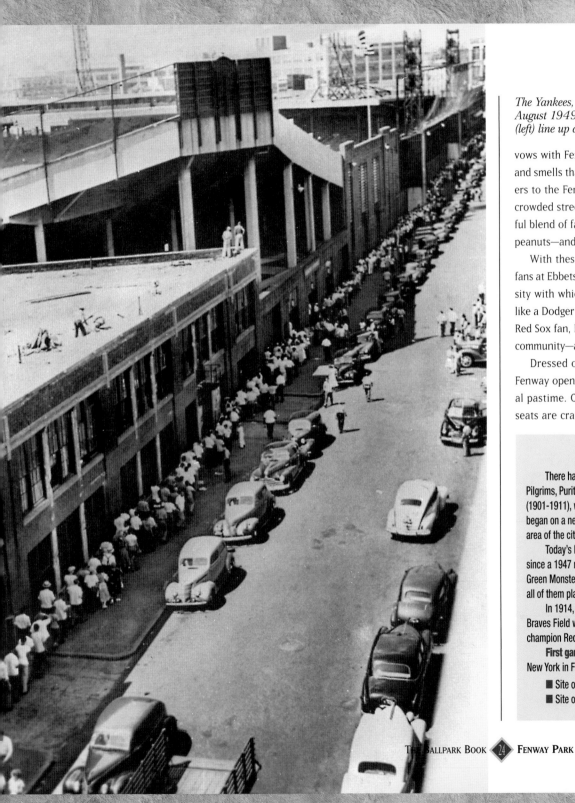

vows with Fenway every game day since 1912, a ritual of exciting sights, sounds and smells that fill the packed subway cars, trolleys and buses transporting rooters to the Fenway area and eventually come together in a festive mania on the crowded streets around the park. Pregame activity on Yawkey Way is a wonderful blend of fans, vendors, baseball banter, scalpers, hot dogs, sausages, roasted peanuts—and a deep-rooted, single-minded passion for the beloved Red Sox.

With these people, it's personal, much like it was decades ago for Brooklyn fans at Ebbets Field. The fervor is reflected in their eyes, their dress and the intensity with which they discuss the Red Sox and bat around their strong opinions, like a Dodger Stadium beach ball. To the 21st century fan, Fenway is a shrine. To a Red Sox fan, Fenway is an important piece of Boston's fabric and an extension of community—a corner supermarket where he can get a basic necessity of life.

Dressed on the outside like one of the city's finest, red-brick institutions, Fenway opens into an incongruous Norman Rockwell-like portrait of our national pastime. Concourses are narrow and dingy, aisles are difficult to navigate, seats are cramped and uncomfortable, pillars block some views and your eyes

FENWAY PARK (1912-)

There have been two homes in the history of the Boston Red Sox, who also were known as Pilgrims, Puritans and Somersets in earlier days. The first was the Huntington Avenue Grounds (1901-1911), which served as site for the first World Series game in 1903. In 1911, construction began on a new ballpark that opened in 1912 at the corner of Brookline and Jersey—in a marshy area of the city known as the Fens.

Today's Fenway is the oldest ballpark in the major leagues. It has not changed all that much since a 1947 renovation in which lights were added and advertising removed from the 37-foot Green Monster wall that dominates left field. Fenway has been the site for seven World Series, not all of them played by the Red Sox.

In 1914, the N.L.-champion Boston Braves used Fenway as their World Series base while Braves Field was under construction. In 1915 and '16, the Braves reciprocated by letting the A.L.-champion Red Sox use bigger Braves Field as their World Series home.

First game: April 20, 1912. In a precursor to the great Red Sox-Yankees rivalry, Boston beat New York in Fenway's debut, 7-6, in 11 innings.

■ Site of seven World Series (1912, '14, '18, '46, '67, '75 and '86)
■ Site of three All-Star Games (1946, '61 and '99)

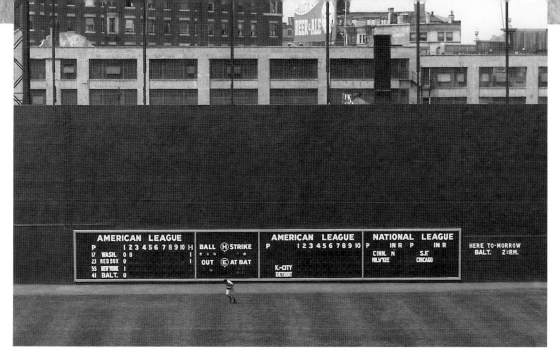

The Green Monster (above) comes complete with manual scoreboard, ladder and a doorway (above right) to its inner thoughts. The right field corner (right) is more like a loop that quickly expands home run distance from 302 feet at the pole to 380 at the bullpen marker.

have trouble coming to terms with one of the most absurd ballpark configurations ever conceived. When they do, you fall head-over-heels in love.

"I don't know anything about classical music," said former Yankees manager Buck Showalter, "but if there's a baseball symphony, this is it."

A symphony of cheers, boos, insults, shrieks and agonizing epithets, accompanied by the drumbeat of balls bouncing off a 37-foot left field wall nicknamed, appropriately, the Green Monster. The wall, by baseball standards, is intimidating—a mere 310 feet (or so they say) from home plate—and mesmerizing. No single ballpark feature has influenced games more consistently and dictated more thoroughly the personality of a franchise.

On one hand, it can eat up scorching line drives that would sail out of most other ballparks and shoot them back onto the field like a pinball machine. On the other, it can coax lazy fly balls into its 23-foot home run screen, like a spider enticing a fly into its web. Many casual baserunners have been cut down at second base by a Williams, Yaz or Jim Rice throw off a friendly carom. Championships, subtly and obviously, have been decided by not-so-routine fly balls.

This is a monster that has wrecked the careers of horrified lefthanded pitch-

Expectant kids, gloves at the ready, are bleacher regulars during batting practice before any game at Fenway Park. Not far below their center field perch is the Triangle.

ers, ruined the stroke of power-hitting wannabes and shattered the defensive confidence of bewildered left fielders. This is a house of offense and it's no coincidence that the Red Sox hold the major league records for runs in a game (29 in 1950) and an inning (17 in 1953).

If you can wrest your eyes away from the Green Monster, you'll discover a green-tinted baseball world full of interesting quirks. Aside from the Wall, there's the Ladder, the Scoreboard, the Door, the Triangle, the Yellow Line and the Jimmy Fund sign, to capture attention within the park. Beyond the walls are more sizeable landmarks like the Citgo sign (located several blocks away in Kenmore Square) in left and the Prudential building in right. The newest scene stealer, a slap in the face for Boston traditionalists, is the three-Coca Cola bottles advertisement perched atop the light standard in left field.

Most of the quirks are part of a zigging and zagging outfield fence that has more angles than a 500-piece jigsaw puzzle. The vertical yellow line rises from the point where the center field fence angles into the Green Monster, a visual reference for umpires to call a home run. The triangle marks another fence angle in right-center where the bullpens jut forward—the deepest point of the park at 420 feet. The large manual scoreboard is a fixture on the left field wall, as is the ladder that allows workers a scenic climb to remove balls from the screen.

It's easy to become entranced with the left field visuals and miss one of the park's most interesting features. There is no right field corner, thanks to a cozy 302-foot foul pole atop a right field fence that rolls quickly backward and levels off at 380 feet. Beyond the right field bullpens, high in the bleachers that back the right and center field fences, is a single red seat that marks the spot where Williams hit the longest measured home run in Fenway's history—a 1946 blast that traveled 502 feet.

Contrary to popular belief, this was not a ballpark designed by out-of-work architects in one of Boston's friendly corner pubs. Like most parks of its era, Fenway was built to conform to a crazy, patchwork neighborhood of strangely angled streets and railroad lines in a marshy area of Boston known as the Fens. Lansdowne Street, only 300-plus feet on the left field side of the park from where home plate would be located, was banked by the Boston & Albany Railroad, meaning there wasn't room for stands and the fence could not be moved out.

That was not a problem in the dead-ball era to which Fenway Park was introduced in 1912—with a brick facade patterned after Philadelphia's Shibe Park. There was no monster in left, but there was a 10-foot incline that rolled up to the

Seats near the left field corner are coveted (top photo), as are seats near the first base dugout where 1999 All-Star Game attendees got good looks at Derek Jeter (2), a dreaded Yankee, and hometown favorite Nomar Garciaparra (right).

The Fenway corner of Brookline Avenue and Yawkey Way is a beehive of activity before Red Sox games—a throwback to the excitement that has been gripping ballpark neighborhoods for decades.

The left field screen appeared in 1936, a concession to businessmen and home owners on Lansdowne who tired of broken windows. In 1940, the bullpens were added in front of the right field wall, shortening the home run distance by 23 feet for second-year man Williams. Lights came in 1947, the same year advertising was removed from the Green Monster, the Citgo sign went up in 1965 and in 1970 the flagpole, a fixture on the left-center field warning track for more than half a century, was moved out of play.

The final serious additions were an electronic scoreboard atop the right-center field scoreboard in 1976, padding for the outfield walls after star rookie Fred Lynn crashed into the center field fence in

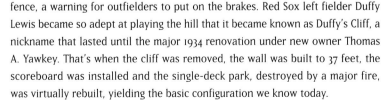

fence, a warning for outfielders to put on the brakes. Red Sox left fielder Duffy Lewis became so adept at playing the hill that it became known as Duffy's Cliff, a nickname that lasted until the major 1934 renovation under new owner Thomas A. Yawkey. That's when the cliff was removed, the wall was built to 37 feet, the scoreboard was installed and the single-deck park, destroyed by a major fire, was virtually rebuilt, yielding the basic configuration we know today.

the 1975 World Series, luxury boxes in 1982 and the 600 Club boxes behind home plate in 1989, a reconstruction that forced relocation of the press box. Through all of its makeovers, Fenway has always been charming, intimate, charismatic and a perfectly tinted backdrop for baseball's whitest uniforms and the most colorful fans this side of Brooklyn.

Former Red Sox stars, who have felt the tenderness of their affection and the sting of their wrath, might call them fanatics. They don't watch the game, they participate. Fenway allows them that luxury and refrains from the frills and distractions that entertain fans at other parks. Red Sox rooters are interested only in the game and anything beyond the background organ will not be tolerated. Everybody at Fenway keeps score, everybody knows the team's roster and everybody offers their verbal opinions, knowing full well they probably will be heard. Woe to any fan of the hated Yankees who dares enter Fenway's gates and shame on anybody who might leave early, an obvious character flaw. Baseball is serious business here—and disappointment an annual rite.

The Red Sox of Tris Speaker, Ruth, Harry Hooper, Smoky Joe Wood and Dutch Leonard won World Series in 1912, 1915, 1916 and 1918—but no Boston team has won one since. A Williams, Johnny Pesky and Bobby Doerr-led team won the A.L. pennant in 1946 and three other pennant-winners have been cut down in the World Series. The 1986 Red Sox, featuring Rice, Dwight Evans and Wade Boggs, put a dagger into the heart of their fans when they came within one out of the elusive championship, only to lose on a 10th-inning error.

Disappointment is a relative term at Fenway Park. It's hard to go there and feel any emotion other than exhilaration. Many exclusive nuances only enhance the feeling.

This is the only ballpark where you can get Fenway Franks and clam chowder.

It's the home of baseball's worst sun field—"The sun rises in the east and sets in right field at Fenway"—unpredictable breezes, occasional fogs, pesky pigeons and the smallest foul territory in baseball, which means more souvenirs—and more scrapes and bruises—for the fans. Did you ever notice the vertical morse code inscription on the right side of the scoreboard (the initials of Yawkey and his wife)? And how can anybody forget the distinctive public address announcements of (6-second hesitation) the late Sherm (14-second hesitation) Feller ... Feller?

It's crazy and intense, fun and serious, happy and sometimes sad. It's Fenway Park, where baseball is still the king.

The Green Monster was decked out in red, white and blue during a 2002 memorial for victims of the September 11 terrorist attacks.

Wrigley
Field

Also known as Cubs Park (1916-1926)

Wrigley finally saw the light on
Aug. 9, 1988, when it played host
to its first official night game

Where Stan Hack's hit skipped over
Hank Greenberg's shoulder, winning
Game 6 of 1945 World Series

Where Banks hit 500th homer, May 12, 1970

Fergie Jenkins
(left) and Andre
Dawson (right):
1971 Cy Young
winner and
1987 MVP

Where Cardinals
star Stan Musial
lined a double
for career hit
No. 3,000,
May 13, 1958

Where Gabby Hartnett hit his "Homer
in the Gloamin' " in 1938

Rookie Kerry Wood
strikes out record-tying
20 batters in one-hitter
vs. Astros, May 6, 1998

Gary Gaetti homer keys 5-3 win over
Giants in one-game playoff to decide
wild-card berth, Sept. 28, 1998

Site of Fred Toney
(Reds) and Hippo
Vaughn (Cubs) double
no-hitter, May 2, 1917

Second baseman
RYNE SANDBERG
posted a record 123-game
errorless streak, 1989-90

Billy
Williams
ends his
playing
streak at
1,117 games,
Sept. 3, 1970

You can't escape its
allure, that tantalizing
aura that wafts through
the residential
neighborhoods on Chicago's North
Side. Wrigley Field sneaks up on you,
pulls you into its embrace and hugs
you until your baseball senses are
squeezed dry. Resist if you want,
but prepare to be coddled, charmed
and enchanted when you enter
the friendly confines of the most
affectionate little ballpark in
North America.

Wrigley has been coddling,
charming and enchanting baseball
fans since 1914, when it opened as a

Mark Grace: 11-for-17, 8 RBIs in NLCS loss to Giants, 1989

Wrigley traditions: Ivy-covered walls, flags that fly after every game—white flag with "W" after win, blue flag with "L" after loss

Where broadcaster Harry Caray stayed out of tune from 1982-97, much to the delight of raucous Wrigley bleacher bums. Holy Cow!

Where Babe Ruth's "called shot" landed in 1932 World Series

The wind's blowing out and Mike Schmidt goes deep four times in Philadelphia's 10-inning, 18-16 win, April 17, 1976

1998 MVP Sammy Sosa: only player in history with three 60-homer seasons (66 in '98, 63 in '99, 64 in 2001); N.L. home run champ in 2000 (50), 2002 (49)

Jon Lieber, Kerry Wood fire back-to-back one-hitters in 3-0 and 1-0 wins over Reds and Brewers, May 24 and 25, 2001

Cubs beat Phillies 26-23 as teams combine for record 49 runs, Aug. 25, 1922

Pete Rose ties baseball's all-time hits record with two singles in game vs. Cubs, Sept. 8, 1985

Pirates' Rennie Stennett goes 7-for-7 in 22-0 victory over Cubs, Sept. 16, 1975

Home of Hack Wilson, who drove in big-league-record 191 runs in 1930

Mr. Cub ERNIE BANKS holds franchise records for games (2,528), home runs (512) and total bases (4,706). "Let's play two!"

No pennant has flown at Wrigley since 1945, when Cubs lost their last World Series to Tigers

14,000-seat Federal League base under the alias of Weeghman Park. It stands today, almost nine decades later, as a stately 39,059-seat baseball time machine, one of the few places you can go to experience the game as it was presented a half century ago. Billed nonchalantly as "Home of the Cubs," Wrigley more accurately is a sanctuary for the entire baseball world and one of the last bastions for many of the game's fading traditions.

That's a perception Chicago's North Siders take seriously. This is neighborhood ball, the kind where venue, team and surroundings live in perfect harmony with each other and with the city of which all are an intricate part. Wrigleyville is all about the Cubs; the Cubs are all about the mystique fans associate with baseball through their childhood memories. Lovable, affable, colorful, entertaining and frustrating underachievers, they light up a com-

You know you've reached Wrigley Field when you see the colorful red sign (left) at the main entrance. Life is fine, friendly and fun in the outfield bleachers (below, above left) at any Cubs game.

munity and are rewarded with a shower of loyal, undying affection.

Wrigleyville buzzes on game day—a tunnel-vision baseball experience that includes corner taverns, an old-fashioned red-brick fire station, narrow residential streets, the rumble of nearby elevated trains, noisy bleacherites lining up for tickets, expectant fans waiting on Waveland Avenue for batting-practice home runs, vendors hawking their wares, a lifesize statue of Harry Caray and voices from the rooftops of brownstone apartments, some of which provide free views into the ballpark below.

For a first-time visitor, a pregame refresher at Murphy's Bleachers or the Cubby Bear Lounge might be needed to prepare for the unexplainable shiver that's sure to come with a first sighting of the giant red "Wrigley Field: Home of Chicago Cubs" sign that has marked the corner of Clark and Addison streets for generations of fans. Everything around the park's white, blue-trimmed exterior cries out baseball, from the corner hot dog and ice cream stands to the team flags that blow in the breezes along the stadium's outer rim.

The outside of Wrigley is nostalgia; the inside is pure, unadulterated ambience. The open, green-grass field spreads out before you like a Norman Rockwell painting—pure Americana, not as quirky or cozy as Boston's Fenway Park, but intimate and refreshing in ways Fenway cannot match. In a burst of Ernie Banks-like enthusiasm, you have an immediate yearning to "play two." No matter where you sit, you're part of the game—you can almost reach out and touch someone in a white, blue-striped uniform.

If Wrigley's not the most visual ballpark in the major leagues, it's close. From ivy-covered walls and distinctive wooden bleachers to the largest manual scoreboard still in use, baseball is played here with old-time flavor and the kind of charisma the new-era retro parks aspire to, but somehow never quite attain.

Nothing in baseball can compare to the thick, green ivy that covers the red-brick outfield wall, a brainstorm of young Bill Veeck during a 1937 ballpark renovation. Patches of brick peek out from ivy cutouts, revealing big yellow numbers that mark the outfield distances. The wall, uncovered in foul territory, circles the rest of the perimeter, providing a distinctive brick divider for player and fan.

Above the outfield wall, rising before you in all their rowdy glory, are the

Big yellow numbers on the red-brick wall, telling the distance down the left field line, offer a striking contrast to Wrigley's thick green ivy.

most famous bleachers in the game, another product of the 1937 makeover. The boomerang-shaped bleachers begin at a narrow point in both corners, widen symmetrically as you move through the outfield and then crest dramatically in center field—a melting pot for partiers, shirtless sun worshipers and the park's most boisterous rooters.

Perched atop the bleacher crest is a 27-foot manual scoreboard, slightly off-kilter with home plate and topped by a round clock that brings the board's height above the field to 85 feet. Inside that hollow structure toil Wrigley's most anonymous statisticians and the rear of the board marks the outside corner of Sheffield and Waveland—with a photo of a pennant and the words "Chicago Cubs."

Amazingly, no one has ever driven a ball off the face of the scoreboard—even with the infamous home run-aiding wind gusting over the fence toward nearby Lake Michigan. Pittsburgh's Roberto Clemente and former Cub Bill Nicholson came close, but prodigious home runs are measured here by their landing points on Waveland and Sheffield—streets frequently visited by such power hitters as Banks, Billy Williams, Nicholson, Ron Santo, Dave Kingman, Ryne Sandberg and, of course, current record chaser Sammy Sosa.

It was during the bleacher construction that the park gained its most unusual feature—an inward jog of both the left and right field fences, resulting in an odd situation in which home runs hit 30 or 40 feet inside the foul poles have to travel shorter distances than those hit down the lines. Those lines measure a hefty 355 to left and 353 to right, not too much different than friendly power alleys of 368. But dimensions are irrelevant when the wind blows out—or the ill, cold winds off the lake turn Wrigley into a pitcher's paradise.

The Cubs have always been vulnerable to the unpredictable whims of Lake Michigan. After being acquired by Charles H. Weeghman in 1916, they moved into his lakeside ballpark and began a long North Side association that would blossom under the eventual ownership of chewing gum magnate William Wrigley. Cubs Park was renamed Wrigley Field in 1926, the same year the facility's first important makeover took place—a second deck was added to the entire foul-territory grandstand, almost doubling the park's capacity.

Wrigley's wild-and-crazy bleacher fans have formed an understandably close relationship with Cubs right fielder Sammy Sosa.

WRIGLEY FIELD (1916-)

Also known as Cubs Park (1916-1926)

For a park long identified by a single name — it has been Wrigley Field since 1926 — the history of baseball at Clark and Addison has not been so simple.

Baseball at that North Side corner predated even the Cubs. Ground was broken for the site in 1914 for Charlie Weeghman's Federal League team. Originally named North Side Ball Park, it was changed in 1914 to Weeghman Park and again in 1915 to Whales Park—reflecting the nickname of Weeghman's Federal League team.

In 1916, Weeghman headed a group that included William Wrigley Jr. and purchased the Cubs. The team played its first game that year in newly named Cubs Park. Weeghman sold controlling interest in the team to Wrigley in 1918 and the new owner renamed the park Wrigley Field in the middle of the 1926 season.

The outfield ivy and famed bleacher seats became part of Wrigley Field's lore during an extensive 1937 ballpark makeover.

First game: April 20, 1916. Cubs Win! ... Cubs Win! ... Gene Packard gets credit for a 7-6 victory in 11 innings over the Cincinnati Reds.

■ Site of six World Series (1918, '29, '32, '35, '38, '45)
■ Site of three All-Star Games (1947, '62 and '90)

The back of Wrigley is notable for its 'Chicago Cubs' pennant and flags that blow in the Lake Michigan breezes atop the scoreboard.

That soon paid dividends. The 1929 Cubs won a National League pennant and began a run that would net five more pennants through 1945. Players like Hack Wilson, Nicholson, Gabby Hartnett, Charlie Grimm, Charlie Root, Claude Passeau, Bill Lee and Stan Hack passed through the friendly confines, as did any Cubs' championship hopes. The team would never win another pennant, much less a World Series title.

The big renovation of 1937 came under the direction of Philip K. Wrigley, William's son. He added the bleachers, installed a new scoreboard on its current center field perch and created many of the physical nuances that have become so much a part of the ballpark's lore. Wrigley, home of baseball's first organ and the first Ladies Day promotion, has maintained its basic personality since that renovation and many of those nuances still exist as visible reminders of years gone by.

Reminders such as the flags, banks of which fly atop the scoreboard, representing every National League team in order of that day's standings. Centering those banners is an American flag that is replaced after each game by either a white flag with a blue "W" signaling victory, or a blue flag with a white "L" sig-

naling defeat. Two Hall of Fame numbers fly atop the foul-pole flags—Banks' 14 in left, Williams' 26 in right, and team flags circle the inner rim of the park.

Wrigley also has been known for two things you didn't see.

For many years, the Cubs refused to add lights, giving the ballpark distinction as the champion of daytime baseball—a Wrigley trademark embraced by fans and baseball locals. Baseball in the sunshine, the way "it was meant to be played," endured until 1988, when Cubs officials finally gave in, installed light standards and played the first night baseball on Chicago's North Side.

The team always has refused to plaster advertisements all over the park,

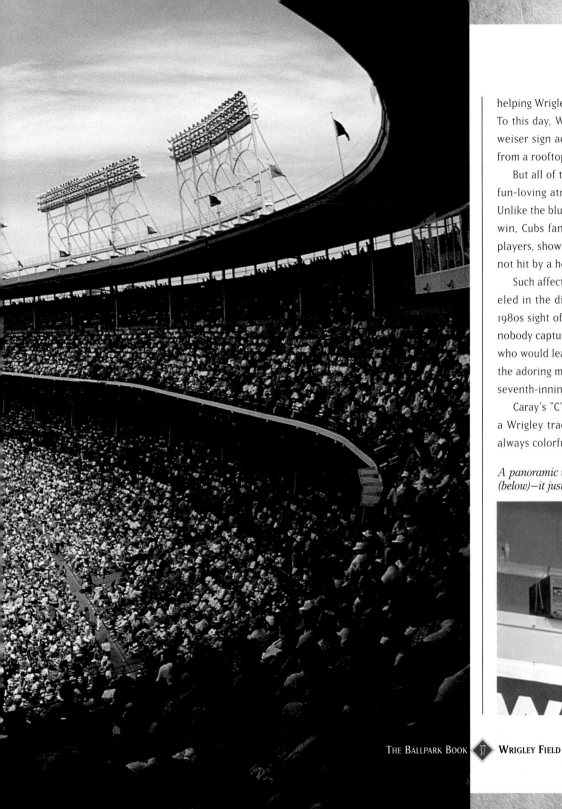

helping Wrigley maintain a clean, natural look that few other parks can claim. To this day, Wrigley remains relatively advertisement free, except for a Budweiser sign across the foot of the scoreboard and a "Torco" sign that hangs from a rooftop beyond the right field wall.

But all of that Wrigley ambience would be cosmetic without the laid-back, fun-loving atmosphere created by some of the most social fans in baseball. Unlike the blue-collar South Siders who go to a White Sox game to watch them win, Cubs fans are interested in having a good time. They heckle opposing players, shower affection on their favorite Cubs and throw back any home run not hit by a hometowner—like a fish that's too small.

Such affection is not reserved just for Cubs in uniform. For years, fans reveled in the distinctive "Hey, heys" of broadcaster Jack Brickhouse and the 1980s sight of retired—and shirtless—Bill Veeck in the outfield bleachers. But nobody captured Wrigley's flavor more than the colorful, beer-drinking Caray, who would lean out of his broadcast-booth perch behind home plate, wave to the adoring masses below and exhort them to join in one of the most popular seventh-inning stretch traditions in baseball history.

Caray's "C'mon everybody! Let me hear you now!" exhortation lives on as a Wrigley tradition, now delivered by guest celebrities who lead fans in an always colorful rendition of "Take me out to the Ballgame."

A panoramic view of packed Wrigley Field with Harry Caray at the microphone (below)—it just couldn't get any better for Chicago North Siders.

Yankee
Stadium

Joe McCarthy managed 8 pennant-winners, 7 champions ... Joe Torre has claimed 5 pennants, 4 World Series titles

Reggie Jackson, a k a Mr. October, hits three home runs in Game 6 of '77 Series . . . all on first pitches

Where Dodger Sandy Amoros raced into corner to rob Yogi Berra and save Game 7 of 1955 World Series

MONUMENT PARK Miller Huggins, Ruth, Lou Gehrig, DiMaggio and Mickey Mantle

A's second baseman Randy Velarde turns 10th regular-season unassisted triple play in game against Yankees, May 29, 2000

Grover Alexander comes out of bullpen to face Tony Lazzeri in '26 Series

Where Dodger Al Gionfriddo made spectacular catch of DiMaggio's long drive in Game 6 of '47 World Series

Where Johnny Lindell's slide into Whitey Kurowski was turning point of '43 Series

She stands as a cathedral, a monument to glories past—made over, spruced up and overhauled beyond the recognition of many old-timers who worshiped there. Yankee Stadium might not be the grand old lady she used to be, but her eloquence stretches well beyond the borders of baseball time. Her patrons have witnessed more drama, her heroes have inspired more prose and her championship banners have produced more emotion than any athletic arena in the world.

To walk through her gates is a religious experience. An aura of greatness, an unexplainable mys-

BABE RUTH, the Sultan of Swat, 714 life-time home runs, .690 career slugging average, 60 home runs in '27, 177 runs scored in '21

Yankees post A.L.-record 114 wins and overall 125-50 mark en route to record 24th World Series crown and second in three years, 1998

THE PERFECT PLACE Don Larsen shocked the baseball world with his perfect game in 1956 World Series. David Wells also was perfect on May 17, 1998, and David Cone on July 18, 1999

Remodeled Yankee
Stadium opened
April 15, 1976

1999 Yankees close out century
with another World Series win
... 2000 Yankees beat Mets in
Subway Series, win 26th
championship

Where Roger Maris hit
homer No. 61, Oct. 1, 1961

CASEY STENGEL managed
10 pennant winners:
'49,
'50,
'51,
'52,
'53,
'55,
'56,
'57,
'58,
'60

Mickey Mantle hits shot
off facade, May 22, 1963

K.C.'s George Brett
hits third-deck
homer that cooks
Yankees' Goose in
Game 3 of the 1980
ALCS

Mickey Mantle hits
500th career homer,
May 14, 1967

Where Chris Chambliss hit
ALCS-winning home run in 1976

Where 12-year-old Jeffrey
Maier made the catch of his
life on Derek Jeter's home run
bid in Game 1 of 1996 ALCS

Where Roger Clemens
raised ire of Mets and
Mike Piazza in 2000
... claimed record 6th
Cy Young in 2001

Site of K.C. third
baseman George
Brett's Pine Tar tirade,
July 24, 1983

JOLTIN' JOE DIMAGGIO,
center fielder for
9 World Series
champions. He started
56-game hitting streak
here, May 15, 1941

Lou Gehrig Day, July 4, 1939
A farewell to the Iron Horse,
"the luckiest man on the face
of the Earth"

Tino Martinez, Scott Brosius hit two-out,
two-run, game-tying, ninth-inning
home runs on consecutive nights to stun
Diamondbacks in Games 4 and 5 of 2001
Series ... Jeter, Alfonso Soriano provide
game-winning hits

Grand, pennant-filled Yankee Stadium provided the perfect backdrop for Babe Ruth's farewell to New York fans in 1948.

tique hangs over the great edifice like a thick fog. This is the Temple of Sport, where the New York gods created a masterpiece and dressed it in pinstripes.

This is where Babe Ruth hit 60 home runs while leading the charge for the most feared team in baseball history. This is the former home of Murderer's Row, the Iron Horse, the Yankee Clipper and the Old Professor. This is where Don Larsen pitched his perfect World Series game, Lou Gehrig delivered the Gettysburg Address of baseball, Mickey Mantle launched a stadium-threatening rocket and Roger Maris set off a record-shattering bomb.

"Where have you gone Joe DiMaggio?" wasn't merely a line from a song here—it was a lament that drifted through the Bronx for years after his 1951 retirement. "Mr. October" wasn't just a nickname here, it was Reggie Jackson's ticket into New York's elite postseason society.

"Elite" is an adjective that fits Yankee Stadium, the home of 26 championship teams and stage for 103 World Series games. More than a quarter of the 98 World Series played have been won by the Yankees, which explains the dignified, almost-arrogant aura that grips every visitor who walks through the turnstile.

The tradition has been a constant, from that April 18, 1923, day when "The House That Ruth Built" opened its gates for the first time. But this is actually a tale of two stadiums, one reflective of the quiet elegance inspired by Jacob Ruppert, Tillinghast Huston, Ed Barrow, Miller Huggins, Joe McCarthy and all the workmanlike Yankees championship teams through the 1973 season, and another featuring the Bronx Zoo atmosphere of a

A 1950s bullpen view shows the park's imposing grandstand and trademark facade. Fans (below) were warned about the team's strict rules of conduct.

refurbished Yankee Stadium, inspired by George Steinbrenner.

The Good Old Days

Early Yankee Stadium commanded a reverence that differentiated it from other arenas of its generation. Whereas Ebbets Field, located across the East River in Brooklyn, was known for its rollicking fun and zany characters, visitors to Yankee Stadium behaved with a more reserved dignity, a "we're better than you" arrogance supported by the quiet, businesslike manner in which their team went about winning pennants and championships. Ebbets was a cozy, home-style ballpark; Yankee Stadium was a massive, corporate-minded stadium.

It was expansive beyond the imagination of anybody setting foot through its gates for the first time. It rose up around you like a baseball canyon, its farthest third-deck seat about three or four echoes distant. It was big, like the city that surrounded it and the egos of the baseball teams that competed there.

Quirks and personality were exhibited in many forms. The roof that jutted over the upper stands was rimmed by a pale green facade that gave the park a distinctive, almost regal look. A scoreboard rose from ground level above the open right-center field wall, where passengers on the elevated train could get quick glimpses of action and freeloaders on rooftops and a train station platform could watch an entire game. Green wooden seats seemed to blend into a lush grass carpet that was maintained with obsessive diligence.

The Yankees added a huge helping of character in 1932 when a monument to former manager Huggins was erected in dead center field, in fair ground under the flagpole, about 10 feet in front of the wall. Gehrig and Ruth monuments joined Huggins in 1941 and '49, with plaques of former owner Ruppert and others adding to the mystique. The Yankees further charmed their fans by allowing them to exit every game through the center field gate, after pausing and paying homage to their departed heroes.

Over the years, the team's proud tradition became more and more a part of the Yankee Stadium experience through championship photos that greeted visitors outside the gates and expansive action photos of individuals that grabbed their attention once inside.

But nowhere were the Yankee Stadium quirks more pronounced than on a playing field tailored to the power stroke of Ruth. True to form, the Bambino dedicated the giant structure in 1923 with a three-run homer into a short right field porch that measured only 296 feet down the line.

"The biggest crowd in baseball history rose to its feet and let loose the biggest shout in baseball history," reported the New York Times, accepting an official record fan count of 74,200 that officials later admitted was padded.

The overview (above) shows old Yankee Stadium with the Polo Grounds in the background, just across the Harlem River. Improved transportation helped make Yankee Stadium a New York showplace by 1925 (right).

While lefthanders were taking shots at the short right field porch, righthanders were losing would-be home runs in the vast left-center field pasture known as "Death Valley." The left field line was only 301 feet, but the fence arced deeply toward a distant center field wall that measured 461. That's where the monuments were positioned, forming a frustrating obstacle for center fielders who allowed balls to get over their heads.

That didn't happen often to the Yankees, who spoiled fans for more than three decades with the superior center field play of DiMaggio and Mantle.

Something New

You stand at the main entrance of refurbished Yankee Stadium, in the

Monuments of Huggins, Gehrig and Ruth once stood in fair territory at Yankee Stadium. Now they're part of a Monument Park display beyond the left-center field fence.

shadow of a giant bat that stands majestically on one end, and you're filled with the same sense of awe that greeted fans of yesteryear. It still rises above you in all of its expansive glory, it still reeks of success and heroic deeds and it still smells and feels like the Yankee Stadium of Ruth and Gehrig and Gomez must have felt decades ago.

But make no mistake, this is not the Yankee Stadium of Ruth and Gehrig. It's a younger, sleeker, prettier and more modern Yankee Stadium, the championship playground of Jackson, Munson, Guidry, Nettles, Randolph and Jeter.

There are reminders. Nostalgic team and individual photographs still overpower you when you step through the turnstiles, the expanse and atmosphere still trigger emotions and the calming, perfect-diction words of public address announcer Bob Sheppard still provide elegant respites. They're illusions that mask what really

Ticket booths were plentiful and grandstand prices were right outside old Yankee Stadium.

is a facsimile of the old Stadium.

Patrons no longer are subjected to coronary-inducing climbs to the upper deck, thanks to a series of escalators and elevators. Gone are the sight-impeding pillars that supported the two upper tiers, giving every seat in the house a near-perfect sight line. Gone, too, is the roof and the facade that once gave the facility its regal air.

It's hard to keep your eyes off a massive 560-foot-long scoreboard that covers a wall blocking view of the once-prominent elevated trains and neighboring rooftops. The new wall is topped by a concrete facsimile that reminds fans of the old facade. Also missing are the center field monuments, which now reside in a special "Monument Park" located behind the left-center field fence.

While the general shape of the field has been retained over the years, the fence distances have become much less imposing for righthanded

hitters and the coloring of the stadium has changed from green to bright blue with a stately white trim. Even the feel of the games is different.

With the makeover has come a different breed of team and a new, less-patient generation of fan. Gone is the dignified approach of those amazingly consistent championship teams featuring Ruth, Gehrig, Lefty Gomez, Waite Hoyt, Bill Dickey, Yogi Berra, Whitey Ford and Mantle. The Steinbrenner Yankees have featured more volatile personalities like Billy Martin, Thurman Munson, Ron Guidry, Jackson, Sparky Lyle, Graig Nettles, Willie Randolph, Don Mattingly and Dave Winfield. The Bronx Bombers have given way to the Bronx Zoo and fans, suffering through the first serious pennant drought in the Stadium's 50-year history, have become impatient, loud and occasionally rowdy.

The defining moment of 1976, new Yankee Stadium's first season, came in

Yankee Stadium's scoreboard operator in 1948 viewed games through small slots, hidden from general view inside the giant right-center field structure.

Game 5 of the American League Championship Series against Kansas City, when Chris Chambliss secured the first Yankee pennant in 12 years with a home run, then feared for his life as he attempted to circle the bases while being mobbed by crazed fans.

The end result is a different kind of Yankee Stadium—still the House of Champions, but now catering to a rowdier, younger crowd that is tougher for opposing players and those Yankees not performing up to expectations. Through the transformation, the winning mystique continues. World Series titles in 1996, '98, '99 and 2000, with players like Derek Jeter, Bernie Williams, Paul O'Neill, Tino Martinez, David Cone and Mariano Rivera operating with the businesslike efficiency of old, brought the curtain down on an incredible eight decades of baseball excellence.

In the proudest, grandest stadium the sports world has ever produced.

YANKEE STADIUM (1923-)

Facing eviction from the Polo Grounds, a home they had shared with the rival Giants since 1913, Yankees owner Jacob Ruppert purchased the land on which Yankee Stadium stands in 1921. It took only two years to build baseball's showcase arena, which opened its gates for the first time in 1923.

Original plans called for a three-deck grandstand to encircle the stadium, but that was scaled back with the original grandstand not even reaching the foul poles. In 1928, the grandstand in left field was extended to its current point, and in 1937, the right field grandstand was expanded around the foul pole.

In 1946, lights came. In 1967, the green grandstand seats were painted blue. And in 1976, after two seasons in Shea Stadium to allow for major renovations, a new Yankee Stadium, one without supportive steel pillars that obstructed the view of the fans, opened.

The greatest legacy of Yankee Stadium is its 26 World Series championships, the last four under manager Joe Torre (right).

Through it all, one element has remained constant— the facade, Yankee Stadium's most-recognizable feature. The stately, elegant green facade once adorned the rim of the grandstand; today's replica version spans the top of the scoreboard from the left field to right field grandstand.

Even with all of that history oozing at you from every corner of the ballpark, there's nothing like Monument Park, a memorial that today resides behind the wall in left-center field and honors Yankee greats Miller Huggins, Lou Gehrig, Babe Ruth, Joe DiMaggio and Mickey Mantle.

First game: April 18, 1923. Babe Ruth christened the new stadium with a home run in the Yankees' 4-1 victory over the Boston Red Sox.

■ Site of 36 World Series (1923, '26, '27, '28, '32, '36, '37, '38, '39, '41, '42, '43, '47, '49, '50, '51, '52, '53, '55, '56, '57, '58, '60, '61, '62, '63, '64, '76, '77, '78, '81, '96, '98, '99, 2000, 2001)

■ Site of three All-Star Games (1939, '60, '77)

The Middle Ages

They were products of baseball's Middle Ages, that period from 1953 through 1969 when the game relocated and expanded to parts unknown.

Los Angeles' Dodger Stadium and the Oakland Coliseum were either built or renovated for teams shifting operations from other cities; Anaheim Stadium, New York's Shea Stadium and San Diego's Jack Murphy Stadium were built for expansion teams.

All have undergone cosmetic changes, even major surgery, to help them make the transition to a new millennium. Some have even changed their personality, from baseball-only to multi-purpose.

But their time is fleeting, some with more immediacy than others, as plans are being drawn and votes are being cast. They're starting to hear the whispers, sometimes shouts, of inadequacy, that it's time to rebuild for a new generation of fan.

Anaheim
Stadium

Also known as Edison International Field of Anaheim (1997-)

Destination of Dave Henderson homer off Donnie Moore in Game 5 of 1986 ALCS—a stunning blow that denied Angels first pennant

Where Rod Carew (left) drove a pitch from Minnesota lefty Frank Viola for 3,000th career hit, Aug. 4, 1985

Alex Johnson becomes Angels' only batting champion . . . .329 in 1970

Lefthanded complement: Frank Tanana, Chuck Finley, Mark Langston, Clyde Wright, Jim Abbott find success in Anaheim

NOLAN RYAN struck fear into opposing hitters with his powerful right arm, 1972-79

Don Baylor and Fred Lynn power Angels in Games 1 and 2 of 1982 ALCS, but Brewers rally for three straight wins at Milwaukee

A.L. West champs 1979, '82, '86 — always an ALCS bridesmaid

The Big A, banished to a corner of the Anaheim Stadium parking lot, still towers majestically over the mortality below. Long removed from its perch beyond the left field fence, it now flashes its giant halo at passing motorists, spreading the good news of Angels' victories. At first glance, the 230-foot, A-framed former scoreboard seems over-qualified for such work. But in this world of retro-fitted, fan-friendly, throwback ballparks, it provides a powerful and necessary reminder of humble beginnings.

Anaheim Stadium is perfect testimony to the adage, "What goes

The "Big A" undergoes facelift, changes from open to enclosed stadium, 1981

Bobby Grich's 11th-inning single completes big comeback in Game 4 of 1986 ALCS and gives Angels three-games-to-one edge over Red Sox

Reggie Jackson hits 500th career homer on Sept. 17, 1984—same date and place where he hit first major league homer 17 years earlier for A's

Ryan blows away 383rd batter in Sept. 27, 1973 game vs. Twins, sets major league single-season strikeout record

George Brett collects fourth hit of game, 3,000th of career, off Tim Fortugno, Sept. 30, 1992

Don Baylor
(36 homers, 139 RBIs)
1979 A.L. MVP

Bo Jackson, Wade Boggs hit back-to-back homers leading off game, trigger 5-3 A.L. All-Star win, July 11, 1989

Yankees reliever Ron Davis strikes out eight straight Angels, May 4, 1981

Tony Perez's 15th-inning homer off Catfish Hunter ends longest game in All-Star history, July 11, 1967

2000 A.L. leaders: third baseman Troy Glaus 47 homers; outfielder Darin Erstad 240 hits

Angels finally win one for the Cowboy. ... Garret Anderson's three-run double secures 4-1 win over Giants, team's first championship, Oct. 27, 2002

Where Ryan posted two of his four Angels' no-hitters, beating Twins 4-0 in 1974 and Orioles 1-0 in 1975

Don Sutton (left) pitches Angels to 5-1 win over Rangers, notches 300th career victory, June 18, 1986

BRIAN DOWNING:
Angels' career leader in runs, hits, home runs, total bases, RBIs and extra-base hits

Three Angels top 100 RBIs in 1995—Jim Edmonds (107), Tim Salmon (105), J.T. Snow (102)

around, comes around." It opened in 1966 as a baseball-only facility, was enclosed in a 1979-80 cookie-cutter renovation that added 20,000 seats for football's Los Angeles Rams and was given a 1996-97 Disney makeover that knocked out 20,000 seats, reopened the outfield and transformed the stadium back into a ballpark—with splashy Camden Yards and Coors Field-type retro trimmings.

You don't get the glitzy, Hollywood feel of Los Angeles neighbor Dodger Stadium, but you quickly get the idea that Anaheim Stadium is a production—choreographed and directed like the visitor-friendly Disneyland, which is located only two miles away in suburban Anaheim. You are greeted at the gate by two giant caps and the main-entrance awning is supported by huge baseball bats. The exterior has been modernized, garden-like greenery and palm trees circle the facility and everything is immaculately clean, from the outdoor plazas to the well-lit concourses and precisely-placed concession stands.

And, of course, you are served by the most courteous attendants and ushers in baseball. "Convenience, Comfort and Courtesy" has always been the Anaheim Stadium motto and that hasn't changed. But the Disney Angels also are obsessed with the park's visual impact—much of which has been borrowed from other facilities.

Intimacy is the goal and Anaheim Stadium was originally designed with that in mind. Limited foul territory puts seats close to the field and a well-designed three-tiered grandstand stretches from foul pole to foul pole, with the highest seats seemingly close to the action. On a clear day, the newly-opened outfield provides a wonderful view of the San Gabriel Mountains and The Pond, the arena where Disney's Mighty Ducks play hockey, can be spotted over the left-center field fence.

This park can make out-of-towners feel at home. A Coors Field-like retro scoreboard looms over outfield bleachers in right-center, complete with video board, JumboTron display and other state-of-the-art goodies. A Jacobs Field-like out-of-town scoreboard is built into the right-center field fence, Camden-like terraced bullpens are visible in left and a rock pile in left-center is a clever disguise for a Kauffman Stadium-like water display. Behind-the-plate dugout suites offer a field-level view, similar to Dodger Stadium.

Two Anaheim Stadium quirks have remained constant through all of its makeovers—a 4.75-foot high home run fence in both corners, where the ends of the grandstand jut into play, and the laid-back, late-arriving Southern California fans who often seem more interested in the social experience and less passionate about winning and losing than fans in other ballparks.

The distances down both lines are 330 feet, but that's where the symmetry ends. Both short fences, which sometimes force outfielders to wrestle eager fans for potential home run balls, roll out quickly to deep power alleys that turn Anaheim into a pitcher's park. The power alley in right-center is 370 feet, 26 shorter than its counterpart in left center. The 408-foot center field crest fronts an 18-foot fence and a dark

When Anaheim Stadium opened in 1966, the halo-topped Big A was a hulking presence over the left field fence (below, right), a combination scoreboard and landmark. During a later renovation, the Big A, no longer a scoreboard, was relegated to its current location in the stadium's parking lot (right inset).

hitter's backdrop. A small bleacher section in left and extended bleachers in right offer prime views of the action.

Anaheim Stadium has come a long way since its 1966 debut—when the Los Angeles Angels, then under the fatherly direction of "Singing Cowboy" Gene Autry, relocated there and changed their name to California Angels. The grandstand layout and beautiful grass carpet were much the same then and the outfield was open, without the retro frills of today. Light standards and the Big A, which served as the park's original scoreboard, were the only obstructions for balls launched toward the nether reaches of Anaheim.

"The first chill I ever received in this game came when I walked into the Polo Grounds for the first time. I received another when I walked into this park," said then-Angels manager Bill Rigney after getting his first look at what soon would become known as "the Big A."

This was the Anaheim Stadium of Jim Fregosi, Alex Johnson, Bobby Knoop, Frank Tanana, Clyde Wright and a young, flame-throwing Nolan Ryan. The later, 65,000-seat enclosed version belonged to the Rod Carew, Don Baylor, Fred Lynn, Brian Downing, Bobby Grich, Wally Joyner, Doug DeCinces, Bobby Witt and Mark Langston teams that won three division titles and even came within one pitch of securing the Angels' first

ANAHEIM STADIUM (1966-)

Renamed Edison International Field of Anaheim (1997-)

When awarded an expansion franchise in 1960, the "Los Angeles" Angels began looking for a place to call their own. Their dream wouldn't be realized until 1965, after playing their 1961 inaugural season at tiny Wrigley Field in Los Angeles and the next four as tenants—unhappy tenants—of the Dodgers at Dodger Stadium.

Farmland in Anaheim, with easy access to major highways, was finally selected as the ballpark site, in part because of population studies that showed it would be the center of a growing metropolitan area. Another candidate, Long Beach, was eliminated in part because the team objected to the city's demand that the club be renamed "Long Beach" Angels.

The team existed as the Los Angeles Angels through 1965 and as the "California" Angels from 1966-96, at which point the Walt Disney Company took control. Disney renamed the team "Anaheim" Angels.

First game: April 19, 1966. Chicago White Sox pitcher Tommy John, who would play for the Angels 16 years later, was the winning pitcher in a 3-1 Chicago victory.

■ Site of one World Series (2002)
■ Site of two All-Star Games (1967 and '89)

Two giant caps and a baseball bat-supported awning greet visitors at the main entrance (above) of the renamed Edison Field. A rock pile water display (right) dresses up the scenery over the left-center field fence.

World Series appearance—a hope that was denied by Boston center fielder Dave Henderson's 1986 ALCS home run, one of the most shocking blows in baseball history.

It was the kind of drama that appeals to today's impact-minded Disney Angels, complete, at last, with a happy ending. Sixteen years after that disappointment, Anaheim Stadium played host to its first World Series championship—a seven-game Angels triumph over the San Francisco Giants.

Dodger Stadium

Montreal's Dennis Martinez retires all 27 Dodgers he faces in perfect 2-0 victory, July 28, 1991

Ironman Mike Marshall (a record 106 games) becomes first reliever to win Cy Young, 1974

Jack Clark's ninth-inning, three-run homer off Tom Niedenfuer shocks Dodgers in Game 6 of 1985 NLCS

In short there's simply not a more congenial spot, for happily ever-aftering than here in Ca-me-lot.

Back-to-back seventh-inning homers by Pedro Guerrero, Steve Yeager give Jerry Reuss 2-1 win over Yankees in Game 5 of 1981 World Series

Where Cubs' Rick Monday snatched American flag away from protestors who were trying to burn it, April 25, 1976

Walter Alston won his 2,000th game as manager, July 17, 1976

King Arthur would have approved of Dodger Stadium. He would have liked the laid-back atmosphere of the place and the way color literally explodes before your eyes. And the trees and the flowers and its near perfect harmony with nature. And, of course, the weather—it couldn't rain until after sundown in Camelot; in Chavez Ravine, it seldom rains at all.

But unlike Camelot, Dodger

SANDY KOUFAX: Dominated N.L. hitters here from 1961-66 with five straight ERA titles, four strikeout titles, one MVP and three Cy Youngs

1965 switch-hitting infield: Wes Parker 1B, Jim Lefebvre 2B, Maur Wills SS, Jim Gilliam 3B

Where Orel Hershiser compiled many of his record 59 consecutive scoreless innings in 1988

Giants score four runs in ninth, defeat Dodgers 6-4 in third game of playoff to determine N.L. pennant, Oct. 3, 1962

Orioles reliever Moe Drabowsky strikes out 11 Dodgers in Game 1 of '66 World Series

Rookie Fernando Valenzuela becomes baseball sensation en route to 1981 Cy Young

Cardinal Fernando Tatis goes where no player has gone before—two grand slams in one inning, April 23, 1999

Shawn Green sets franchise single-season home run record with 49 in 2001, including three in Aug. 15 win over Expos

World Series champs in 1963, '65, '81, '88 World Series losers in 1966, '74, '77, '78

Where gimpy Kirk Gibson hit dramatic two-out, two-run, ninth-inning homer off Dennis Eckersley to beat A's in Game 1 of 1988 World Series

Four balls have been hit out of Dodger Stadium: Willie Stargell 1969, 1973; Mike Piazza 1997; Mark McGwire 1999

Where Willie Davis made three errors in fifth inning of World Series Game 2 vs. Orioles, Oct. 6, 1966

Where Phillies' Garry Maddox dropped Dusty Baker's line drive, setting up winning run in 1978 NLCS

Maury Wills finishes record-breaking 1962 season with steals 103 and 104 in finale of pennant playoff series vs. Giants

Site of Koufax's perfect game vs. Cubs, Sept. 9, 1965 . . . Where he set N.L. single-season strikeout record with 382 in 1965

1974 MVP STEVE GARVEY: Top gun of long-running infield that included Ron Cey, Bill Russell and Davey Lopes

Don Drysdale shuts out Yankees on three hits, posts club's first World Series win at Dodger Stadium, Oct. 5, 1963

Huge photographic 'banners' of current Dodgers decorate the outside facade at Dodger Stadium, providing an inspirational beginning to a fan's baseball experience.

Stadium is no mythical wonderland. Its one brief shining moment has been sustained for almost four decades in one of the most pristine baseball settings imaginable. Nestled in the tree-lined Elysian hills, with the purple San Gabriel Mountains standing guard to the north and a breathtaking view of downtown Los Angeles available to the south, it looks like an Arthurian castle, perched on a pedestal for approaching visitors to look up to and admire.

The approach, from the network of expressways that feed into 21 terraced lots, is a memorable part of the Dodger Stadium experience. It glitters high above you in the bright sunlight; it offers a beautiful light show at night. Your eyes become locked on the structure, oblivious to the magnificent landscaping—more than 3,400 trees, grassy landings, colorful flowers—that surrounds you as you ride the escalator up, up, up.

The Dodgers take great pride in the look—and the almost obsessive cleanliness—of their summer playground. The concourses of Yankee Stadium and Fenway Park are old, dingy reminders of baseball past. The corridors of Dodger Stadium are colorful, freshly-painted hallways, with floors so clean you could eat off them.

It almost becomes too much—that antiseptic sense of perfection. But then you step into the field area and back to reality—baseball reality, complete with sparkling green grass, rich brown dirt and all the sights and sounds you might expect from a ballpark visit.

From the parking lot behind the right field bleachers (top), approaching fans can get a close look at palm trees and the wavy pavilion roof that is distinctive to Dodger Stadium. This panoramic view (right) shows colorful Dodger Stadium looking out on the tree-lined Elysian hills beyond the outfield fences.

DODGER STADIUM (1962-)

Dug out of a hilly section of earth known as Chavez Ravine two miles from the center of downtown Los Angeles, colorful, sparkling, symmetrical Dodger Stadium was hailed as baseball's Taj Mahal when it opened its gates to startled fans in 1962.

Those fans had been more intuned to the dingy, oddly configured nuances of the Los Angeles Memorial Coliseum, the converted football edifice in which the Dodgers played four seasons after relocating from Brooklyn in 1958. The Coliseum's left field foul pole was an inviting 251 feet away from home plate and not even a 40-foot screen could discourage the inevitable—lots of cheap, fly-ball home runs.

But four unpredictable seasons at the Coliseum would be followed by more than four decades of ballpark bliss. Dodger Stadium, a pitcher's park with a baseball-only intimacy, still offers fans an outstanding baseball experience, complete with ideal weather conditions and sweeping, picture-postcard views.

First game: April 10, 1962. The Reds defeated the Dodgers, 6-3.

■ Site of eight World Series (1963, '65, '66, '74, '77, '78, '81 and '88)
■ Site of one All-Star Game (1980)

Dodger Stadium struggles with the intimacy issue, but it's a huge, five-tiered, aging arena that still manages to retain most of the classic ballpark feel. An upper tier wraps from just beyond first base to just beyond third. The other four levels stretch from foul line to foul line, cut off from single-level fair-territory bleachers by bullpens shaded by palm trees. Distinctive wavy-topped roofs hang over the back few rows of the outfield bleachers, a challenging target for gargantuan home runs in what has always been a pitcher's park.

For anybody who has watched a Dodgers game on television, the sight of radar gun-toting Mike Brito is locked in memory. Brito is always standing behind home plate, clocking pitches, in the dugout-level boxes that wrap behind home plate, giving fans a field-level view of the game. Fans in the outfield areas are kept abreast of game progress by field-level auxiliary scoreboards on the sides of both dugouts.

This has been the basic look of Dodger Stadium since 1962, the year it opened as "the Taj Mahal of baseball"—a symmetrical 330 feet down both lines,

the open feel of the outfield, expansive foul territory, especially the area between the dugouts and the infield foul lines, state-of-the-art score and video boards in left- and right-center and 3-foot right and left field fences that connect the foul lines to the bullpens, making shots into the corners a test of restraint for souvenir-hungry fans.

"This edifice is one of the important steps in a new era of the game," raved baseball commissioner Ford Frick after his first look at the facility in 1962. "I expected it would be great. But my wildest imagination did not foresee anything this remarkable."

Attention to detail and Dodgers class have kept it among the best parks in the game. Little things matter here, from the bright, perfectly-pressed uniforms of ushers to comfortable plastic seats and the precise efficiency of the grounds crew between innings. The powerful voice of former public address announcer John Ramsey, Vin Scully at the mike, Dodger Dogs and the trick-shot peanut-delivery artistry of vendor Roger Owens add to the color. But fans are the dimension that sets Dodger Stadium apart from contemporary parks.

They arrive late and leave early, partly because of the horrid Los Angeles traffic and partly because this is the California way. The entire Dodger Stadium experience is very Los Angeles, a stereotypical laid-back, fun and trendy thing to do, complete with stars, starlets and other pretty faces. There's a definite Hollywood feel. Forget the baseball, what better place to watch the sunset on a clear summer night?

But that's not to say fans don't support their Dodgers—and that they aren't rewarded for doing so. This was baseball's first 3-million attendance ballpark, and it's usually full. The Dodgers have rewarded them with eight National League pennants, four World Series winners, eight N.L. West Division crowns and a Who's Who player roster that includes such names as Koufax, Snider, Drysdale, Wills, Sutton, Garvey, Cey, Guerrero, Gibson, Hershiser and Piazza.

Say what you want, but it's hard to ignore the diversity of a ballpark that speaks to you from as many levels as Dodger Stadium. It's beautiful, it's painfully clean, it exudes an old-style charisma, it mimics the personality of its fans and it reeks of success. A real Dodger-blue Camelot in the City of Angels.

Shea Stadium

Tug McGraw's "You Gotta Believe" motto rallies Mets to '73 pennant

Dodgers' Kirk Gibson settles Game 4 of 1988 NLCS in 12th inning with solo home run

Aging Willie Mays celebrates New York return debut with game-winning homer vs. Giants, his former team, May 14, 1972

Phillies' Johnny Callison ends 1964 All-Star Game with dramatic three-run, ninth-inning homer

Phillies' Jim Bunning pitches perfect game on Father's Day, June 21, 1964

Where Cincinnati's Pete Rose was pelted with garbage after his Game 3 fight with shortstop Bud Harrelson in 1973 NLCS

Where Yankees played their home games in '74 and '75

Mike Hampton stops Cardinals, 7-0, on three hits and Mets win first pennant since 1986, Oct. 16, 2000

New York's first Subway World Series since 1956 ends on sour note when Yankees post 4-2 Game 5 win over Mets, Oct. 26, 2000

DWIGHT GOODEN: Doc, 20, became youngest pitcher to win Cy Young and youngest 20-game winner in century, 1985

1999 infield as good as gold: John Olerud (1B), Edgardo Alfonzo (2B), Rey Ordonez (SS), Robin Ventura (3B)

Lenny Dykstra's two-run, ninth-inning homer beats Astros 6-5 in Game 3 of 1986 NLCS

It was a child of the '60s, home of the Amazin' Mets, "New Breed" fans and the craziest kind of baseball ever conceived. Shea Stadium is all grown up now, more mature and sophisticated, but age cannot wipe away the memories. This was the house of Casey Stengel and no-holds-barred fun, where ineptitude didn't matter, wins and losses were meaningless and there was always reason to smile.

That early innocence is long gone now, the smiles have become jaded and, like it or not, winning does matter. But today's Shea Stadium delivers a more enduring kind of charm. Many New Yorkers

Ninth-inning rally beats Marlins, ends Anthony Young's record 27-game losing streak, July 28, 1993

Mets lose to Cardinals in 25th inning when wild pickoff throw to first allows Bake McBride to scurry around bases, Sept. 11, 1974

Casey Stengel called shots for Amazin' Mets. Gil Hodges guided Miracle Mets. Davey Johnson choreographed 1986 championship.

Where Robin Ventura hit game-winning, bases-loaded "single" in 15th inning, ending 1999 NLCS Game 5

Where Seaver struck out 10 straight Padres and 19 total, April 22, 1970 . . . . where he topped 200 strikeouts for nine straight seasons

The Big Apple celebrates Mets home runs

Where Ron Swoboda made his diving catch in Game 4 of '69 Series

Where Tommie Agee robbed Orioles Elrod Hendricks, Paul Blair with game-saving catches in Game 3 of '69 World Series

Where Boston's Bill Buckner missed Mookie Wilson's (right) grounder, allowing Ray Knight to score winning run in World Series-saving Game 6 miracle in 1986

Where masked man Mike Piazza harasses opponents

Where six-time Mets Gold Glover Keith Hernandez (below) dazzled fans . . . Home of power men Gary Carter, Howard Johnson

TOM SEAVER: Three-time Cy Young winner provided anchor for '69 World Series champs, '73 pennant-winners

Mets

still view it as a big, blue, concrete bowl in the heart of Queens—a distant challenger to the incredible New York ballpark legacies of Ebbets Field, Yankee Stadium and the Polo Grounds—but what Shea lacks in history and charisma, it more than makes up for with personality.

To fully appreciate Shea Stadium, you need to understand the context of its first six seasons—a rollicking stretch of fun and unadulterated joy. When Shea made its major league debut in April 1964 as a spectacular showcase stadium in Flushing Park, it was located only a long fly ball or two from the World's Fair, which would draw millions of tourists through 1965. And it offered a different kind of baseball, the bumbling, sometimes-bizarre kind played by the expansion Mets, who had lost 231 games in two seasons under Stengel. Shea was fun and trendy, a place, unlike Yankee Stadium, where younger fans could cut loose.

It was a comedy act that played to rave reviews through 1968, thanks also

Shea glowed (above) in 1964 when it opened amid the hoopla surrounding the nearby World's Fair, the grounds of which can be seen in the upper left and center of the photograph. Shea is much more than a big, blue, concrete bowl, although that wasn't obvious from this 1999 parking lot view (right).

to the shifting of allegiance by jilted Dodgers and Giants fans. There was something going on here and, unlike anywhere else, losing was acceptable. The Mets drew 1.7 million fans in their first Shea season, 400,000 more than the pennant-winning Yankees. And so the fun continued.

But then, just as the comedy was wearing thin, the Amazin' Mets transformed into the Miracle Mets and Shea Stadium played host to its first World Series. Ironically, the 1969 Mets, managed by former Dodgers hero Gil Hodges and led by Cy Young winner Tom Seaver, posted the team's first winning record, won the first of the franchise's two championships—and changed the way Mets fans would view their teams forever.

Shea was a grand showcase when it opened, a high-tech curiosity and the trigger for the so-called cookie-cutter ballpark explosion of the late 1960s and '70s. Pirates manager Danny Murtaugh, who watched his team beat the Mets in the Shea inaugural, called it "a showplace. This will become one of the must visiting places for all tourists to New York, like the Empire State Building, Radio City or the Statue of Liberty," Murtaugh raved.

But later reviews were not so kind. Shea was fingered as a leader in the age of round, symmetrical, turf-covered, multi-purpose facilities that briefly changed the face of baseball. But it dodged much of the criticism that relentlessly dogged later stadiums in Cincinnati, Pittsburgh and Philadelphia. Shea was never enclosed by grandstands, which camouflages its circular shape; its open outfield gives it a baseball-only feel; and real grass and several distinguishing features make it easy to forgive its symmetrical lack of imagination.

The first thing you notice is the openness, a baseball characteristic the National Football League's Jets had to live with for 20 seasons. But your eyes drift quickly to the giant scoreboard that commands much of the right-center field view. The scoreboard, one of baseball's biggest in 1964, now is balanced by a Diamond Vision video display in left-center, a backdrop for the park's few bleacher seats. Next to the scoreboard in center field is the "Big Apple", which celebrates Mets home runs.

More than 90 percent of Shea's blue, red, orange and green seats are located in foul territory, which adds to the open feeling. But that is offset by the five-tiered grandstands that climb precipitously high above the field. A curious architectural quirk can be found down both lines, where the grandstands edge inside the 338-foot foul poles, providing small fair-territory home run targets.

A visit to Shea is not complete without the roar of passing planes into and

The Mets' 1969 title triggered a wild celebration that resulted in serious damage to Shea Stadium (above).

out of nearby La Guardia Airport—a noise so deafening that players often step out of the batter's box until the roar subsides. Over the years, other recognizable sounds have been provided by organist Jane Jarvis and the rhythmic chant of "Let's Go Mets, Let's Go Mets."

Signs have always been an important part of the Shea landscape, encouraged by the Mets in deference to Yankee Stadium's no-banner rule. Big white-letter slogans adorned the stadium's exterior in the early years—"Watch the Stars Come Out", "Catch the Rising Stars", "Ya Gotta Believe"—and fans have always been willing to contribute their own expressive work. Who can forget Shea regular Sign Man, wearing his distinctive pie-hat, or Doc Gooden's "K"

SHEA STADIUM (1964-)

Left without a National League team when the Dodgers and Giants departed after the 1957 season, New York, primarily because of the efforts of young attorney William Shea, was awarded an expansion franchise in 1960. The Mets opened play in 1962 and called the Polo Grounds home for two seasons while their new ballpark—appropriately named Shea Stadium—was being built in the borough of Queens.

Shea opened its gates in 1964 and has withstood the test of time. A product of the round, symmetrical, multi-purpose ballpark craze of the 1960s and '70s, Shea resisted the gravitation toward artificial turf and enclosure, giving it a baseball-only feel. It has remained open and friendly, an oasis in a desert of New York City concrete. Fans attending games at Shea have to endure the noise of airplanes taking off and landing at nearby LaGuardia Airport.

First game: April 17, 1964. Willie Stargell's second-inning home run, the first hit at the new stadium, sparked the Pirates to a 4-3 victory over the Mets.

■ Site of three World Series (1969, '73 and '86)
■ Site of one All-Star Game (1964)

count? Shea's annual Banner Day promotions have ranked among the most popular in baseball.

At night, the exterior of Shea is like a wonderful Christmas light show for travelers on the network of expressways that connect Queens with the distant skyline of Manhattan and surrounding areas. Part of that show is provided by a series of lights that form the outline of bigger-than-life players in various poses (batting, pitching, catching, etc.) on the stadium facade. Part also comes from the distinctive lighting system that rims the inside of the grandstands and the two towers beyond left- and right-center fields.

Shea will not be named on many most-beautiful-stadium lists, but it's a good place to watch baseball and it has always been fun. From the craziness of Stengel and the Mets' improbable 1986 World Series comeback victory to the idiosyncrasies of coach Joe Pignatano's bullpen tomatoes and broadcaster Lindsey Nelson's wild and crazy sports jackets, fans have always gotten their money's worth.

And that, the Mets will assure you, is what baseball's all about.

The Big Apple (above) celebrates Mets home runs. Almost four decades after Shea Stadium's opening, its outfield remains open (left) and its right-center field scoreboard (right) still dominates the view of fans.

AMERICAN			
	NYY		23
N	ANA		55
	CLE	0	34
6	BAL	3	55
	MIN	5	41
4	TB	3	34
	BOS		41
D	SEA		54
	CWS		40
N	TEX		32
	DET		36
N	OAK		40

GIANTS	
14	CF
32	3B
25	LF
21	2B
23	RF
6	1B
35	SS
19	C
26	P

METS	
24	LF
13	2B
5	1B
31	C
4	3B
19	RF
10	SS
73	P

NATIONAL		
	COL	5 3
5	MON	3
	SD	3 4
7	PIT	2 4
	CIN	1 5
2	CHI	1 5
	LA	
0	FLA	
	HOU	
N	PHI	
	STL	
N	ATL	

Arbitron
AMERICA'S WATCH

3:05

BALL	STRIKE	OUT		KENNY ROGERS		
			AVG	HR	RBI
2	1	2	.188	0	1
			2B	3B	R
AB: #73 ROGERS			0	0	2

	1 2 3	4 5 6	7 8 9	10	R	H	E
GIANTS	0 0 0	0 0			0	1	0
METS	0 0 0	0			0	1	0

UMPIRES
PL 8 97 2B
1B 43 24 3B
RF   LF

371 THE W DVD

Oakland
Coliseum

Also known as Oakland Alameda County Coliseum; Network Associates Coliseum (1999-)

Scott Hatteberg's pinch-hit homer gives A's 12-11 win over Royals and A.L.-record 20-game win streak, Sept. 4, 2002

It's a tough, imposing baseball factory, placed strategically in the hard, rigid, industrial community it serves. The Oakland Coliseum tries hard not to be flashy, hip or beautiful—and succeeds on all counts. Comfort and convenience are overrated accessories; charisma and charm are frivolous values. This is working-class baseball, the kind you have to labor, sweat and fuss over to appreciate.

You sense the need for such pain well before you even see the Coliseum complex. A gray, drab, rundown industrial neighborhood surrounds it, a sprawling parking lot and train tracks add to its isolation. At first

CHARLES O. FINLEY: A's colorful and controversial owner, 1960-80

A's bat around three times and set team record for runs in 23-2 win over Texas, Sept. 30, 2000

1973 A.L. MVP Reggie Jackson hit 269 home runs in Athletics uniform

1972-73-74 world champions— The Mustache Gang

Where Henderson slid safely into record books with 939th career steal, passing Lou Brock, May 1, 1991

Finley tries to "fire" Mike Andrews after second baseman makes two errors in Game 2 of '73 World Series

Tim Raines' 13th-inning triple snaps scoreless deadlock and gives N.L. 2-0 All-Star Game win, July 14, 1987

A.L. MVP Jose Canseco becomes baseball's first 40-40 man, 1988

2000 MVP Jason Giambi (43 homers, 137 RBIs) and 20-game winner Tim Hudson lead A's to first division title since 1992; Miguel Tejada (.308, 34, 131) and 23-game winner Barry Zito help A's claim division honors in 2002

Joe Rudi's seventh-inning, Game 5 homer off Dodgers ironman Mike Marshall decides 1974 World Series

1988-89-90 pennant winners—The Bash Brothers

Where Reds completed shocking World Series sweep of A's in 1990

Where Catfish Hunter pitched perfect game vs. Twins, May 8, 1968

Catfish wins 25 games, claims 1974 Cy Young

Where Mark McGwire launched his amazing career with rookie-record 49 homers in 1987

Four A's combine for no-hitter vs. Angels, Sept. 28, 1975 (Vida Blue, Glenn Abbott, Paul Lindblad, Rollie Fingers)

Big pitch: Dave Stewart records four straight 20-win seasons, 1987-90; Bob Welch claims Cy Young with 27-6 record, 1990; Dennis Eckersley wins MVP and Cy Young, 1992

Sprinter Herb Washington serves as Finley's "designated runner" in 1974-75

Darold Knowles pitches in all seven games of 1973 World Series

Where Bert Campaneris hurled his bat at Detroit pitcher Lerrin LaGrow in Game 2 of 1972 ALCS

RICKEY HENDERSON: Baseball's all-time and single-season (130 in '82) basestealing king ... 1990 A.L. MVP

The Coliseum, dressed to the hilt for the 1990 American League Championship Series, still had its open outfield and a much more friendly feel.

glance, the huge, bowl-shaped Coliseum seems to rise up out of the pavement, overpowering its surroundings and the smaller, sleeker Oakland Arena, home of the NBA's Golden State Warriors.

It's no illusion. The floor of the Coliseum is dropped 21 feet below sea level, making its gray, nondescript facade less imposing than it could have been. But not even a tree-lined pathway around the structure can disguise what it really is—a monument to exposed concrete. It still is huge, it still rises up, up and away and it still overwhelms a first-time visitor, not unlike a first viewing of Yankee Stadium or the Los Angeles Coliseum.

Your first real sense of baseball is a powerful one—a symmetrical, lush, green,

grass carpet that spreads out below and sweeps you away. You enter the stadium at mid-level, between the first and second decks, to a panoramic view that suggests important things happened here. There is little physical evidence and the A's do little to promote their championship aura, but you are bombarded by subliminal reminders that great teams—rough-edged, hard-working, raw-power teams with Oakland-style personalities—competed here.

You can almost see the faces of Reggie, Rudi, Campy, Sal, Catfish, Vida and Rollie as they feuded with owner Charlie Finley, fought among themselves and battled their way to five consecutive division titles and three straight World Series championships in the early 1970s. You can feel the arm-throbbing pain

delivered by the Bash Brother teams of Jose Canseco, Mark McGwire and Rickey Henderson as they powered their way to three straight division titles and another Series win in 1989. This wasn't corporate America bottom-lining another championship; this was baseball with an old-fashioned mentality.

As hard as the Coliseum tries to maintain its edge, there's an ample supply of subtle charms and idiosyncracies to win over the toughest fan. Baseball has always been a pleasant experience here, especially before a 1995-96 football renovation enclosed the center field area and blocked a scenic view of a grassy knoll and the distant East Bay Hills.

It doesn't take long for your eyes to connect with the park's signature features. Expansive foul territory down both lines turns normally harmless out-of-play popups into easy outs. The backstop, which has been shortened from 90 feet to 60 behind the plate, appears to be notched into the box seats with side runways that provide a working area for photographers and feed directly into the dugouts and player clubhouses. Mirrored areas of sectioned steps over the left and right field fences—apparently going nowhere—send well-targeted home runs pinballing wildly in unpredictable directions.

The triple-decked grandstand wraps from foul pole to foul pole, curving away from the lines to create the large foul territory. For years, the Coliseum boasted one of the most raucous bleachers in baseball—two sections of single-decked seats, separated in center by an open runway, that connected the left and right field grandstands. The retainer wall above the bleachers was decorated by a line of pennant and team flags and three separate scoreboard units—including one of the first and best Diamond Vision boards in baseball—were perched atop the outer wall.

The entire center field structure changed with the 1995 renovation to accommodate the prodigal Raiders, who were making a triumphant return from Los Angeles. Now a massive wall of seats and skyboxes rise above the stadium rim, creating an edifice known among baseball fans as "Mount Davis," a sarcastic reference to Raiders owner Al Davis. The bleachers are gone, as are the flags and a concourse that allowed fans to pass above the bleacher sections. New video boards are perched on the stadium rim down the left and right field lines.

Mount Davis, the massive wall of seats and skyboxes that rise above the stadium rim in center field (bottom left), is equipped with retractable seats that can extend forward for football (center left). Like all modern stadiums, the Coliseum has its share of luxury boxes (above left) filled with amenities.

The stadium now has a football feel and small crowds get lost in its cavernous sprawl. When the house is full, fan enthusiasm makes the place jump. When it's not, baseball can be a lonely experience.

These are fans who know how to have fun and celebrate. They cut their major league teeth on the always-controversial Finley and his creative promotions when the team relocated there in 1968, and they survived the late-1970s, when Finley's tight-fisted management helped turn the stadium into the "Oakland Mausoleum." This is the reputed birthplace of video dot racing and the current or former home of drum-beating Crazy George, Charley O. the Mule, deep-voiced public address announcer Roy Steele and the wave. Bay Area bragging rights are locked safely away in a Coliseum vault, thanks to the A's 1989 World Series victory over the Giants.

What Oakland doesn't have—thankfully, A's fans will tell you—is San Francisco flavor or Candlestick Park weather. Coliseum patrons can put up with chilly night games and occasional wind-blown pop flies—as long as baseball is played there with old-fashioned values like hustle and hard work.

OAKLAND-ALAMEDA COUNTY COLISEUM (1968-)

Renamed Network Associates Coliseum (1999-)

After years of threatening to move his Athletics out of Kansas City, Charles O. Finley finally pulled the trigger in the fall of 1967. Oakland was selected over Seattle, in part, because it had a stadium already in place.

Although the Coliseum already was home to the NFL's Raiders when the A's made their move, the stadium had a nice baseball feel—an open outfield that allowed fans a view of the distant East Bay Hills. The Raiders accepted that configuration when they played there from 1966-81, but they demanded more seating when they returned in 1995.

To satisfy the Raiders, the stadium underwent a major transformation. It was enclosed with the addition of center field stands and skyboxes that blocked out the view, giving the facility a multi-purpose feel. The stands also affect wind patterns and help fly balls to carry better.

First game: April 17, 1968. With California Gov. Ronald Reagan on hand to throw out the first pitch, the A's lost their Oakland debut, 4-1, to the Orioles.

■ Site of six World Series (1972, '73, '74, '88, '89, '90)
■ Site of one All-Star Game (1987)

The circular Coliseum provided a spectacular panorama from center field (right) in 1991, before Mount Davis took away its tree-lined view (below).

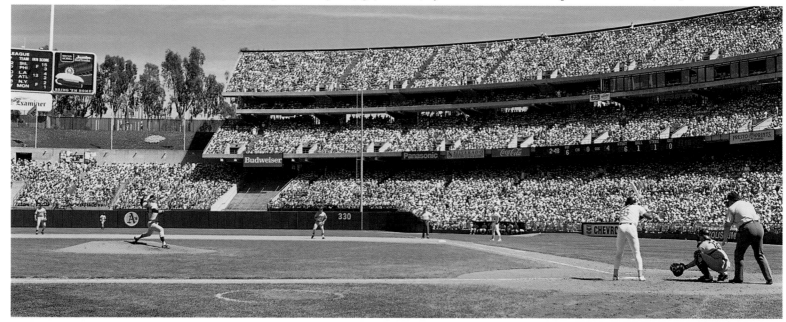

Jack Murphy Stadium

Site of 1978 and 1992 All-Star Games

Also known as San Diego Stadium (1969-1980); renamed Qualcomm Stadium (1997-)

It's situated in the lush, rolling Mission Valley countryside, a few miles from where Father Junipero Serra established the first California mission more than two centuries ago. Beautiful downtown San Diego lies about six miles to the southwest, the Pacific Ocean eight miles to the east and the San Diego River four or five long fly balls to the south, diverted from its natural banks. If there's such a thing as sunshine heaven, it's in the right field bleachers, where you can get a tan while offering strategy and advice to the Padres right fielder.

What's not to like about Jack Murphy Stadium?

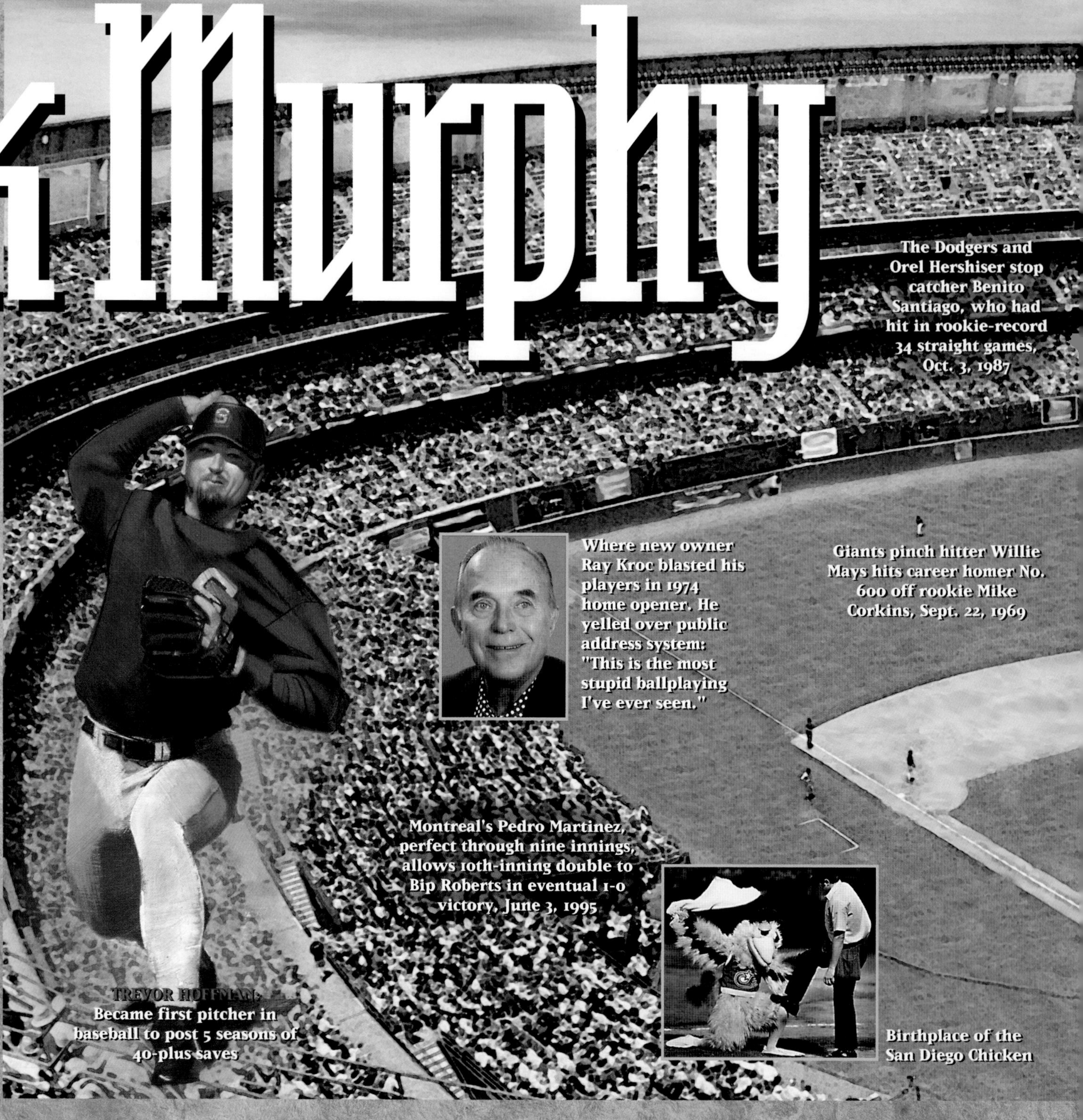

The Dodgers and Orel Hershiser stop catcher Benito Santiago, who had hit in rookie-record 34 straight games, Oct. 3, 1987

Where new owner Ray Kroc blasted his players in 1974 home opener. He yelled over public address system: "This is the most stupid ballplaying I've ever seen."

Giants pinch hitter Willie Mays hits career homer No. 600 off rookie Mike Corkins, Sept. 22, 1969

Montreal's Pedro Martinez, perfect through nine innings, allows 10th-inning double to Bip Roberts in eventual 1-0 victory, June 3, 1995

TREVOR HOFFMAN: Became first pitcher in baseball to post 5 seasons of 40-plus saves

Birthplace of the San Diego Chicken

Cardinals' Lou Brock sets modern major league record with 893rd stolen base, Aug. 29, 1977

Padres beat Braves 4-1, take shocking 3-0 lead in NLCS en route to second N.L. pennant, Oct. 10, 1998

Dodgers' ace Orel Hershiser works 10 scoreless innings vs. Padres, stretching record streak to 59, Sept. 28, 1988

Clay Kirby, who trails 1-0 after pitching eight hitless innings vs. Mets, is lifted for pinch hitter in controversial conclusion to eventual 3-0 loss, July 21, 1970

Three Cy Youngs: Randy Jones (left) 1976, Gaylord Perry (right) 1978, Mark Davis 1989

Where Steve Garvey hit ninth-inning, Game 4-winning home run vs. Cubs in must-win 1984 NLCS battle

2001 milestones: Rickey Henderson scores 2,246th run Oct. 4, breaking Ty Cobb's career record; gets 3,000th hit, a double, in Oct. 7 season finale

Tigers storm past Padres in five-game 1984 World Series; Yankees sweep Padres in 1998 classic

Where Hoffman converted 53-of-54 save opportunities for a single-season record .981 percentage in 1998

Where Steve Garvey's ironman streak ended at 1,207 games when he dislocated thumb while sliding vs. Atlanta, July 29, 1983

TONY GWYNN: Mr. Padre is a member of baseball's 3,000-hit club and owner of eight N.L. batting titles

There are a few things—a 1997 renovation that enclosed a once-open right field; its multi-purpose feel—but it's hard to escape San Diego without a good baseball experience. It's all about atmosphere and casual fun here, the national pastime with a soft edge. On a perfect, sunshiny spring or summer afternoon, it's like a day at the beach—without the water.

The first thing you notice about Jack Murphy is the pastoral surroundings, once pristine but now more commercial with intruding hotels, restaurants and gas stations. It's a river area, always green and favorable to wildlife if you really take time to look. The 122-acre parking lot is an attraction in and of itself, an expansive area used for events like drag racing and skateboarding and a tailgating paradise for baseball and football fans who have been known to import sand, set up volleyball courts and even flavor their atmosphere with potted palm trees. Trolleys roll in and out of the lot, dropping off passengers from downtown San Diego or nearby Old Town—the historic mission district.

Entrance to the open-air concourses also is an experience. You can take the conventional escalator route to your desired level or you can be more adventurous and walk one of the distinctive concrete swirls that sit outside the main structure—ramps that look like giant springs ready to uncoil skyward. No matter where you're located at Jack Murphy, you can always feel the gentle breezes off the Pacific—the park's natural air-conditioner.

For many years, the field was shaped like a horseshoe, with five-level grandstands wrapping behind home plate from the right field foul pole all the way through left field to center. The open right field, which once offered a nice view of the rolling hillsides, now is closed—with grandstands butting up to a giant, high-tech scoreboard in right-center field. This obviously is a football stadium, but it somehow retains a reasonable baseball feel.

You have to be careful not to overdose on Jack Murphy's colors, a virtual rainbow of blues, reds, oranges and greens that surround you the moment you step into the field area. The green looks like an Augusta putting surface, spread out below on one of the best-kept natural carpets in the game. The coup de grace is provided by miniature palm trees that occupy the dead area between the outfield fences and bleacher retaining walls, inviting targets for home runs.

If you can get past the sense of enclosure and the park's near symmetry (327-405-330), you'll pick up on subtle quirks that make Jack Murphy distinctive. Such as a left field foul pole that stands 2 feet behind the outfield fence, 1 foot in from of the retaining wall—

The sparkling green grass and high-rising grandstands provide the backdrop for San Diego-style baseball.

Horseshoe-shaped Jack Murphy Stadium, renamed Qualcomm Stadium in 1997, is a monument to concrete, complete with giant swirling ramps (above, below) that take visitors to desired seating levels. The outside experience is active and quaint, enhanced by colorful trolleys (right) that deliver and carry away baseball-loving fans.

The Turf Era

T hey survived scorn and ridicule for three decades while filling a basic need for fiscal responsibility. The Turf Era parks always got a bad rap because of the round, cookie-cutter mentality, look-alike symmetry and artificial surfaces that were a shocking departure, technologically and aesthetically, from their charming predecessors.

Now only three remain—Busch Stadium in St. Louis, Veterans Stadium in Philadelphia and Kauffman Stadium in Kansas City—and the Phillies will relocate to a new retro park in 2004. But the Turf Park legacy lives on—for the way these interlopers increased revenue streams for the cities they served and how they affected the way the game was played with their larger dimensions and speed-demanding surfaces.

Purists have welcomed the turf-to-grass switch at Busch and Kauffman and the move to throwback parks in Pittsburgh and Cincinnati. But it seems inevitable—and in a strange way even sad—that this chapter of ballpark history is rapidly approaching its conclusion.

Kauffman Stadium

Also known as Royals Stadium (1973-1993)

Carlos Beltran becomes first rookie since 1975 to drive in and score 100 runs, 1999

Where Cookie Rojas and Fred Patek celebrated Royals' clinching of '76 division championship by jumping into water fountain

Royals

Minnesota's Paul Molitor gets 3,000th career hit, a triple, on Sept. 16, 1996

Brett goes 4-for-4, hits two homers in clutch ALCS Game 3 win over Blue Jays, Oct. 11, 1985

Misplayed fly ball gives Brett inside-the-park homer and allows him to edge teammate Hal McRae for controversial batting crown, Oct. 3, 1976

21-year-old Bret Saberhagen wins first of two Cy Youngs, 1985 ... hometown product David Cone wins award in 1994

GEORGE BRETT: Three-time batting champ wrote his own Royals record book en route to Hall of Fame

How do you spell relief? Dan Quisenberry (1979-88), Jeff Montgomery (1988-99)

I t is an I-70 jewel, a must-look landmark for anybody driving to or from downtown Kansas City. The seats of Kauffman Stadium seem to bristle in the daylight, a reflection of all the lustrous baseball moments they have witnessed since 1973. Hundreds of thousands of drivers zip past the stadium on a daily basis, momentarily distracted by the sudden dash of color and the back of a giant, crown-shaped object that stands guard over the facility.

That's the 12-story-high scoreboard, a replica of the Kansas City Royals' logo and one of the two

Where Mark Quinn belted record-tying two homers in his first big-league game, Sept. 14, 1999

Bret Saberhagen shuts out Cardinals as Royals win all-Missouri Series and claim first championship, Oct. 27, 1985

Hal McRae collects 54 doubles in 1977, a major league DH-record 133 RBIs in 1982

Home of the Lemonade Guy—"Woooooo!"

Where Amos Otis (left) and Willie Wilson patroled for more than two decades

Royals defeat A's, Sept. 15, 1977, for 16th straight win, the longest major league winning streak in 24 years

Where Angels' Nolan Ryan fired first career no-hitter, first at Royals Stadium, May 15, 1973

Where umpire Don Denkinger made his infamous call on Jorge Orta's ground ball in Game 6 of '85 World Series

FRANK WHITE: Winner of eight Gold Gloves as one of premier second basemen in baseball history

Brett's .390 average, MVP exploits help Royals capture first A.L. pennant, 1980

Willie Wilson ties switch-hitting records with 230 hits and 100 hits from each side of plate, 1980

Brett kisses home plate, to delight of fans attending his final Kauffman Stadium performance, Sept. 29, 1993

signature features of a ballpark that somehow escaped the depressing cookie-cutter stigma of the 1970s. You see the scoreboard coming, you see it going—and it commands your attention for significant spans during every game.

Kauffman Stadium has always been a structure of vision, and that becomes apparent the moment you enter a massive parking lot that serves two masters. Kauffman, a k a Royals Stadium, was built as a baseball-only ballpark in the era of sterile, nondescript, multi-purpose facilities that sprung up in St. Louis, Philadelphia, Cincinnati and Pittsburgh. Next door, a couple of football fields away, stands Arrowhead Stadium,

The trademark crown-shaped scoreboard (above) dominates the view of Kauffman Stadium, home of the Royals, from Interstate 70. The stadium (right) has always been known for its beauty, both during its turf and grass eras.

the equally impressive home of Kansas City's Chiefs.

On Sunday mornings during the fall, this parking lot would be filled with the aroma of the best barbecue any taste bud could hope to savor and the sights and sounds of fans who have turned tailgating into an art-form. But baseball appetites are less demanding and the real experience begins with your first gaze on a travelogue-like playing area.

You can't avoid the giant JumboTron video board stationed on the left field hillside or the vertical scoreboard, which rises up, up, up on the sta-dium's outer wall in dead center field, framed by towering light standards and flanked on both sides by a 322-foot-long waterfall that covers most of the area beyond the fences in both left and right. The water is mes-merizing, whether shooting skyward, cascading or merely reflecting a variation of colored lights.

It's hard to sit anywhere in the ballpark, gaze upon the open outfield expanse and not appreciate what a distinctive backdrop the fountain provides. You might understand the charm of Ebbets Field or Fenway Park, the charisma of Yankee Stadium or Wrigley, but it's still hard to imagine baseball in a brighter, cleaner or more beautiful setting. The park's pastoral effect was punctuated before the 1995 season, when the Royals finally replaced their artificial surface with grass.

The geometrically-perfect and symmetrical Kauffman (330 feet down both lines, 400 to center) looks and feels almost like a painting, unlike the quirky and colorful atmospheres of many old-time ballparks. It lacks the colorful frenzy of some parks, the boisterous cheers and jeers of others. Kauffman has the feel of a small community relationship with a serenity that can almost lull you to sleep. But the Royals teams of the late 1970s and early '80s inspired as much fervor and baseball passion as you'll find anywhere in the country.

These were the Royals of George Brett, Hal McRae, Amos Otis, Frank White, Willie Wilson and Paul Splittorff—the six-time West Division champions who provided a blueprint for expansion success. This was a team filled with warriors who stood toe-to-toe and traded punches with the powerful Yankees in four memorable American League Championship Series.

Colorful, high-rising fountains form a spectacular backdrop for hitters and a scenic view for Kauffman visitors.

KAUFFMAN STADIUM (1973-)

Also known as Royals Stadium (1973-1993)

When the Royals began play as an expansion franchise in 1969, they spent four seasons at cozy Municipal Stadium, the former home of the Kansas City Athletics.

Since opening in 1973 as Royals Stadium, Kauffman has undergone remarkably few major changes. The stadium was renamed after former owner Ewing M. Kauffman in 1993, a large video board was added in left field, the fountains were extended into left field and the artificial surface was replaced by natural grass before the 1995 season.

Lighted, bustling Kauffman Stadium is visible to passing traffic on I-70, an unmistakable jewel in the Kansas City landscape.

First game: April 10, 1973. John Mayberry homered and the Royals beat the Rangers, 12-1, behind lefty Paul Splittorff.

■ Site of two World Series (1980 and 1985)
■ Site of one All-Star Game (1973)

It's hard to visit Kauffman without getting a special sense of Brett, the multi-talented third baseman who helped make the small-market Royals a nationally respected championship contender. You can still see him, standing on second base, tipping his cap to a delighted crowd as the scoreboard flashes ".401" in the background. He's at the plate, crouched, weight back, ready to uncoil into another pitch. He's making that "in your face" home run trot in the first inning of Game 5 of the 1980 World Series.

But other images are just as prominent. Who can forget Cookie Rojas and Freddie Patek jumping into the fountains to celebrate a division title? Or Bo Jackson's titanic home run over the center field fence? Or a Patek-to-White-to-Mayberry double play, a Bret Saberhagen no-hitter, a U.L. Washington toothpick, an Otis running catch?

The pain still burns deep from that 1977 ALCS loss to the hated Yankees, but the joy still bubbles

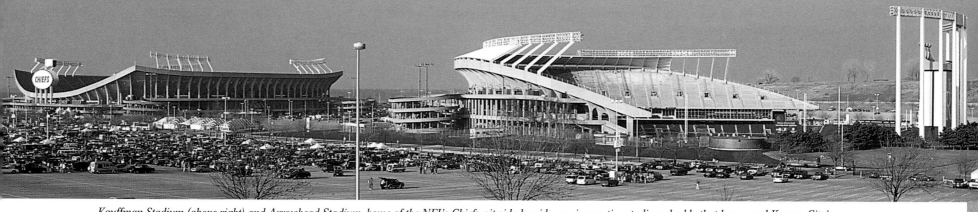

Kauffman Stadium (above right) and Arrowhead Stadium, home of the NFL's Chiefs, sit side-by-side—an innovative stadium double that has served Kansas City's professional sports needs since 1973. A sunset over Kauffman (below) is as good as it gets in baseball.

over from that incredible Game 6 comeback win over Whitey Herzog and the cross-state Cardinals in the 1985 World Series. Fans will never forget Dick Howser, hugging his players after the Game 7 championship-sealing victory, a smiling, waving Ewing Kauffman or the sight of reliever Dan Quisenberry, hose in hand, showing compassion for sweltering fans hanging over the side wall of the right field bullpen.

Kauffman Stadium is a place of community, a reflection of the Midwest values that often are scorned by the more hard-core fans of other regions.

But that laid-back approach also is a big part of the flavor that makes it so special. Through the Royals' 1976-85 run, the facility stood as a Camelot among ballparks, that near-perfect blend of success, beauty and personality.

Maybe the most appropriate tribute to Kauffman Stadium was made, fittingly, by Brett in his final career home game in 1993 when he sent the crowd into a frenzy by getting down on his knees to deliver a goodbye kiss to home plate—the final stop on his path to the Hall of Fame.

Veterans Stadium

It opened in 1971 to rave reviews, a baseball showcase mirroring state-of-the-art facilities already in use at St. Louis, Cincinnati and Pittsburgh. Almost three decades later, Veterans Stadium stands as a monument to nondescript, one of the ultimate cookie-cutter stadiums that have drawn the everlasting scorn of ballpark purists. Somewhere between those extremes is the real Vet, the home of three National League pennant winners, the franchise's only World Series champion and the most emotional, vocal fans in baseball.

The only real problem with Veterans Stadium is perception—it was built for comfort and multi-purpose durability, not as a charming reflection of a city or team's personality.

The "Bull Ring", where Greg Luzinski bought tickets for various youth organizations

Where smooth-fielding shortstop Larry Bowa patroled for 11 seasons

Carlton wins 15th straight game, Aug. 17, 1972

Blue Jays score six runs in eighth inning and claim wild 15-14 win in Game 4 of 1993 World Series

STEVE CARLTON won Cy Youngs in '72, '77, '80 and '82

Carlton finishes 1977 season with 17-3 record at Veterans Stadium

Gary Matthews' three homers, eight RBIs help Phillies to a four-game NLCS win over Dodgers and fourth pennant, 1983

National

Dave Johnson hit
two pinch-hit
grand slams
in 1978

Where Greg Luzinski
drove a 500-foot
homer off old
Liberty Bell,
May 16, 1972

Greg Luzinski's homer
wins Game 1 of 1980
Championship Series

Eddie Murray crashes
two Game 5 homers as
Orioles dash Phillies'
hopes for 1983 World
Series championship

Curt Schilling
shuts out Blue
Jays, gives
Phillies
temporary life
after five
games of 1993
Series

Home-field advantage?
N.L. pitchers hold
A.L. batters to
a single run in
7-1 (1976) and 6-0 (1996)
All-Star Game wins

Home of 1983
and 1987 Cy
Young winners—
John Denny,
Steve Bedrosian

Tug McGraw
holds off
Royals
in sixth
1980
World
Series game,
giving
Phillies first
championship

Bake McBride's
three-run homer
helps Phillies beat
Royals in Game 1 of
'80 World Series

Schmidt ties
N.L. record
with 11th
home run in
April of 1976

Three-time MVP
third baseman
MIKE SCHMIDT
owns numerous
team offensive
records and 10
Gold Gloves

Pete Rose
singles for
N.L.-record hit
No. 3,631,
Aug. 10, 1981

It lacks the quirks and nuances of the baseball-only parks of yesteryear, it doesn't have a lot of distinctive features and it's not Camden Yards, the blueprint for today's retro parks. What it does have is simplicity—Veterans Stadium is a comfortable place to watch baseball for demanding patrons who would gladly substitute success for beauty.

To appreciate the Vet, you first have to put it in perspective. The stadiums of the 1970s were built in the shadow of Houston's Astrodome, the biggest, baddest, most wondrous superstructure ever erected—the sports arena that lifted the concept of multi-purpose practicality to a new level. This was not the age of ballparks—it was the era of high-tech, durable, no-nonsense facilities that could serve two masters, baseball and football, while attracting non-sports events ranging from revivals and concerts to rodeos and tractor pulls.

For many years, the Big Three venues in Philadelphia sports were (right to left) Veterans Stadium, the Spectrum and John F. Kennedy Stadium.

When Veterans Stadium opened its doors, it was hailed as a masterpiece, a circular, enclosed, concrete-based sports nirvana located within a few dribbles of two other South Philadelphia sports arenas—the Spectrum and John F. Kennedy Stadium, now the site of First Union Center. Not only was the Vet splendid and hip, its baseball field was a symmetrical work of art (330 feet down both lines, 371 to the power alleys, 408 to center), covered with a durable, low-maintenance AstroTurf carpet that had dirt cutouts around home plate, the bases and the pitcher's mound.

"It's got to be the best new park in baseball," raved then-Montreal manager Gene Mauch. "It looks like they've taken the good things from all the other new parks, added some things of their own, and whipped them into a pretty good place."

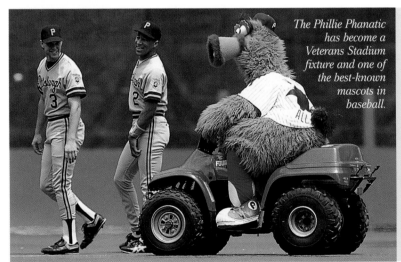

The Phillie Phanatic has become a Veterans Stadium fixture and one of the best-known mascots in baseball.

VETERANS STADIUM (1971-)

Talk about a new stadium began as early as 1953 but ground-breaking for a facility to replace aging Shibe Park did not take place until 1967. Further delays plagued the project and pushed back the unveiling of new Veterans Stadium to 1971.

Newspaper public opinion polls showed a preference for such names as Philadium and Philadelphia Stadium, but legislation was passed in Philadelphia's city council to dedicate the stadium to the city's war veterans—hence, Philadelphia Veterans Stadium.

Hailed as a state-of-the-art masterpiece when it opened, the Vet now is chastised as a member of the sterile, personality-devoid cookie-cutter ballpark craze of the 1960s and '70s. Nondescript in design and without many of the nuances cherished by today's fans, the multi-purpose Vet does have the Phillie Phanatic—a 1978 marketing creation and now one of the most-recognizable mascots in American sports behind the San Diego Chicken.

First game: April 10, 1971. Jim Bunning pitched the Phillies to a 4-1 victory over the Expos.
- Site of three World Series (1980, '83 and '93)
- Site of two All-Star Games (1976 and '96)

THE GREAT WALLENDA

The brilliance of that 1970s Vet is contrasted by today's perception of a big, sterile sports amphitheater. It's simply a matter of bad timing. As the 1970s notions of hip and trendy died away, words like "atmosphere," "charm" and "character" began creeping back into the ballparks vocabulary. Your first sense when gazing over the still geometrically-perfect, personality-challenged Vet is that this could be the model stadium if a mathematician became baseball commissioner and decided to standardize all playing fields.

Veterans Stadium, while comfortable, has no skyline and few other distinguishing characteristics. A statue of Connie Mack, the venerable ruler of Philadelphia baseball for a half century, stands guard on the corner of Broad Street and Pattison Avenue and an unidentified player remains locked in mid-slide, elevated on the outside of the stadium near the Phillies offices. But few of the original inside landmarks remain.

Opening day, Veterans Stadium-style, has featured everything from misguided parachutists to tight rope-walking Karl Wallenda (above). Phil and Phyllis (left) were early mascots, modeled after mechanical dolls that were part of a Liberty Bell display in center field. A Connie Mack statue (right) is still a fixture outside the Vet.

The "Bull Ring" was a former special section of the left field stands named in honor of longtime Phillies star left fielder Greg "Bull" Luzinski.

The Liberty Bell, once part of the Phil and Phyllis display that celebrated home runs at the base of the upper deck in dead center field, now rests on the stadium roof in center, a moonshot away from the plate. Phil and Phyllis, a pair of huge, computer-controlled dolls dressed in colonial garb, are gone, as are the massive twin scoreboards in left and right-center fields and the team logos that formerly decorated the black backdrops just above the outfield fences. Two state-of-the-art video boards entertain fans from high in the blue-seated center field bleachers and two recently installed scoreboards catch your attention from behind the open, glass-fronted, ground-level bullpens in left and right field. The "worst turf in baseball" is faded and the outline of the football field never completely disappears.

What the Vet lacks in personality it tries to make up for with promotional gimmicks. The Phillie Phanatic has become one of the best-known mascots in baseball and the team is constantly entertaining fans with promotions ranging from its one-year American Phanstand to its long-standing tradition of delivering first balls on opening day in creative ways—by air, horseback, cannon and even by Karl Wallenda, who crossed boldly above Veterans Stadium on a high wire.

One of the enduring images of the Vet came from Game 6 of the 1980 World Series, as the Phillies were on the verge of wrapping up the first championship in the franchise's long history. Surrounding the field from corner to corner, positioned on the foul-territory warning track, were helmeted police on horseback, nightsticks at the ready and snarling attack dogs ready to pounce. Phillies fans, already regarded as the most antagonistic in baseball, never lived it down.

But Phillies fans also are among the most enthusiastic and loyal, when the players give them a reason to care. And the lack of Veterans Stadium atmosphere, a major contrast to Camden Yards less than two hours away, is never a problem when the baseball is right.

It simply doesn't get any better than Mike Schmidt facing Tom Seaver, no matter where the game is played. And how can you improve on Steve Carlton vs. Dave Parker or Curt Schilling staring down Barry Bonds? A Greg Luzinski home run would be impressive in any ballpark, as would a Larry Bowa diving stop or a Lenny Dykstra running catch.

There's no doubt Veterans Stadium has lost its cutting-edge appeal—it exists as a relic from better times. But memories are in the eyes of the beholder and Phillies fans have plenty to choose from. Love it or hate it, there's no place like home—even if it is Veterans Stadium.

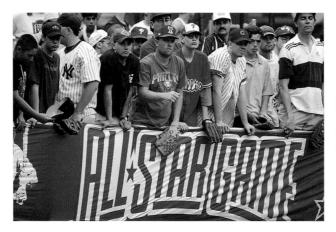

Phillies fans can be antagonistic, but they also are among the most enthusiastic and loyal in baseball. That enthusiasm was on full display during 1996 All-Star Game festivities.

Busch Stadium

Big Mac Land

Keith McDonald becomes second player in history to homer in first two major league at-bats— July 4 and 6, 2000, vs. Reds

Landing pads for Mark McGwire homers Nos. 62 and 70 during historic 1998 season

Mark McGwire hits career homer No. 500 (Aug. 5, 1999), follows up record-breaking 1998 season with 65

Tom Lawless' second career homer, a three-run shot, helps Cardinals beat Twins, Frank Viola in Game 4 of 1987 World Series

OZZIE SMITH! The Wizard of Oz performed magic on left side of Cardinals' infield from 1982-96

Steve Carlton strikes out 19 Mets but loses game 4-3, Sept. 15, 1969

The Gateway Arch towers in the skyline above Busch Memorial Stadium, an ever-vigilant sentry guarding its St. Louis treasures. Jewels, past and present, like Bob Gibson, Lou Brock, Joe Torre, Ted Simmons, Bob Forsch, Ozzie Smith, Willie McGee and Mark McGwire. Diamond memories of Cardinals, Clydesdales, baseball magic and World Series moments, all colored in a sea of red.

Rumor has it the Arch sways to every beat of the Budweiser song, which has filled the downtown St. Louis air around 250 Stadium Plaza for more than three decades. So do the bronze statues of Stan "The Man" Musial, Gibson, Brock, Enos Slaughter, Red Schoendienst, Dizzy Dean, Rogers Hornsby, George Sisler, Jack Buck,

Where Albert Pujols became first major league player to top .300, 30 homers and 100 RBIs in first two seasons, 2001 and 2002

N.L. prevails 2-1 on 105-degree afternoon in hotly-contested All-Star Game, July 12, 1966

Lou Brock sets single-season record with 104th and 105th steals en route to 118, Sept. 10, 1974 . . . slashes 3,000th career hit off hand of Cubs pitcher Dennis Lamp, Aug. 13, 1979

Joe Torre put up MVP numbers here in 1971 . . . Willie McGee did the same in 1985

Keith Hernandez: 1979 co-MVP and big gun in 1982 World Series championship

Where Mark McGwire's 545-foot blast off Marlins' Livan Hernandez dented sign, May 16, 1998

Site of Gibson's overpowering 17-strikeout performance in Game 1 of 1968 World Series vs. Tigers

Ozzie Smith's first career lefthanded homer shocks Dodgers in Game 5 of 1985 NLCS

BOB GIBSON: Five-time 20-game winner, two Cy Youngs, 1.12 ERA in 1968

Where Curt Flood misjudged Jim Northrup's fly ball, opening gates to seventh-game Tigers win in 1968 World Series

Roosting place of "Cha Cha" Cepeda, MVP cheerleader for 1967 El Birdos

Pennantless in the '90s, Cardinals fall just short with NLCS losses in 1996, 2000, 2002

Where "Mad Hungarian" Al Hrabosky meditated before striking out another batter

Where Larry Jaster shut out Dodgers for fifth straight time in remarkable 1966 performance, Sept. 28

Where Vince Coleman, the Cardinals' 110-steal rookie, was gobbled up by automatic tarp before Game 4 of NLCS, Oct. 13, 1985

Line drive by Pirates slugger Roberto Clemente breaks Gibson's leg, July 15, 1967

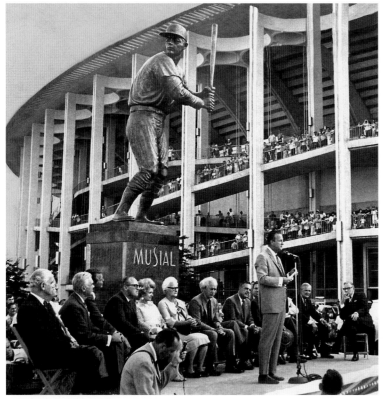

Cool Papa Bell and Ozzie Smith, strategically placed outside the stadium to offer inspiration—to properly prepare visitors even before they walk through a gate.

Inspiration is everything for St. Louis fans, who have always blanched at the nonstop verbal shots Busch Stadium has endured from ballpark purists. From its 1966 opening through its impressive 1990s facelift, Busch has carried the tag of "cookie-cutter" original—the first of the sterile, plastic, boringly symmetrical, Astro-Turf, multi-purpose facilities that sprang up in the late 1960s and '70s. "I stand at the pitcher's mound in Philadelphia and I don't know if I'm in Pittsburgh, Cincinnati, St. Louis or Philly," former major leaguer Richie Hebner once complained. "They all look alike."

Critics took one look at the nearly-round, cavernous, bowl-like Busch in 1966 and labeled it an "airport"—with seats, a scoreboard and little by way of personality. They were appalled when it became the assembly-line blueprint for a wave of unimaginative stadiums affected by the desire for big seating capacities and the need to convert back and forth between baseball and football.

But fans who have worshiped there, who have experienced five World Series and countless memorable moments there, remember early Busch for a subtle beauty that emanated from its proud Cardinals tradition and a personality supplied by special players and successful teams.

The Cardinals know how to celebrate their heroes. The 15-foot Stan Musial statue, a Stadium landmark since its dedication (above) in 1968, has been joined by statues (below) of Bob Gibson, Lou Brock, Enos Slaughter, Jack Buck, Red Schoendienst, Dizzy Dean, Rogers Hornsby, George Sisler, Ozzie Smith and Cool Papa Bell on the Plaza of Champions.

BUSCH MEMORIAL STADIUM (1966-)

The bowl-shaped facility, a charter member of the multi-purpose stadium craze of the 1960s and '70s, was named after August A. Busch Jr., the former chairman of Anheuser-Busch, Inc., when the St. Louis-based brewery owned the Cardinals from 1953-1995. The Busch Stadium name had also been used by former Cardinals home Sportsman's Park from 1953-1966.

For many years, Busch Stadium endured a negative reputation as part of baseball's cookie-cutter ballpark era—lookalike facilities with turf, symmetrical fields, sterile atmospheres and football-friendly seating arrangements. But recent renovations have transformed it into a personable, fan-friendly baseball theater. Busch actually opened with a grass field, changed it to artificial turf after the 1969 season and returned to natural grass in 1996.

One of the stadium's most endearing features is a 15-foot bronze statue of Cardinals great Stan Musial outside its northeast stands—a meeting place for fans attending games. It has been joined in recent years by statues honoring other Cardinals greats in the Plaza of Champions.

First game: May 12, 1966. Atlanta's Felipe Alou hit two home runs, but the Cardinals posted a 4-3 victory over Phil Niekro and the Braves in 12 innings.

■ Site of five World Series (1967, '68, '82, '85 and '87)
■ Site of one All-Star Game (1966)

Career Home
HANK AARON   5
BABE RUTH   573
WILLIE MAYS
FRANK ROBINSON   563
H. KILLEBREW
REGGIE JACKSON   548
MIKE SCHMIDT
MARK McGWIRE   543
MICKEY MANTLE   5
JIMMIE FOXX   5

The outer wall at Busch has been spruced up with replay screens, out-of-town scoreboards and a list of baseball's all-time top home run hitters.

The early Busch Stadium experience was Gibson and McCarver, Maxvill and Javier, Torre and Cepeda, Brock and Coleman, Smith and Herr, Clark and Hernandez, Pendleton and Simmons, Hendrick and McGee, Tudor and Andujar. It was waves of red, the color of choice for the self-professed "best baseball fans in America," line drives into the gap, a man-eating automatic tarp, the Wizard of Oz, Whitey Ball, Harry Caray, Buck and Mike Shannon in the broadcast booth and the Budweiser song, which never failed to whip Cardinals supporters into frenetic fits.

It was a massive two-sectioned scoreboard, one side occupied by an Anheuser-Busch eagle that flapped its magnificent wings in approval, the other by an electronic Redbird that flew back and forth during a seventh-inning stretch or in recognition of a Cardinals home run. It was team owner August A. Busch triumphantly circling the stadium in a beer wagon pulled by a team of Clydesdales, an Ozzie Smith body flip or a seat in the left field bleachers, as close as a young fan could get to childhood hero Brock.

Busch Stadium was proactive, which allowed fans to ignore unfavorable comparisons to ballpark favorites Wrigley Field, Fenway Park and the Polo Grounds. There were no unusual angles, dimensions or nuances to spice up play—little personality beyond that supplied by the people who played and cheered there. Dimensions were a standard 330 feet down both lines and 386 to the power alleys. Center field was 414 (later 404) and the AstroTurf, installed in 1970, was hard and fast, features that fit the profile for a team dependent on speed and defense.

Supporting the Cardinals meant appreciating aggressive, fundamental play—and, of course, the stolen base, which Brock and Vince Coleman turned into lethal offensive weapons. The home run, which would become such an important factor in the 1990s, was a 1970s and '80s afterthought. Whitey Herzog's 1982 world champions hit 67 homers, three fewer than McGwire hit in his record-setting 1998 season, while recording 200 steals.

But Big Mac wasn't the only thing new about the 1990s Cardinals. New ownership, no longer content to let one of baseball's premier franchises play in a no-frills setting, retro-fitted Busch Stadium into one of the fan-friendliest playgrounds in the game. For St. Louis baseball fans, the Cardinals' house became a home.

The turf, at long last, was removed and replaced by grass. The outer walls in left- and right-center field were spruced up, one area, decorated by flags, celebrating all the retired numbers in Cardinals history. The bullpens were moved from the first and third base foul lines to areas behind the left and right field fences. And a more modern scoreboard in left-center was mirrored by a replay/highlights screen in right-center.

New interactive attractions, picnic areas, extended bleachers and an upper-deck seating area named Big Mac Land became hot locations, primarily because of McGwire's headline-generating home run prowess.

A fan who had not been to a game since the 1970s might not have recognized the new Busch. Sleek, modern and attractive to the first-time visitor, the stadium became an attraction on its own merit—an eye-pleasing structure and a fitting depository for the moonshot blasts launched by McGwire into the outer limits.

The house that a beer baron had built in 1966 was officially transformed into a warm, inviting corporate showcase for one of the greatest baseball shows on earth.

The Dome Era

They were heralded as technological wonders and for awhile regarded as offensive to our baseball senses. What the dome really gave us was relief from game-inhibiting elements and a sense of what baseball luxury could become.

They came to us with good intentions—baseball Utopia, where it was never too hot or too cold, too wet or too dry, too rainy, too snowy or too breezy to play. Whether permanent or retractable, the roof meant the show would always go on in Houston's Astrodome, Seattle's Kingdome, Minnesota's Metrodome, Toronto's SkyDome or Montreal's Olympic Stadium, which finally was crowned after more than a decade of political hassling.

The Astrodome and Kingdome are gone now, and their legacies, ironically, are less about what was above than what was below. The most significant measure of dome ball has been the artificial surface it introduced to the sport.

Baseball has never been the same since.

The Metrodome

Tom Kelly managed Twins to 1,140 wins and two World Series titles from 1986-2001

Where Twins' Dave Winfield (left) and Orioles' Cal Ripken collected 3,000th career hits in 1993 and 2000 seasons

Indoor baseball, complete with fiberglass roof, lighting and acoustical problems, artificial turf and a "Hefty Bag" lining that serves as right field wall

Consecutive at-bat popups by Detroit's Rob Deer ricochet off ceiling to shortstop Greg Gagne, May 30, 1992

Dan Gladden's grand slam sparks 10-1 win over Cardinals in first indoor World Series game, Oct. 17, 1987

U nimpressed writers have nicknamed it the Hump, Humpty-Dump, Homerdome, Thunderdome, Sweat Box, Sweatrodome and Metrodish. More generous visitors observe diplomatically that it looks like a big, rectangular-shaped mushroom—without the stem. By any name or description, the Hubert H. Humphrey Metrodome is a baseball anomaly, an indoor ballpark that still stirs passion in much of the outdoor-loving community it has served for almost two decades.

Twins players and hard-core fans have another nickname for the white-topped structure that sits defiantly on the east edge of downtown Minneapolis, guarded by one of the

KIRBY PUCKETT:
Popular Kirby was .318 career hitter and six-time Gold Glove center fielder

Atlanta's Lonnie Smith commits Game 7 baserunning gaffe that helps Twins win worst-to-first World Series . . . Gene Larkin gives Jack Morris 1-0 Series-clinching win with 10th-inning single, Oct. 27, 1991

Roof suffers slight tear due to high winds, causing nine-minute delay in game vs. Angels, April 26, 1986

Surprising Twins rebound from contraction talk, win 2002 A.L. Central Division title before upsetting A's in Division Series

Site of 1985 All-Star Game—a 6-1 N.L. victory

Milwaukee's Ben Oglivie hits longest homer in Metrodome history—a 481-foot rocket into second deck, July 27, 1983

Gary Gaetti homers twice vs. Tigers in ALCS opener and Twins win first postseason game since 1965, Oct. 7, 1987

Puckett goes 3-for-4, makes sensational leaping catch and hits 11th-inning homer to beat Braves in Game 6 of World Series, Oct. 26, 1991

Where Hrbek hit his Game 6 grand slam in 1987 World Series vs. Cardinals

Frank Viola (right) goes 24-7, wins 1988 Cy Young . . . Scott Erickson wins 20 in 1991, Brad Radke 20 in 1997

Where Hrbek gave Atlanta baserunner Ron Gant a lift and tagged him out in Game 2 of 1991 World Series

Chili Davis hits towering fly ball that bounces off speaker and caroms to Orioles second baseman Mark McLemore, transforming sure homer into pop out, July 5, 1992

Oakland's Dave Kingman hits ball into one of roof's drainage holes and it never comes down, resulting in ground-rule double, May 4, 1984

First baseman KENT HRBEK: 293 homers, 1,086 RBIs from 1981-94

Home Sweet Home for Twins, who win all eight World Series games played there in 1987, 1991

The Metrodome was packed and dressed to the hilt for the 1987 World Series, one of the two fall classics that would be decided there over the most prosperous five-year period in Twins history.

friendlier skylines in big-city America. They call it "home" and, putting aside the frustrations you must endure as a player there, you will not find a greater field advantage for any team in professional sports.

"The Twins have a very good ballclub—in their park," manager Whitey Herzog grumbled after watching his Cardinals lose four times at the Metrodome in a seven-game 1987 World Series. "But their guys didn't look all that good down in our park, did they?" The Twins, 85-77 during the 1987 regular season, won all six of the postseason games they played at the Metrodome and five of six they played there en route to the 1991 Series championship. No question, the world's largest air-supported dome does have its advantages.

The exterior roof is coated with Teflon, giving the outer building a white glow. But the inner lining, made of fiberglass, is a dirty white color that combines with the lighting system to swallow balls hit into the air. The Twins play there regularly and have learned how to deal with the problem of disappearing fly balls, but it's more of a problem for visiting teams. "This ballpark is a joke," Yankees manager Billy Martin said in a 1985 moment of anger. "It should be banned from baseball. Why don't they spend a hundred grand to paint the ceiling blue and this stuff won't happen?"

Teams, especially when the Metrodome is filled, become overwhelmed by the noise, which reverberates around the dome and almost makes the building rock.

HUBERT H. HUMPHREY METRODOME (1982-)

Faced with the problem of a decaying facility in Metropolitan Stadium, the city announced its desire to provide a new home for the Twins and NFL Vikings. Plans for a new indoor stadium were approved in 1979 with financing to be provided by the state of Minnesota. Ground-breaking followed in December of that year.

Named in honor of Hubert H. Humphrey, a former mayor of Minneapolis, U.S. Senator and U.S. Vice President, the facility opened in 1982 as baseball's third dome (behind Houston's Astrodome and Seattle's Kingdome) and the largest air-supported dome in the world.

The oft-criticized Metrodome, where outfielders have trouble picking up fly balls against the dirty-white ceiling, was the first facility to play host to a World Series, All-Star Game, Super Bowl and NCAA basketball championship game.

First game: April 6, 1982. Foreshadowing the offense-favoring nature of the dome, the Seattle Mariners beat the Twins, 11-7.

■ Site of two World Series (1987 and '91)
■ Site of one All-Star Game (1985)

Twins fans waved their Homer Hankies in 1987 and created such a din that noise experts measured Game 2 at an average of 98.5 decibels and equated it to three straight hours without earplugs in a printing plant or standing behind a running Lawnboy. The Cardinals in '87 and the Braves in '91 were clearly affected by the numbing Thunderdome atmosphere.

The Metrodome, while artificial and sterile when compared to many outdoor ballparks, is filled with quirky nuances you normally don't find in domed stadiums or the multi-purpose facilities. You can't come into Minneapolis once or twice a year and expect to play baseball with any degree of efficiency.

Variations of the outfield fences (an irregular 343-408-327) are both fascinating and frustrating. The park's signature feature is a 7-foot padded right field wall topped by a 16-foot piece of stretched canvas that has been dubbed the "Hefty Bag." Balls hitting the hard padding shoot back toward the infield but balls hitting the Bag drop straight to the ground.

For years, the 7-foot padded left field wall was topped by a 6-foot section of plexiglass, providing an outfield view much like you find at a hockey game. The recently removed glass, erected to cut back on ground-rule doubles off the hard turf, made for fast and difficult bounces as well as impaired viewing. The 7-foot center field fence, immortalized by the home run-stealing catches of Kirby Puckett, is made from a thin sheet of canvas that gives on impact, allowing center fielders to snag balls actually hit 2 or 3 feet beyond the barrier.

Another oddity is an irregular curvature behind the plate that creates a right field lean and forces passed balls to bounce off the backstop toward first base. A secondary result is that fielders have more foul-territory room on the right side than the left and fans in the third base boxes are closer to the action than those on the first base side.

Nothing about the Metrodome is conventional, from the way the roof is supported to the shape of the field, a result of the building's rectangular form. It is

Umpires still feel the heat under the air-conditioned dome (left) and a plexiglass barrier (below) once gave left field fans a hockey-like feel. Homer Hanky-waving fans (below left) made the dome rock during the 1987 World Series.

covered by more than 10 acres of Teflon-coated fiberglass and the dome requires 250,000 cubic feet of air pressure per minute to remain inflated. You enter through revolving doors, getting a quick rush of air that makes you feel like you're walking against the wind. That department-store feel is reversed when you exit, the air rush practically vaulting you through the doors and onto the stadium plaza.

The inside experience feels cozier, less imposing, than what you found at Houston's Astrodome or Seattle's Kingdome. The ceiling has a puffy, quilted look and looms overhead with speakers dangling precariously in a high-wire act. From those speakers come all the sounds of a high-tech ballpark and the perpetually angry-sounding voice of public address announcer Bob Casey, a local celebrity dating back to the Twins' Metropolitan Stadium days.

The three-level stands circle the field, awash in a dark blue coloring matched by the outfield walls and the Bag, which covers some of the 7,600 retractable seats that are unfolded for football. The long, paneled scoreboard and videoboard dominate most of the left field view atop the upper grandstand and a 200-foot-long curtain stretches from deep left-center to the right field corner, covering seldom-used upper-deck seats and giving the dome less of an empty feel. The curtain, 51 feet high, is decorated with massive portraits of former stars and banners that highlight the Twins' postseason accomplishments.

There have been many such highlights since 1982, when the Metrodome opened without air-conditioning (the Sweat Box, Sweatrodome) and quickly gained renown as one of the friendliest home run parks in the game (Homerdome). Many focus on Puckett, one of the most popular players in Twins history, and stars like Kent Hrbek, Frank Viola, Greg Gagne, Gary Gaetti, Jack Morris, Chuck Knoblauch and Brad Radke. Others revolve around the Metrodome and the numerous special effects—like them or not—it has brought to the game.

The Metrodome's Teflon-coated roof provides a quilty cushion for the Minneapolis skyline (right) and a protective cover for Twins baseball (above).

Olympic Stadium

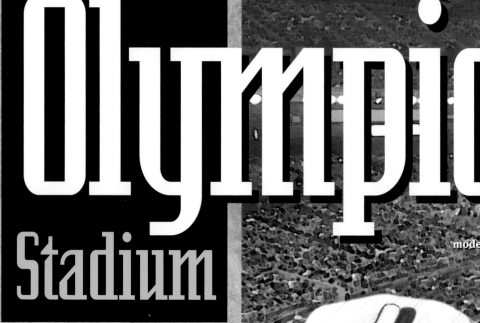

Steve Carlton and Phillies ruin Montreal's Olympic Stadium debut and disappoint 57,592 fans with a 7-2 victory, April 15, 1977

Big crowd watches Expos shell Red Sox and former hero Pedro Martinez in 13-1 victory, June 9, 1999

Tim Raines (right) sets modern rookie stolen base record with 71 in 1981

Padres star Tony Gwynn joins baseball's exclusive 3,000-hit club, Aug. 6, 1999

The Reds end Vladimir Guerrero's team-record 31-game hitting streak, Aug. 27, 1999

Guerrero falls just short of elite 40-40 club with 39-homer, 40-steal 2002 season

ANDRE DAWSON
(225 homers) was Expos' offensive anchor from 1976-86

I t has been criticized, scorned, ridiculed, mocked, despised and laughed at—in two different languages. Some locals call it a white elephant; others think it looks like a white spaceship, ready to transport an alien sport back into the galaxy from which it came. It's a good thing Olympic Stadium has a thick, concrete skin because no venue in sports history has endured more controversy and received less affection.

Strip away all the political posturing, miscalculations, unforeseen costs, bad decisions and untimely mishaps and what you have left is a friendly ballpark. Look past all the contempt and you see a facility with

N.L. wins 4-1, records 11th straight All-Star Game victory, July 13, 1982

Ron LeFlore (below) leads N.L. with 97 stolen bases in 1980

Where Pirates' slugger Willie Stargell hit 535-foot shot on May 20, 1978—the longest homer in Olympic Stadium history

Pete Rose accentuates his short Montreal career with hit No. 4,000, April 13, 1984

The stadium was built for 1976 Summer Olympic Games before being converted to baseball

Steve Rogers (1973-85) holds franchise records in most pitching categories

Rookie Bill Gullickson strikes out 18 Cubs, Sept. 10, 1980

Where Rick Monday drove a two-out, ninth-inning pitch from Steve Rogers in Game 5 of 1981 NLCS, winning a pennant for Dodgers

Where Warren Cromartie's drive caromed off wall, hit Dodgers center fielder Rick Monday on head and bounced into stands for ground-rule double, May 10, 1977

Third baseman Tim Wallach: Career leader in games, hits, at-bats, doubles, total bases and RBIs

No. 10 Rusty Staub: One of three Expos numbers to be retired.

Carter allowed only one passed ball in 152 games in 1978

Where San Francisco lefty Dave Dravecky collapsed in pain with broken arm after delivering pitch to Expos hitter Tim Raines, August 15, 1989

GARY CARTER: Former catcher ranks near top of Expos career lists in many offensive categories.

a proud sports heritage—site of the opening ceremonies and all track and field events at the 1976 Summer Olympic Games, home base for the Expos, one of the two major league baseball franchises that play their home games outside the continental United States.

This is a stadium that lives in two dimensions. In one you can't dispute the two-plus decades of well-publicized financial problems (it has cost more than $1 billion so far) and ill will the structure has generated among French Canadians in the province of Quebec—and its awkward physical appearance, which has shaped the perception of outsiders. In the other, you discover that baseball is not an unpleasant experience in this east Montreal stadium, which once entertained Queen Elizabeth while serving as the centerpiece for a world of athletes in the Olympic Village.

The former Olympic complex still serves as a nostalgic backdrop. Just northwest of the stadium is one of the world's largest botanical gardens, complete with the largest insectarium in North America. Directly north is attractive Park Maisonneuve, perfect for pregame picnics, and next door is a world-class biodome, on the site of the former Olympic cycling track. The area is attractive, clean and largely residential—10 minutes from downtown Montreal. The stadium's trademark feature, of course, is the tower—that 552-foot leaning monstrosity that has been at the center of every Olympic Stadium debate from day one.

The tower, only three feet shorter than the Washington Monument,

The orange roof at Olympic was replaced in 1998 with a roof that is beige on the outside but deep blue inside, giving the impression of a night game under the sky.

leans at a 45-degree angle—considerably more than the Tower of Pisa—and is the world's tallest inclined structure. It hulks over the stadium, huge cables dropping from its apex. Original plans called for the cables to hoist and drop an

Olympic Stadium, with its tower and flying saucer-like look, has become a fixture in east Montreal, on the former site of the 1976 Olympic Village.

umbrella-like top over the structure—baseball's first retractable roof—as weather dictated. But it would take more than a decade of bickering and financial dickering before anything close to that plan could be implemented.

From 1977 through 1986, fans endured the unpredictable whims of spring and fall weather in Montreal—much as they had since 1969 when the expansion Expos, baseball's first non-U.S.-based team, began play at open Jarry Park. The three-tiered Olympic oval was completely enclosed with a steel-and-concrete rim that extended over the seats like a protective roof, leaving only an oval hole at the top. Through the hole, beyond center field, stood the half-finished tower in all its intimidating glory.

The roof, a high-tech synthetic cloth-like material called Kevlar, remained in storage for a dozen years before finally being installed in 1987. But generator problems kept the roof—a gaudy orange umbrella that looked like the meringue on top of a pie—in place for two years before it finally became retractable in 1989. It worked only briefly, because of tears, leaks and other persistent problems. The stadium was closed for 72 days in 1991 when a concrete beam the size of a locomotive fell off the exterior of the stadium onto a concrete walkway.

The orange roof finally was removed in 1998 and the Expos played a full season in open air while a permanent-top dome was being installed. Baseball, 1999-style, came with a plastic fiber cover coated in Teflon—beige to outside viewers on the top, blue (like the sky) to inside viewers from below. The new blue roof, which coordinates well with the blue and yellow seats and a navy blue tarp that covers much of the upper deck to relieve a sense of emptiness that comes with small crowds, can be inflated to keep water from building in heavy pockets on its top.

It is symmetrical baseball (325-404-325) with air-conditioning, 12-foot walls and artificial turf, but everything here has a fresh and curious feel. Where else can you find coatrooms, mixed-drink vendors and the dressiest crowd on the major league circuit? The theater-like lobby that houses ticket booths is distinctive, as is the Jackie Robinson (he played with the minor league Montreal Royals before the Dodgers) statue outside the main entrance. Two national anthems (the fans here really sing) are played, all announcements come in two languages

Since starting play at Olympic Stadium in 1977, the Expos have worked under the ominous shadow of the hulking tower (left), a leaning roof support that is almost as tall as the Washington Monument. The Olympic tower is the tallest inclined structure in the world.

and every Expos rally is saluted with chair-banging fervor. This is baseball with a French accent.

The Big O is really a reasonable place to watch a game. Among the best visual features are an attractive, horizontal scoreboard that dominates your view just above a dead area beyond the center field fence and retired-number logos that adorn the outfield walls. Among the

The bright yellow seats at Olympic are especially noticeable because of the traditionally sparse crowds.

best seats are the left and right field bleachers and the field-level Catcher's Club behind the plate.

Through all the mishaps and unfortunate publicity, Montreal fans maintained a nice relationship with baseball and their teams, most of which have fallen well short of championship-caliber, but have usually been entertaining. Only once have the Expos captured a division title (in the strike-shortened 1981 season) and

only three postseason games have been played on the Olympic Stadium turf.

But just mention names like Rusty Staub (Le Grande Orange), Gary Carter, Tim Wallach, Tim Raines, Andres Galarraga, Steve Rogers, Larry Parrish, Andre Dawson, Pedro Martinez and current favorite Vladimir Guerrero and watch some eyes light up. It's much more fun than discussing political maneuvering, cost overruns and best-laid plans gone awry.

OLYMPIC STADIUM (1977-)

For their first eight years, from 1969 through 1976, the expansion Expos played at Jarry Park—a small, stopgap field that would be used only until the promise of a large covered stadium could be fulfilled. The team topped 1 million in attendance in each of its first five years at the inadequate facility while hopes for a new stadium were bogged down in red tape.

Unable to find funding for a covered stadium, the Expos moved into Olympic Stadium in 1977, the year after it had served as a centerpiece for the Summer Olympics in Montreal. The bowl-shaped cookie-cutter stadium came with artificial turf, symmetrical design, sterile atmosphere and a 552-foot leaning tower (a potential roof support) that gave it distinction.

A high-tech, cloth-like, orange roof finally was installed in 1987 but did not become retractable until 1989—and then only briefly. Problems persisted and the roof was replaced in 1999 by a permanent Teflon dome.

First game: April 15, 1977. The Phillies, behind Steve Carlton, beat the Expos, 7-2.

■ Site of no World Series
■ Site of one All-Star Game (1982)

During the 1998 season, while the roof was being repaired, fans got to watch Rondell White (above) and the Expos play baseball outdoors.

SkyDome

Where an Aug. 27, 1990 game vs. Brewers was delayed 35 minutes when bugs swarmed field

Where Carter blasted his World Series-ending home run off Philadelphia's Mitch Williams, Oct. 23, 1993

Call it a Magic Kingdom of sports, a massive complex that houses a 348-room hotel, a Hard Rock Cafe, several restaurants, a 300-foot bar and enough other amenities to make your Toronto baseball experience, well ... comfortable. SkyDome is not a ballpark, it's an urban megastructure with a split personality, thanks to the inside-outside magic of a remarkable four-paneled retractable roof. This is baseball with frills, the glitzy, high-tech side of America's national pastime.

That glitz is a perfect fit for Toronto, a cosmopolitan, vibrant city that takes pride in its social and cultural diversity and reputation as an architectural pioneer. SkyDome is located in the heart of Canada's largest city, within easy walking distance of the entertainment district,

Oakland's Mark McGwire reaches fifth deck with 488-foot bomb on July 25, 1996 . . . Carter follows two days later with 483-footer

ALCS losers in '89, '91 at SkyDome before two-year championship reign

Oakland's Jose Canseco launches 480-foot rocket into fifth deck of SkyDome in Game 4 of 1989 ALCS

1996 Cy Young winner
PAT HENTGEN

Home runs by Carter, Candy Maldonado in Game 6 of ALCS gives Canada its first pennant and World Series team, Oct. 14, 1992

(Left to right) Carlos Delgado (44) and Shawn Green (42) combine for team-record 86 home runs in 1999 ... Delgado reaches 100-RBI plateau five straight years, 1998-2002

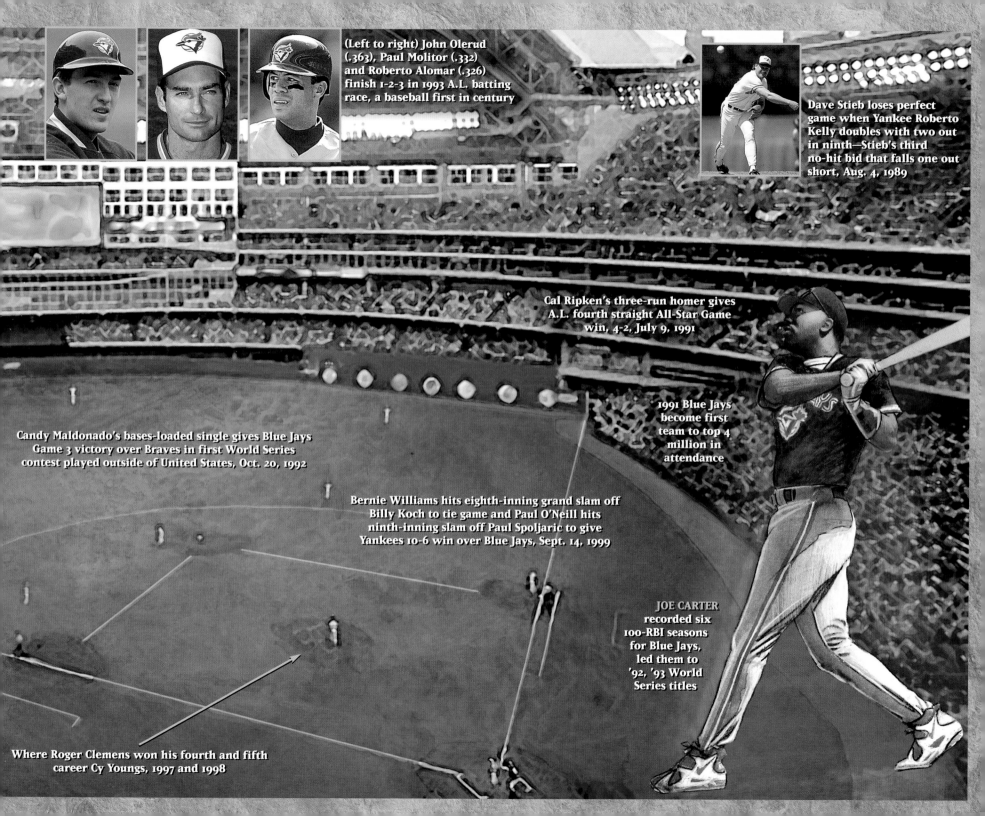

(Left to right) John Olerud (.363), Paul Molitor (.332) and Roberto Alomar (.326) finish 1-2-3 in 1993 A.L. batting race, a baseball first in century

Dave Stieb loses perfect game when Yankee Roberto Kelly doubles with two out in ninth—Stieb's third no-hit bid that falls one out short, Aug. 4, 1989

Cal Ripken's three-run homer gives A.L. fourth straight All-Star Game win, 4-2, July 9, 1991

Candy Maldonado's bases-loaded single gives Blue Jays Game 3 victory over Braves in first World Series contest played outside of United States, Oct. 20, 1992

1991 Blue Jays become first team to top 4 million in attendance

Bernie Williams hits eighth-inning grand slam off Billy Koch to tie game and Paul O'Neill hits ninth-inning slam off Paul Spoljaric to give Yankees 10-6 win over Blue Jays, Sept. 14, 1999

JOE CARTER recorded six 100-RBI seasons for Blue Jays, led them to '92, '93 World Series titles

Where Roger Clemens won his fourth and fifth career Cy Youngs, 1997 and 1998

SkyDome provides an architectural balance for the CN Tower, which rises majestically above Toronto's elegant skyline.

masked by a business-office look and interesting distractions like the gigantic sculptures depicting cheering, booing, pointing and binocular-viewing fans on its north facade.

It's not until you step inside that you get a true sense of SkyDome, the last of baseball's multi-purpose stadiums to be built. Open or shut, the roof overwhelms you—a lurking, hovering protector of the green artificial turf expanse below. When open, it rises up over center field like a giant whale preparing to swallow its prey. When closed, you get a sense of what Jonah must have felt like after the meal. The open roof exposes 100 percent of the field and 91 percent of the seats and it's worth the price of admission just to watch the sliding, rolling, twisting panels work their way open or shut in a fascinating 20-minute sideshow.

If you're not careful, baseball and the Blue Jays can get lost in this remarkable entertainment maze. The symmetrical, turf-covered field (330-400-330) is cookie-cutter ordinary with uniform 10-foot fences surrounding the outfield. But foul territory behind the plate is major league minimum, five-level circular grandstands offer a variety of viewing options and the Jumbotron video board (33-by-110 feet) provides near-perfect reproduction from its high center field perch.

The board is framed by windows of the 70 SkyDome (renamed Renaissance) Hotel rooms that overlook the field—the same hotel Roberto Alomar once called home. Several times those windows have provided shocking outside-in views for Blue Jays fans who caught hotel patrons in amorous encounters. Hard Rock dancers have similar window perches over the right field wall and bar patrons can watch the game without leaving their seat at the center field club level.

SkyDome is not an intimate ballpark experience—on its best days, it's a stadium without bleachers. But, surprisingly, it does not have the sterile, amusement park feel you might expect. When the roof is open on a sunny afternoon or clear summer night, it becomes a pleasant place to watch a game. When the roof is closed because of rain or cold, you're thankful for the wonders of modern technology.

SkyDome becomes a pitcher's park when the roof is open, the stationary panel serving as a wind scoop that causes a home run-hindering downdraft. The ball carries better with a closed roof, a result of the building's climate-controlled predictability. Joe Carter's 1993 World Series-deciding drive into SkyDome's left field seats off Philadelphia's Mitch Williams—one of baseball's most memorable home runs—came with the roof shielding appreciative fans from the cold winds of October.

the appealing Harbourfront Centre and Lake Ontario. It opened in 1989 as a companion to the world's tallest self-supporting structure—the 1,821-foot CN Tower, which challenges the stratosphere from its sentry point beyond the right field corner.

The contrast between the huge, white-topped oval dome and the towering needle is striking—visual counterpoints that help define the largeness of both. SkyDome is big and tall enough to hold a 31-story building inside its dome, which measures 282 feet (87 feet higher than Minnesota's Metrodome) at its apex and weighs 11,000 tons. But its hulking size and drab, concrete grayness are well

The hotel facade is adorned by a gigantic sculpture depicting cheering, booing, pointing and binocular-viewing fans.

The Blue Jays like to brag about their 150-plus private skyboxes and that most of their 50,516 blue plastic seats are located in foul territory. But that results in a steep climb to distant upper decks for fans who are not the most vocal or enthusiastic baseball supporters to begin with. The crowd noise is minimal at a packed SkyDome game, an atmosphere that sometimes ranges between heavy breathing and excited applause. Some of the perceived lack of enthusiasm can be attributed to the park's status as one of baseball's biggest tourist attractions.

You can never really escape the sense that this is an incredible piece of architecture, an engineering breakthrough with a cleanness and luxury never before witnessed in a sports venue. Other amenities include a health club with squash courts, a glass-enclosed promenade that circles much of the stadium, providing wonderful views of the city, a home clubhouse with health spa, weight complex and recreation room and dugout monitors that allow coaches to check activity in the bullpens, which were out of sight behind the left and right field fences before windows were installed for the 1999 season.

You are constantly reminded of baseball's American ties (McDonald's was the supplier of SkyDome concessions for the park's first 10-plus seasons). But banners honoring former Toronto Argonauts (CFL) stars give the place a Canadian feel as well. SkyDome's official baseball stamp of approval was delivered in 1992 and '93 when the expansion Blue Jays (1977) rose up to avenge 1985, '89 and '91 ALCS losses and give Toronto consecutive World Series championships—the first ever for a Canadian-based team.

Cutting through the glitter of SkyDome has never been easy, but Toronto fans have been entertained by a succession of great players and pitchers—Alomar, Carter, John Olerud, Paul Molitor, Rickey Henderson, Devon White, Tony Fernandez, Fred McGriff, Dave Stewart, Dave Stieb, Pat Hentgen, Todd Stottlemyre, Juan Guzman, Roger Clemens—who have kept the wandering spotlight on the field rather than the many distractions that surround it. That hasn't always been easy.

Ballpark comfort is a lounge chair and drinks inside your luxurious room at the Renaissance Hotel, within full view from left-center field of all the action on the field.

SKYDOME (1989-)

Almost 3 1/2 years in the making, SkyDome (no "the" and capital D) rests on a site under which a main water tunnel traveled. During excavation for the facility, a number of artifacts, primarily bottles, were uncovered.

The site for the retractable-roof facility, the last of the multi-purpose stadiums, was a subject of much debate. Chief concerns surrounded aesthetics of the area and prospective traffic difficulties. Ultimately, the government of then-premier William Davis selected the site.

SkyDome's name was the result of a contest that attracted 12,879 different name suggestions. SkyDome was a popular choice, forcing officials to put contest entries into a drum to draw the winner— an Ontario resident named Kellie Watson. Why SkyDome? "It was a dome where you could see the sky," she told the Toronto Globe and Mail.

First game: June 5, 1989. The Brewers' Paul Molitor, whose career would eventually take him through Toronto, opened the park with a first-inning double and the Brewers beat Toronto, 5-3.

■ Site of two World Series (1992 and '93)
■ Site of one All-Star Game (1991)

The New Wave

They are the New Wave ballparks, feel-good venues that borrow the textures, feelings and emotional characteristics of their early-century predecessors.

A seat in Comiskey Park gives you the feel and visual impact of Old Comiskey; Camden and Jacobs give you a sense of Fenway and Wrigley; Minute Maid Park has a Crosley-like hill and Coors Field hits you over the head with its Ebbets Field-like facade; The Ballpark in Arlington offers visual tributes to Tiger and Yankee. Bank One is SkyDome with grass and Tropicana is, well, a dome, not unlike the one that covers the Metrodome.

Some refer to them as retro parks—modern facilities that try to combine all the modern conveniences and technologies with old-time charm and charisma.

Only time will tell if they can accomplish that goal.

The Ballpark
in Arlington

One was a North Texas dinosaur, tough, functional and lacking in the frills and grace of today's modern sports venues. The other is a baseball oasis, a sparkling, quirky and refreshing breeze in the scorching Texas heat. The Ballpark in Arlington stands only a quarter of a mile from the site of old Arlington Stadium, but it's a world or two away from Arlington's oppressively hot, friendly-but-unsophisticated, minor league-like atmosphere.

It's not that old Arlington was a bad place to watch baseball. But The Ballpark was beautiful, upscale, charismatic and filled with amenities long-suffering Rangers fans had never dreamed possible. This was a mansion replacing a one-bedroom apartment—

1996 West Division champions: 35 years of frustration ends as franchise takes first postseason plunge

Perfecto: Kenny Rogers retires all 27 Angels he faces in 4-0 masterpiece, July 28, 1994

Home of Alex Rodriguez, who blasted all-time shortstop-record 52 homers in 2001, 57 in 2002

Ivan Rodriguez, Gonzalez and Rafael Palmeiro (left) combine for 121 homers, 389 RBIs as offense enjoys prolific 1999 season

West Division titles in 1998, 1999 are followed by Division Series sweeps by Yankees . . . Texas scores one run in 1999 Division Series

JUAN GONZALEZ: Two-time MVP and team's career leader in runs, homers, total bases and RBIs

Odd configuration of Rangers bullpen makes for some crazy bounces

Palmeiro's inviting right field porch.

Gonzalez drives in six runs, Dean Palmer (left) and Kevin Elster five apiece as Rangers blow away Orioles 26-7, April 19, 1996

N.L. manages only three hits, but all are home runs in 3-2 victory in first All-Star Game at The Ballpark in Arlington, July 11, 1995

The Ballpark plays host to first interleague game in major league history: Giants 4, Rangers 3, June 12, 1997

After grueling 6 hours, 35 minutes, Rangers beat Red Sox 8-7 in 18-inning thriller, Aug. 25, 2001

Gonzalez ties postseason single-game record with fifth home run, but Rangers still fall to Yankees in fourth and final game of 1996 Division Series

Rangers, en route to third A.L. West title in four years, get three-run homer in ninth from Lee Stevens (right) and game-winning homer in 10th from Gonzalez in 4-3 win over Royals, May 31, 1999

Catcher IVAN "PUDGE" RODRIGUEZ, the Man with the Golden Glove

and a defining commitment for sports in the Dallas-Fort Worth metroplex. With the 1994 opening of the shiny new facility came Arlington's first All-Star Game (1995) and West Division championship (1996) and clear signals that baseball is here to stay, the team will henceforth be competitive and the franchise, after 22 seasons in Texas, finally will be accepted into the major league fraternity.

Arched windows and entryways play a big role in The Ballpark's design (above) and a closeup of the center field office building (right) reveals many architectural nuances as well as a display base for advertisers.

corners is a nice blend of red brick, red granite and cast-stone reliefs of a Lone Star and steer heads alternating between the tops of giant, arched windows. Murals depicting Texas historical scenes circle the park between the upper and lower arches and a brick Walk of Fame rings the perimeter, honoring every Rangers team.

Once inside, you can entertain yourself for hours before even sitting down to watch a game. The concourses are spacious with restaurants, gift shops, a pizza place, an art gallery, a monument to Ryan and a scenic picnic area. But the best attraction is a 17,000-square-foot Legends of the Game baseball museum that might be second only to the facility at Cooperstown. The museum contains a 7,000-square-foot children's learning center with interactive exhibits.

Appearance means a lot in today's sports world and The Ballpark can match any facility in the major leagues, quirk for quirk. Hitters can deposit fly balls into a friendly Tiger Stadium-like right field porch, take aim at the distant Yankee Stadium-like white facade or bounce a line drive off one of the yellow foul poles from old Arlington. Fans can check out the Camden Yards-like brick exterior or the out-of-town Fenway Park-like manual scoreboard on the left field wall.

The Ballpark gives new meaning to the term "retro park." But it's also filled with innovative features and a sense of purpose never experienced by the once-lowly Rangers. The Ballpark, thanks to such stars as Juan Gonzalez, Ivan Rodriguez, Rafael Palmeiro, Will Clark and Kenny Rogers, played host to three West Division titles and the first three postseason series in franchise history—over its first six years. If clothes can make the man, then appearance definitely can make the ballpark.

And this one is an eye-grabber—from the moment you reach Nolan Ryan Expressway in search of a parking space. The square complex with the beveled

The field area, set 22 feet below street level to ease the problem with summer winds, is a frenetic visual wonderland. There's so much to see that visitors often miss the obvious. One thing you can't miss is a four-story office building that dominates the landscape from left-center to right-center, a facility that encloses the normally open center field in most baseball-only parks.

The building, complete with large picture windows and white wrought-iron decor, houses the Rangers' offices (fourth floor), retail shops and ticket offices (first floor) and rental offices (second and third floors). Sitting atop the building are advertising panels and a 42-by-430-foot windscreen. To its right field side is the three-floor museum.

Cast-iron Lone Stars decorate all of the dark green plastic armchairs that make life comfortable for fans at The Ballpark in Arlington.

The park's most appealing feature is the 325-foot, double-deck right field porch that looks very much like the old stands at Tiger Stadium and provides an inviting home run target as well as a sense of intimacy. The state-of-the-art main scoreboard sits high atop the porch pavilion, a nice contrast for the manual board that's part of a 14-foot left field wall that measures 332 in the corner.

Home run hitters also can take aim at a grass incline in straightaway center that serves as the batter's eye, an area backed by the picnic park. It's fun to watch kids scurry onto the grass to chase home run balls, a practice not discouraged by the Rangers. On each side of the batter's eye are bleacher sections (bench-style seats from old Arlington Stadium) and the raised lower-deck seats in left field provide a special bleacher-like view.

One of The Ballpark's quirkiest features is a right-center field fence that angles awkwardly around an elevated Rangers bullpen, creating the possibility of unexpected bounces. The point where the bullpen fence

If attention to detail makes the ballpark, then Arlington can be proud of its baseball-shaped lamps (left) and the baseball-friendly atmosphere it provides for fans.

angles away from the right field wall is 381 feet; it jogs again at 377 feet and connects to the center field wall at the deepest point of the park—407 feet, 7 more than straightaway center.

The park's five levels rise up steeply around you, topped by a white hanging facade that circles the entire rim. The grass field seems to stand up well to the intense Texas heat and it blends well with the 49,166 seats—most of them dark green plastic armchairs adorned with cast-iron Lone Stars.

Everything about The Ballpark fits into one of two themes: baseball and Texas. From the parking lot, you can hear the sounds of the nearby Six Flags Over Texas amusement park and you are constantly confronted by detailed design elements that range from Lone Stars and steer heads to upper-concourse light fixtures shaped like baseballs.

The only detail that's missing is a championship—and that, at least, is more of a possibility now.

THE BALLPARK IN ARLINGTON (1994-)

From its first regular-season game on April 11, 1994, the Rangers' retro home, rising from a suburban landscape dotted with theme parks and restaurants, has oozed "Texas" from its granite-and-brick, Lone Star-decorated facade.

With its quirky, asymmetrical playing field, an inviting home run porch in right field and impressive architectural details that conjure images of classic old-time stadiums, The Ballpark is the crowning achievement of the former ownership group headed by then-managing partner George W. Bush.

If Arlington Stadium was an over-expanded minor league facility, then The Ballpark, located a quarter-mile southeast of its predecessor, is major league in every way— from the four-story office complex looming beyond the center field fence and an on-site baseball museum to the amphitheater and youth field that's a downsized replica of the stadium.

And clearly the Rangers have responded to their state-of-the-art surroundings. Try this on for size: Since moving into The Ballpark, they have won their division three times in nine years and were in first place in 1994 when labor problems halted the season; in their 22 previous seasons, the Rangers had never won the A.L. West.

First game: April 11, 1994. Dave Nilsson's home run spoiled the day as the Brewers' Jaime Navarro outdueled Rangers starter Kenny Rogers, 4-3, before 46,056 fans. Like their first season at Arlington Stadium, the Rangers' first campaign at The Ballpark was shortened by labor problems. Although they were 10 games under .500 when the owners' lockout occurred in August, the Rangers were in first place in the A.L. West, a game ahead of the A's.

■ Site of no World Series
■ Site of one All-Star Game (1995)

Turner Field

Eleven straight division titles, the last six at Turner Field: '91, '92, '93 in West; '95, '96, '97, '98, '99, 2000, 2001, 2002 in East

Javy Lopez (right) hits two-out, ninth-inning homer to tie Cubs 1-1. . . Chipper Jones singles home run in 10th, ending Game 2 of 1998 Division Series

Where Eddie Perez hit game-turning home runs vs. Mets in Games 1 and 2 of 1999 NLCS

Where Danny Bautista lost bases-loaded fly ball in lights during five-run NLCS Game 6 explosion that wrapped up 1998 pennant for Padres

Where Kevin Brown fought off flu and pitched Marlins to Game 6 win over Braves in 1997 NLCS, completing their Cinderella run to World Series

Chipper Jones single-handedly crushes Mets with four homers in three-game sweep of East Division contenders, Sept. 21-23, 1999

1999 MVP CHIPPER JONES

It's one of the classic misnomers in baseball history. Yes, Turner Field is a beautiful place to watch a game, a grass-covered jewel with all the sights, sounds, nuances and feels you associate with the ballparks of yesteryear. But a "field?" No way. This is a complex, a self-advertised "baseball theme park" with all the comforts of home—the kind Donald Trump or Bill Gates might choose to live in.

Turner Field is a gleaming example of baseball's new "it takes a village" philosophy. It's a fenced-off, self-contained suburban neighborhood in the downtown edge of one of the most

Braves christen new Turner Field with come-from-behind 5-4 win over Cubs, April 4, 1997

Tom Glavine (left) goes 20-6 in 1998, wins second Cy Young . . . Denny Neagle joins 20-win ranks in 1997

Cal Ripken goes 6-for-6 with two homers and six RBIs in Baltimore's 22-1 interleague win over Braves, June 13, 1999

Where Sammy Sosa's 444-foot bomb left the ballpark—longest homer at Turner Field, May 22, 1998

Brewers' National League debut is a losing one, 2-1 to Braves in 1998 season opener

Where center fielder Andruw Jones flashes his gold glove at frustrated hitters

Michael Tucker ruins no-hit bid by Cardinals' Alan Benes with two out in ninth . . . Braves win 1-0 in 11th on Andruw Jones' RBI single, May 16, 1997

Four-time Cy Young winner GREG MADDUX

Maddux . . . Tom Glavine . . . John Smoltz (below) — 6 career Cy Youngs, 4 ERA titles for pitching-rich Braves

Converted closer Smoltz posts N.L.-record 55 saves, 2002

The columns that help block off Turner Field's Monument Grove plaza once supported the temporary bleachers for Olympic Stadium at the 1996 Summer Games.

cosmopolitan cities in North America. You enter its gates to a montage of restaurants, shops, picnic areas, video arcades, day-care centers, museums, luxury suites and ATM machines—filled with enough money to ensure many hours of entertainment bliss. Baseball is the overriding theme, but it's not the only game in this town.

The Braves are quick to point out that the food, shops and sideshows scattered throughout the park are merely accessories for the National League's team of the decade, a group that won eight division titles, five pennants and one World Series in the 1990s. But they also know that when the glory days of Greg Maddux, Tom Glavine, John Smoltz, Chipper Jones and Andruw Jones are over, Turner Field—the theme park—will be enough to keep the turnstiles moving.

So far, Turner has been on a massive ego trip. First it was a playground for world-class athletes competing in the 1996 Summer Olympic Games. Then it became a world-class retro-style ballpark for one of the best teams in the game. From Olympic Stadium to Turner Field, it has witnessed world-record-setting performances and baseball excellence that many facilities never achieve.

Turner Field was built with that double personality in mind. Olympic Stadium, located in a former parking lot of Fulton County Stadium, was set up so it could be converted into a state-of-the-art baseball field. The columns that once supported Olympic Stadium's temporary bleachers now serve as posts for the fence that surrounds Turner's outer Monument Grove plaza. There you encounter statues of Hank Aaron, Phil Niekro and Ty Cobb, as well as various retired number statues that front a brick-and-limestone facade not too far removed from Camden Yards.

Adjacent to Monument Grove is a giant entry area that almost overwhelms the unprepared. A one-of-a-kind food court—Bison burgers or moon pies anyone?—works its way toward the Chop House restaurant and there's plenty for everybody, including an arcade area called Scout's Alley, photo kiosks, a retail store, a Hall of Fame and museum and a video wall with monitors broadcasting every in-progress major league game.

The emerald-green field, set 20 feet below street level, is contrasted by patriotic bursts of red, white and blue (the Braves' colors) everywhere you look. Even in the field area you can never really escape the distractions. One of the park's distinctive features is an advertisement—a 42-foot-tall, fireworks-spewing Coke

TURNER FIELD (1997-)

In order to host a world-class event like the Olympics, Atlanta required a new Centennial Olympic Stadium, built just a home run distance from Atlanta-Fulton County Stadium.

After the '96 Summer Games and eight months of retro-fitting, the 1996 Olympic Stadium was converted into Turner Field in time for the start of the 1997 season. While Atlanta-Fulton County Stadium still might have been usable, the new facility was state-of-the-art.

Not only does Turner Field bask in the winning ways of today's Maddux-Smoltz-Chipper Jones teams, it also allows visitors to wallow in the glory of the Braves past—Mathews, Spahn, Niekro and, of course, Aaron. The park is named after team owner Ted Turner.

First game: April 4, 1997. With all of the pitching talent the Braves showcased in the 1990s, the winner in the stadium's opener (5-4 over the Cubs) was Brad Clontz.

- Site of one World Series (1999)
- Site of one All-Star Game (2000)

bottle that commands your gaze from the grandstand roof down the third base line. That's where Coca-Cola's Skyfield area—a 22,000-square-foot grass-covered, attraction-filled pavilion—is located, 80 feet above the outfield.

A three-level grandstand backs the entire foul territory, extending a few feet inside both foul poles, and a video-enhanced scoreboard, topped by a scripted Braves logo over a tomahawk, rises to prominence above the hitter's backdrop in an otherwise open outfield. An out-of-town scoreboard—a relic from Fulton County Stadium—rests atop the Stadium Club in left, topped dramatically by Atlanta's towering skyline. Bleacher-like seats are popular in both left-center and right-center.

Turner's slightly asymmetrical field (335-401-330) does not have the crazy angles that affect play in some of the newer parks, but the grass is meticulously maintained and the surface is one of the most beautiful in baseball. It's hard to find a bad view in the 50,091-seat facility, where first-row fans are 8 feet above the field and minimum foul territory keeps everybody close to the action.

Turner Field, nicknamed The Ted after Braves owner and namesake Ted Turner, also forces visitors to look back, particularly with its many tributes to all-time home run king Aaron. Every seat at Turner is decorated with Aaron's silhouette and his record-setting 715th home run ball can be seen in the Hall of Fame or in an enlarged photo at the main entrance. One of the streets bordering the park has been renamed Hank Aaron Drive and if you park across the street, where Fulton County Stadium once stood, you'll probably run across a memorial plaque marking the spot for homer 715.

It's that attention to detail that marks Turner Field as a new-wave ballpark that offers a glimpse of the past. Aaron, tomahawk chops and a Hall of Fame vs. arcades, interactive stations and ATMs—that's 21st century-style baseball.

Georgia Peach Ty Cobb, in his familiar sliding pose, is one of the statues that greet visitors at the main entrance of Turner Field.

Camden Yards

Also known as Oriole Park at Camden Yards

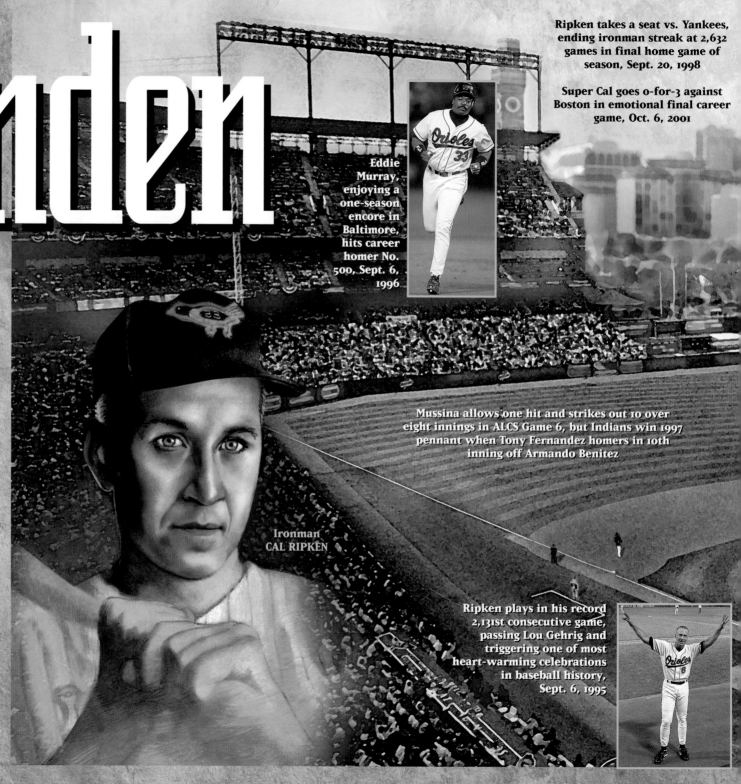

Ripken takes a seat vs. Yankees, ending ironman streak at 2,632 games in final home game of season, Sept. 20, 1998

Super Cal goes 0-for-3 against Boston in emotional final career game, Oct. 6, 2001

Eddie Murray, enjoying a one-season encore in Baltimore, hits career homer No. 500, Sept. 6, 1996

Ironman CAL RIPKEN

Mussina allows one hit and strikes out 10 over eight innings in ALCS Game 6, but Indians win 1997 pennant when Tony Fernandez homers in 10th inning off Armando Benitez

Ripken plays in his record 2,131st consecutive game, passing Lou Gehrig and triggering one of most heart-warming celebrations in baseball history, Sept. 6, 1995

It is nestled snugly within the contours of downtown Baltimore, a comfortable nook in the revitalization of a historic community. Old-timers who remember Camden Yards as a busy former railroad center now marvel at its bustling vitality as a trendy baseball complex. Camden Yards is a reminder of the past, a symbol of renewal and a vision of baseball future—all wrapped strategically in the intricate fabric of a vibrant, growing city.

Camden Yards is, first and foremost, a throwback—an appeal to the charm, charisma and intimacy fans remember from days when baseball

Where center fielder Brady Anderson hit 50 homers in 1996, leading Baltimore's charge to major league-record 257

Mussina, two outs away from a perfect game, surrenders a single to Indians catcher Sandy Alomar before completing his one-hitter, May 30, 1997

Boog's Bar-B-Q is a must-visit spot at Oriole Park

Ken Griffey Jr. went where no one else has gone in 1993, when he crushed a ball off B&O Warehouse during All-Star home run contest

A.L. 9, N.L. 3 in Camden's first All-Star Game in 1993

O's bat around in back-to-back innings and set single-game franchise scoring record in 23-1 rout of Blue Jays, Sept. 28, 2000

Rick Sutcliffe cut the ribbon for Camden Yards' grand opening with a five-hit, 2-0 shutout of the Indians, April 6, 1992

MIKE MUSSINA took center stage as Orioles' ace in 1992

This parking lot behind Camden Yards feeds into Eutaw Street, which becomes a 60-foot-wide promenade that separates the B&O Warehouse (left) from the ballpark. There are amenities for everyone on the promenade, including culinary delights from Boog's Bar-B-Q.

was an extension of community rather than an entertainment extravaganza. It is a marketing strategy, a deliberate attempt to return the game to its ballpark roots. When the park's designers mixed the enchanting nuances of Ebbets Field, Forbes Field, Shibe Park, Fenway Park, Crosley Field, Wrigley Field and the Polo Grounds, they produced a masterpiece of traditions, landmarks and memories that seem to mysteriously multiply with every pitch.

"The smell of Camden Yards is baseball," says admiring Seattle DH Edgar Martinez. And in the case of Camden, the aroma works its way from the outside in.

It starts with the arched brick facade that covers the outside of the stadium and blends subtly with the surrounding neighborhood, matching the field's most distinctive landmark—the all-brick B&O Warehouse that dominates the Eutaw Street skyline beyond the right field wall. You can't take your eyes off the warehouse, an imposing, 1,016-foot, eight-story structure that stretches almost a quarter of a mile and houses the Orioles' offices as well as a cafeteria, sports bar and gift shop.

The ballpark and warehouse are separated by a 60-foot-wide promenade, an extension of Eutaw Street where fans can arrive early to shop, view brass plates that mark landing spots for prodigious home runs, look at plaques honoring Ori-

oles Hall of Famers, take in the batting practice echoes that bounce off the warehouse wall and sample the tasty delight of Boog's Bar-B-Q and Bambino's Ribs.

Boog Powell never played here, but he's a Camden fixture and his barbecue sends tempting odors drifting through the ballpark during the game, luring helpless fans back to the busy concourse between innings. Many give in to its pull, but others are too captivated by what is happening on the emerald green grass field, carved into the ground 16 feet below street level.

It's an irregular-shaped field, framed by the warehouse in right, the downtown skyline in center and triple-decked left field stands that defy the open expanse of the rest of the outfield. A sun roof covers the upper deck, which wraps behind home plate from the right field corner to left field, and an ivy-covered outer wall provides a backdrop in center. An unusual two-tiered bullpen area offers a distinctive look in left-center.

Adding to the nostalgic mix is the knowledge that Babe Ruth, the same Bambino of New York Yankees fame, was born only two blocks from the site of the park, and that his father operated Ruth's Cafe, which was located in what is now center field at Camden Yards. The Babe might have felt right at home here, but

he would have been stunned by the accessories.

Such as the state-of-the-art electronic information boards on the scoreboard in right-center field, which are topped by a double-faced clock you can see from inside or outside the facility. Another electronic board, built into a 25-foot tall right field wall and topped by standing room area, simultaneously posts out-of-town scores.

There is no such thing as a bad seat at Camden, especially for those with tickets in the right-center field bleachers. This is a great place to watch a baseball game, even those that don't end with an Orioles' victory.

The still-youthful Camden Yards has become a symbol for the retro-ballpark mania that is sweeping through baseball, the inspiration for beautiful, old-style

The triple-decked left field stands form a visual barrier, but center field is open to the Baltimore skyline and the ever-present warehouse looms over the right field wall.

facilities that have sprung up in Cleveland, Atlanta, Seattle, Arlington, Phoenix, Denver, Houston, Detroit, San Francisco and Milwaukee. All are spectacular, but so far none have been able to match the ambience and character of Oriole Park.

The only thing missing has been a World Series, but Camden Yards has not been lacking for baseball electricity. Ken Griffey Jr. supplied his share in 1993 when he became the first player to bounce a ball off the warehouse during the All-Star home run competition, Brady Anderson shocked everybody in 1996 when he hit 50 home runs and Mike Mussina helped power the Orioles into postseason play in 1996 and '97. But the national spotlight really focused on Camden Yards during a special September game in 1995.

What baseball fan can forget Cal Ripken, celebrating his new status as the greatest iron man in baseball history, circling the field at Camden Yards, glad-handing with elated fans and introducing millions of television viewers to the charms of a special ballpark. High above right field, hanging from the top of the warehouse, were the massive numbers 2,130, which changed to 2,131 before the eyes of a nation.

The 2130 sign on the warehouse facade paid tribute to Cal Ripken when he tied Lou Gehrig's all-time ironman streak in 1995.

CAMDEN YARDS (1992-)

Also known as Oriole Park at Camden Yards

Its official name is Oriole Park at Camden Yards, but that's often shortened to Oriole Park and, even more often, to Camden Yards.

Camden Yards, opened in 1992 as a state-of-the-art replacement for venerable Memorial Stadium, quickly—deservedly—earned distinction as the blueprint for a new retro ballpark building craze. Many have tried to match the charm and intimacy of Camden—Jacobs Field, The Ballpark in Arlington, Coors Field— but few have captured its overall magic.

One reason is the B&O Warehouse, a historic treasure around which Camden Yards is built. Another is Camden's ability to blend past and present. The cafe owned by Babe Ruth's father once stood in Camden's center field; Cal Ripken Jr. completed his ironman legacy at Oriole Park.

A typical Camden Yards experience might begin with a shopping tour at Baltimore's popular Inner Harbor and a 12-minute walk to the Eutaw Street gate, which gains entrance to the warehouse concourse beyond center field. Fans also can visit the Babe Ruth Museum, located just two blocks away. Browsing not only is permitted at Camden Yards, it is recommended. So are the sights and sounds of batting practice in a baseball atmosphere that literally floats you away.

First game: April 6, 1992. Behind Rick Sutcliffe, the Orioles beat Cleveland, 2-0.

■ Site of no World Series
■ Site of one All-Star Game (1993)

Comiskey Park

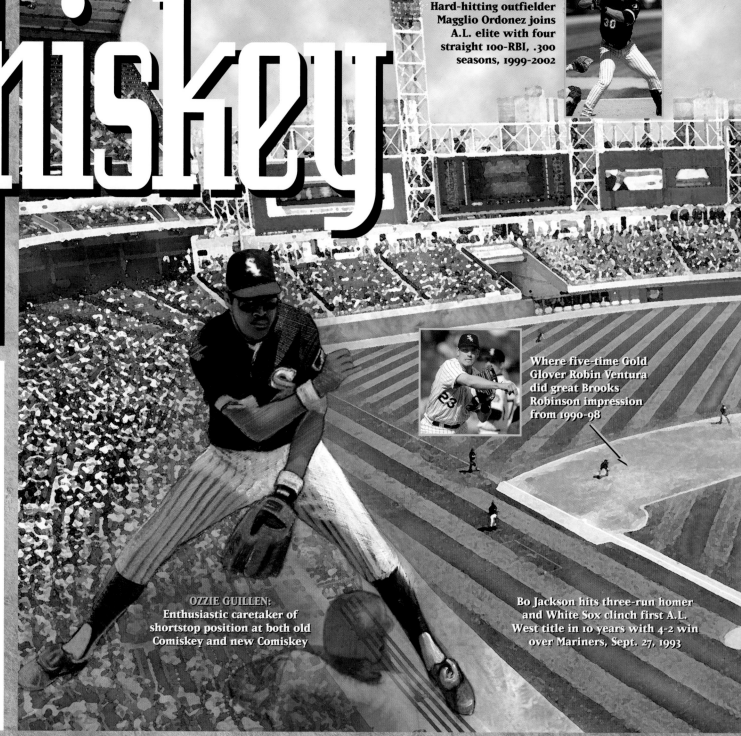

For more than two years, they stood side by side, father and son, on the mean streets of Chicago's South Side. Comiskey Park, the venerable creation of Charles A. Comiskey in 1910; new Comiskey, the evolving protege and successor. This was an honorable passing of the torch, an old story with a new ending. For devoted White Sox fans, it also was an unusual opportunity to respect the past while catching a glimpse of the future.

The future in 1990 was a spiffy, gleaming, state-of-the-art facility

Hard-hitting outfielder Magglio Ordonez joins A.L. elite with four straight 100-RBI, .300 seasons, 1999-2002

Where five-time Gold Glover Robin Ventura did great Brooks Robinson impression from 1990-98

OZZIE GUILLEN: Enthusiastic caretaker of shortstop position at both old Comiskey and new Comiskey

Bo Jackson hits three-run homer and White Sox clinch first A.L. West title in 10 years with 4-2 win over Mariners, Sept. 27, 1993

Thomas (.347) becomes first White Sox player to win A.L. batting title in 53 years and tops 100 RBIs for seventh straight season, 1997

Jack McDowell: 1993 Cy Young winner

Cubs post emotional 8-3 interleague win over White Sox in first regular-season meeting between teams that have competed for loyalty of Chicago fans since 1901, June 16, 1997

Albert Belle obliterates long-standing White Sox single-season records for home runs (49), total bases (399), extra-base hits (99), RBIs (152) and doubles (48), 1998

Rangers' Scott Sheldon becomes third man to play all nine positions in single game during 13-1 loss to White Sox, Sept. 6, 2000

Mariners center fielder Mike Cameron enjoys incredible day against old teammates: 4 solo homers, another near miss and grand slam-saving catch in 15-4 Seattle win, May 2, 2002

Where Dave Stewart shut down White Sox twice in ALCS as Blue Jays set stage for second straight World Series championship, 1993

Where two fans jumped out of stands and attacked Royals first base coach Tom Gamboa, Sept. 19, 2002

Bo Jackson, becoming first major league player with artificial hip, homers with first swing of bat in home opener, April 9, 1993

Tigers 16, White Sox 0 in a disappointing grand opening for new Comiskey, April 18, 1991

FRANK THOMAS:
Two-time MVP first baseman and nine-time 100-RBI man

that would replace the decaying physical structure of old Comiskey, if not the spirit and character that had helped it become baseball's oldest ballpark treasure. New Comiskey was young and alive, dressy and hip. Such qualities as intimacy, charm and charisma would be judged over time.

"Beautiful," marveled Detroit manager Sparky Anderson after watching his Tigers win the new stadium's 1991 debut. "This place feels like a real ballpark. Looks like a real ballpark. ... This place is beautiful, but it's not gaudy. Everybody's going to want one of these now."

It seems ironic, almost a decade later, to hear it judged somewhat harshly — criticism based more on perception than fact. Hailed during its inaugural season as a masterpiece and the first baseball-only major league park to be built since Royals Stadium in 1973, it has become a victim of the very ballpark-building craze it triggered. The only real problem with new Comiskey is that it's not Camden Yards or Jacobs Field.

Eventually, that might not be so bad. As the retro parks continue to pop up around the country, each trying to out-quirk, out-charm and out-

COMISKEY PARK (1991-)

New Comiskey triggered a ballpark-building craze—retro stadiums with all the modern conveniences and clever nuances that allowed visitors to take a trip back in time. But new Comiskey is more than just a ballpark that draws upon Chicago's baseball past. It is the facility that saved South Side baseball for Chicago.

When it became apparent that old Comiskey's days were numbered, rumors surfaced the White Sox would be moved away from their South Side roots to the Chicago suburbs. When those plans stalled, Chicagoans heard whispers the team might be moved to St. Petersburg, Fla., where a stadium already was being built.

When Addison, Ill., voters rejected a move to build a stadium in that suburb, it took a last-minute save by the Illinois legislature to build the new ballpark on the South Side, right next to old Comiskey.

The new ballpark often is criticized for what it isn't—Camden Yards or Jacobs Field. But it is a facility that gives fans a sense of White Sox history.

First game: April 18, 1991. The Tigers' Cecil Fielder hit the park's first home run and the Tigers ran away with a 16-0 victory.
- Site of no World Series
- Site of no All-Star Games

The fireworks-ready scoreboard dominates center field, and fans in the right field picnic area can watch action through a screened, field-level fence (right).

everything the other, new Comiskey stands as a traditional, near-symmetrical park with easy-viewing lines—and a few nice throwback touches mixed in. Comiskey does have a few negatives, but it's a down-to-earth, friendly place to take in a game.

To fully appreciate Comiskey, you have to understand that location and attitude are everything to hard-core White Sox fans, who have been attending games in the rough-edged area between West 35th Street and West 36th for nine decades. Baseball is serious business here, unlike the cuddly, warm-and-fuzzy Cubbies brand played on Chicago's North Side. You approach Comiskey with trepidation and are greeted by an imposing structure that seems much larger than the roofed, compact older version that once stood on the other side of 35th.

Inside, you discover why it looks so huge. The third-tier upper deck, which wraps behind the plate from foul pole to foul pole, sits well back from the field and covers only a small area of the lower grandstands, an architectural quirk that forces a steep rise to the stadium's rim. High upper deck is binocular territory and heavy breathing is encouraged there. Front-row upper-deck seats are located farther from home plate than those in the back row of the upper deck at old Comiskey.

Sections of the upper deck have been closed off when heavy winds come whipping off nearby Lake Michigan, creating potential safety problems. But the steep construction of the upper tier also is what makes the lower grandstand so appealing.

Because the upper deck sits so far back, the lower deck is open and exposed — a behind-the-plate bleacher seat. There are plenty of bleachers in the outfield as well, with four single-decked sections connecting the foul poles, divided in center field by a giant scoreboard and a terraced hitter's backdrop. Some of the outfield openness is blocked, unfortunately, by two video boards and four equal-sized advertising billboards.

Players can enjoy a field-level view of new Comiskey from the bench or top step of the White Sox's third base dugout.

Comiskey has long been associated with its scoreboards and this one is easy to like. Explosive and eye-catching in the Bill Veeck tradition, the board is topped by the familiar pinwheels and responds to White Sox home runs with light-flashing, fireworks-shooting enthusiasm. It is framed on both sides by a white square-pieced, lattice-work design that also tops the outfield billboards and dresses up the light standards, adding a nice visual touch.

Comiskey's charms are demonstrated in other subtle ways. A mid-level concourse circles the stadium, allowing walkers to keep their eyes on the action. The concourse around the outfield has the look of a carnival midway, dotted with stands for cotton candy, hot dogs and other concessions. Right-center field picnickers can watch the action from field level through a screened fence below the bleachers, as can bar patrons in straightaway right. A standing area offers a different perspective from below the scoreboard. Aisles and concourses are wide; ramps protrude from the outer facade, guiding fans to their grandstand destinations.

Comiskey designers at first avoided the temptation to create irregular dimensions, a tribute to the team's symmetrical tradition dating back to the early century, when most parks were nestled into the oddly-shaped contours of their surroundings. Dimensions of 347-400-347 have been altered slightly to 330-400-335, but it remains a roomy pitcher-friendly park with unpredictable winds that can send spring and autumn chills through the sturdiest of bodies.

Nothing sets the tone for a great baseball experience better than the color shock you get the moment you step into the field area. Bright blue seats and fences frame a green grass playing surface that literally explodes before your eyes—a visual wonderland that makes it easy to understand why Ozzie Guillen was always smiling. Also prominent are the sounds of Nancy Faust on the organ, trains that chug and whistle behind the right field grandstands and the crack of the bat on a Frank Thomas, Magglio Ordonez or Paul Konerko line drive.

The only thing missing from a potentially explosive atmosphere are the large, boisterous crowds of old and a team capable of taking the White Sox to their first World Series since 1959.

Jacobs Field

Where Mark McGwire's 485-foot bomb off Orel Hershiser hit left field scoreboard, April 30, 1997

Eddie Murray's 11th-inning single gives Indians 7-6 win over Braves in Game 3 of 1995 World Series—the team's first Series win since 1948

It's an architectural illusion, dropped like a jewel into the center of Cleveland's rehabilitated downtown skyline. Jacobs Field shines, sparkles and glimmers like a diamond, but it feels, smells and sounds like an old-fashioned ballpark. It's an irresistible blending of new and old, a spark that has rekindled a city's love affair with baseball.

The Jake's combination of beauty, character and flashy appeal is no accident. This park wasn't built—it was choreographed. While the exterior is designed to blend into

Jim Thome homers twice, but Indians complete Division Series collapse vs. Red Sox with 12-8 loss, Oct. 11, 1999

Manager Mike Hargrove: Five straight Central Division titles, two pennants, 471 wins from 1995-99

OMAR VIZQUEL: Flashy shortstop with nine straight Gold Gloves to prove it, 1993-2001

Wayne Kirby's 11th-inning single completes comeback, gives Indians 4-3 win in Jacobs Field debut, April 4, 1994

142

Slugging outfielder Manny Ramirez posted baseball's eighth-highest single-season RBI total with 165 in 1999

First-inning ejections of Mike Hargrove, starting pitcher Doc Gooden energize lethargic Indians, who rebound for 9-5 win over Red Sox in Game 2 of 1998 Division Series

Sandy Alomar scores from second on daring baserunning gamble that helps Indians post 8-7 win over Orioles in Game 4 of 1997 ALCS

Cleveland celebrates as Sandy Alomar claims All-Star Game MVP honors with two-run, seventh-inning homer in 3-1 A.L. victory, July 8, 1997

Indians record first postseason win since 1948 when Tony Pena's 13th-inning homer ends Game 1 of Division Series vs. Boston, Oct. 3, 1995

Omar Vizquel fans on suicide squeeze attempt, Baltimore catcher Lenny Webster misses ball and Indians score winning run in Game 3 of 1997 ALCS

Area patroled by Kenny Lofton, five-time A.L. stolen base champion

1999 Indians become seventh major league team to top 1,000 runs in season

Indians score 10 eighth-inning runs, hand Angels shocking 14-12 loss, Aug. 31, 1999

Indians wipe out 14-2 deficit, beat Mariners in 11th on Jolbert Cabrera's single, Aug. 5, 2001

Albert Belle's grand slam off Baltimore's Armando Benitez snaps 4-4 tie and helps Indians post 9-4 win in Game 3 of 1996 Division Series

Albert Belle hits franchise-record 50th home run vs. Kansas City, Sept. 30, 1995

First baseman JIM THOME hits franchise-record 52 home runs, 2002

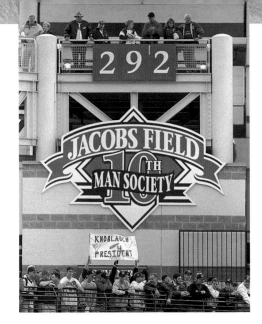

The Indians saluted enthusiastic fans in 1998 (right) with a '10th Man' sign in the left field standing area. The '292' was a running tally of consecutive sellouts that finally ended at 455.

the landscape of Cleveland's downtown renaissance, the interior works hard to combine hip and trendy with charming and old.

You sense that battle the moment you see the intricately crafted white-steel structure, which is nestled into the boundaries of three main Cleveland streets. You can see the inside concourses through the exposed support arms that connect like spider webs to steel buckles, matching the lattice work design of many bridges in the area. The vertical light standards, which tower 200 feet above street level, look like big, white smokestacks, modeled after the factories in Cleveland's industrial zone. Brick, stone and granite also help The Jake blend with its downtown surroundings, a white-steel rim adds a crowning effect and a huge, bronze statue of pitching great Bob Feller guards the Indians Square entrance, adding a nostalgic touch.

Ironically, you can experience the park's signature feature without ever passing through a gate. A large section of the Gateway Plaza entrance across from Gund Arena is closed off only by a wrought-iron fence, allowing visitors a panoramic view of the lush green grass field set 18 feet below street level. Two-thirds of the park is exposed from this unusual sightline over the left field corner, which commands at least a momentary pause for any self-respecting fan—

ballpark regulars and employees as well as occasional visitors.

The ballpark designers sprinkled big helpings of "old" elements throughout Jacobs Field like a cook might garnish his gourmet meal. Concourses are decorated with giant photographs of great Indians players and championship celebrations, the field is asymmetrical with wall irregularities that obviously can affect play and everything seems intimate and close, a vast departure from the feel of the Indians' former home—cavernous Cleveland Stadium.

JACOBS FIELD (1994-)

Jacobs Field, named for Richard E. Jacobs, who with his late brother, David, bought the Indians in 1986, is a symbol for both a city and team's rebirth.

Paired with Gund Arena, home of the NBA's Cavaliers, it forms a downtown Cleveland sports complex that has helped spark economic growth and urban renewal.

The Jake is almost everything its predecessor, Municipal Stadium, was not. Whereas Municipal Stadium was huge, imposing and rarely filled to capacity, the Jake is quaint, intimate and "in"—a park that sold out its first 455 games.

First game: April 4, 1994. An 11th-inning single by Wayne Kirby gave the Indians a 4-3 victory. The stadium's first hit was a home run by Seattle's Eric Anthony.

■ Site of two World Series (1995 and '97)
■ Site of one All-Star Game (1997)

You start your visual tour of Jacobs with the "mini-Green Monster," a 19-foot Fenway Park-like wall that runs from the left field foul pole to center field, at which point it angles away and drops to 8 feet. The wall, which houses an out-of-town scoreboard, fronts a Wrigley Field-like bleacher section and the largest free-standing scoreboard in baseball—a 120-foot-high, 220-foot-wide blitzkrieg of visual effects and advertisements with a giant scripted "Indians" logo on top.

The scoreboard, a Mark McGwire moonshot from home plate, commands most of the left field view, but it doesn't detract from the openness of center field and the left field line—windows to the downtown skyline. Lefthanded hitters take aim at a triple-decked grandstand that rises steeply in right and fans from foul pole to foul pole can watch action

The left field scoreboard with the 'Indians' sign on top provides an inviting home run target—that only the mightiest will reach.

from any of four levels—including luxury boxes and suites.

An oddity of The Jake's asymmetrical configuration is that both foul lines measure 325 feet and straightaway center field (405) is not the park's deepest point. The spot where the little monster connects to the shorter wall in left-center is 410 feet from the plate and provides one of three angles that can result in erratically bouncing balls.

That center field angle marks The Jake's "Back Yard"—a four-tiered, tree and shrub-lined picnic area that offers a panoramic view of the field over the shorter fence. It also overlooks the Indians' bullpen, which is raised above field level for better sightlines—both in and out.

Such nuances only add to the charm of Jacobs Field, which opened to the baseball world in 1994 as a ballpark throwback modeled in the retro image of Baltimore's Camden Yards. The Jake matched up nicely in beauty and intimate detail, but it could not rival the signature-feature warehouse, which became a natural extension of the Camden Yards complex. So Jacobs makes up for that shortcoming with creativity.

Visitors to Camden Yards come away with a feeling of earthy, old-ballpark charm. Jacobs provides a sense of

The overview (left page) shows Cleveland's skyline hulking over Jacobs Field and Gund Arena, home of the Cavaliers. The Jake is all about fans (above, right) and there has been plenty to cheer since the park's 1994 opening.

old—but with all the amenities and comforts of home. The Jake appeals to the family, but it's flashy enough for the young. The music has been carefully choreographed to fit all customers, the electronics are friendly to all eyes and park employees have undergone many hours of Disney training, the better to reach out and touch customers on any level.

But The Jake's greatest appeal might be its complete disassociation from

Cleveland Stadium, the Indians' uninviting, impersonal home for six decades. Jacobs Field (capacity 43,368) is everything the Stadium (74,483) was not—clean, new, vibrant, intimate, noisy and always filled to the brim. It's also filled with expectations, the kind that come from winning teams. Jacobs Field already has played host to six World Series games (more than Cleveland Stadium during its lifetime) and an All-Star Game and its teams ended the millennium with two

pennants and five straight Central Division titles.

Adding to the ballpark flavor are Chris Miltner, the singing beer man (go ahead, ask him what time it is), bleacherite John Adams, the mad drummer, and the Indians' flashy white, red-trimmed uniforms that sparkle under the brightest lights in baseball. The players winning aura fits nicely into a glittering, festive atmosphere that has become one of the best in baseball.

Coors Field

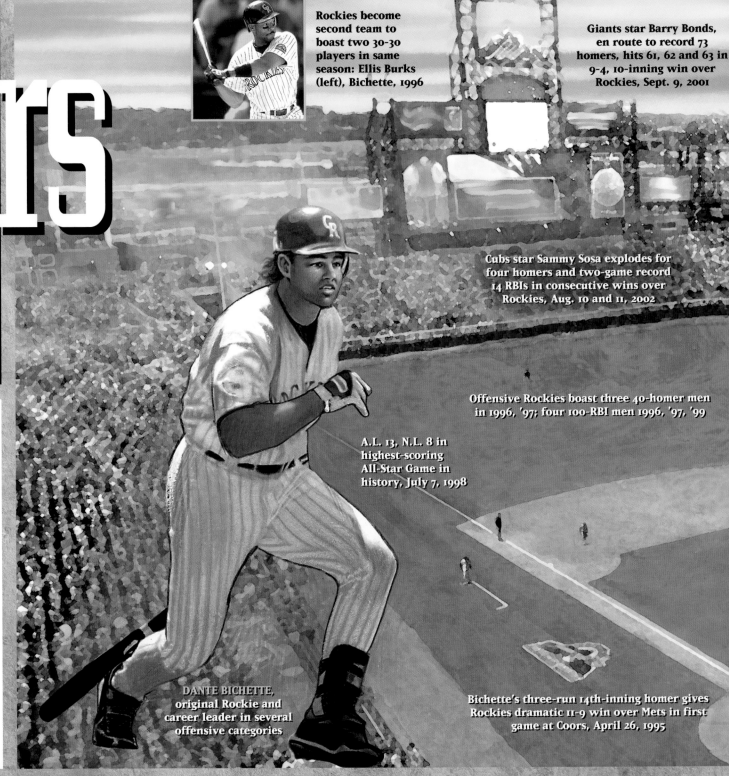

They call it mountain baseball, the kind where home runs zoom up, up and away through the thin air and scores climb up, up and over the limit of our wildest imagination. Coors Field is a launching pad cleverly disguised as a cozy ballpark. You go there to experience its innocence and charm; you leave with a sense of its offensive and unforgiving personality. Coors is a Mile High paradise—with a nasty edge.

The paradise part was planned—choreographed down to Coors Field's most minute details before it opened as new home of the Rockies in April 1995. Not only was baseball's

Rockies become second team to boast two 30-30 players in same season: Ellis Burks (left), Bichette, 1996

Giants star Barry Bonds, en route to record 73 homers, hits 61, 62 and 63 in 9-4, 10-inning win over Rockies, Sept. 9, 2001

Cubs star Sammy Sosa explodes for four homers and two-game record 14 RBIs in consecutive wins over Rockies, Aug. 10 and 11, 2002

Offensive Rockies boast three 40-homer men in 1996, '97; four 100-RBI men 1996, '97, '99

A.L. 13, N.L. 8 in highest-scoring All-Star Game in history, July 7, 1998

DANTE BICHETTE, original Rockie and career leader in several offensive categories

Bichette's three-run 14th-inning homer gives Rockies dramatic 11-9 win over Mets in first game at Coors, April 26, 1995

Andres Galarraga becomes fourth player in history to hit home runs in three consecutive innings, June 25, 1995

Andres Galarraga, The Big Cat: 1996 N.L. home run champ, 1996, '97 RBI champ, 1993 batting champ

Mark McGwire launches ball 510 feet during home run contest prior to 1998 All-Star Game

Trailing 9-2 after 6½ innings, Rockies score 11 in seventh and hold on for 13-12 win over Padres, July 12, 1996

Colorado hitters take aim at Rockpile

Todd Helton explodes into prominence in 2000 with 42 homers and N.L.-leading totals in average (.372), RBIs (147), hits (216), total bases (405), doubles (59) and slugging (.698)

1997 home run champ Walker wins batting titles in '98, '99, 2001 ... percentage triple crown (.379 average, .710 slugging, .458 on-base) in 1999

Dodger Hideo Nomo pitches first no-hitter in stadium history, Sept. 17, 1996

1997 MVP LARRY WALKER: First player to top 400 total bases since Hank Aaron in 1959

Pitcher/pinch-hitter Lance Painter strikes out with bases loaded in ninth as wild-card Rockies drop first postseason game in franchise history to Braves, Oct. 3, 1995

newest retro ballpark an architectural masterpiece of red brick, Colorado sandstone and exposed green girders, it was the magic wand that transformed an old, decaying section of Denver into a vibrant urban village and entertainment center.

The nasty edge was a byproduct of a simple scientific fact: A ball hit in the thin mountain air of Denver will travel 10 percent farther than the same ball hit at sea level. Beautiful new Coors Field was a dark, ugly nightmare for pitchers, a statistics-skewing anomaly for baseball and a career-enhancing blessing for 98-pound-weakling second basemen and shortstops.

This split personality is what gives Coors Field a special niche among such retro contemporaries as Camden Yards, Jacobs Field, The Ballpark in Arlington and Safeco Field. No other park has made such a dramatic impact on both its community and the game. You can feel the buzz of a suddenly active Denver downtown, you can see the explosion of restaurants, nightclubs, shops, art galleries and lofts in LoDo (lower downtown), the warehouse district where Coors is located, and you can calculate the inflated home runs, batting averages and run totals that are redefining the historical perspectives of our national pastime.

The first thing you notice about Coors Field is how it blends into the neighborhood—a warehouse kind of look enhanced by the red-brick facade and low-key design. The main entrance, topped by a distinctive clock tower, rekindles memories of Brooklyn's Ebbets Field and every detail suggests old. Coors Field's height is not overpowering (thanks to the sunken field inside), its coloring is not distinctive to the area and only the light towers and signs reveal its true identity to the casual passer-by.

The Denver skyline towers over the home plate grandstands of Coors Field like a protective mother and the rugged Rocky Mountains provide a scenic backdrop for fans in the first-base-side upper deck and right field stands. Spectacular sunsets over the Rockies are well worth the price of admission, but so are the many quaint, fan-friendly nuances that

Coors Field occupies a significant area of LoDo in full view of the Denver skyline.

give Coors an early-century ballpark feel.

The most captivating is a huge state-of-the-art scoreboard that rises out of the single-deck, open left field bleachers, piggybacking a steel-framed light standard that towers well above the playing field. The latticed light stanchions, designed to reflect LoDo's railroad heritage, also rise periodically from the grandstand rim that circles the park from center field clockwise to the left field foul pole.

Circling the lower-level perimeter of the park is a wide concourse that invites fans to take a leisurely stroll past a playground, a huge mural, an on-site micro

COORS FIELD (1995-)

Without commitment from a major league team, plans for a baseball-only facility preceded the arrival of big-league baseball in Denver. When it was announced on June 10, 1991, that Denver would be home for an expansion franchise, a new stadium already was in the works.

In 1993 and '94, before Coors Field was ready, the Rockies toiled in Mile High Stadium, a facility that had served as home for the Class AAA Denver Bears and Zephyrs as well as the NFL's Broncos.

Tickets to Coors Field are a hot commodity, so take what you can get. But if you do have a choice, try the seats in section 330, where the view and the proximity to amenities is unrivaled.

First game: April 26, 1995. Dante Bichette hit a three-run homer in the 14th inning to give the Rockies an 11-9 win over the Mets in a trend-setting Coors Field inaugural.

■ Site of no World Series
■ Site of one All-Star Game (1998)

short fences and a confined playing area. Not so. Coors Field is spacious, with lines measuring 347 feet and 350, power alleys 390 and 375 and a 415-foot center field that isn't even the deepest point of the park. That honor goes to a right-center field jag that measures 424.

The combination of thin air and spacious field has made Coors Field a tough place for shellshocked pitchers. "I pitched there my second start of the year and for five starts after that I had brain damage," said Expos righthander Jim Bullinger in 1996. That's understandable. Balls

brewery and distinctive concession stands—without ever losing sight of the field. The coup de grace—a feature no other ballpark can duplicate—is a single row of purple seats (upper deck, row 20) that snakes around the grandstand and marks 5,280 feet, or one mile above sea level.

Rising above the center field backdrop is Coors Field's famous bleacher section—the 2,300-seat Rockpile, which admits children and seniors for the unbeatable price of $1 and everybody else for $4. To the right field side of the backdrop is a water spectacular (set within a tree-and-rock-covered mountain scene), side-by-side elevated bullpens and a long manual scoreboard that serves as a big section of the right field fence, raising its height from 8 to 14 feet.

All of this is backdrop for a sparkling grass field (a perfect centerpiece for the park's green hue) with quirky dimensions. A common perception is that Coors Field is a bandbox, a place where lack of outfield speed is neutralized by

leave Coors like rockets and fall in front of deep-playing outfielders, creating softball-like scores. The Rockies, built offensively around such former and current power hitters as Andres Galarraga, Ellis Burks, Vinny Castilla, Dante Bichette, Larry Walker and Todd Helton, produced four 30-homer men in four of Coors Field's first five seasons and the park's single-season team home run record was broken in 1996 (271) and 1999 (303). The faces change, but the results stay the same. Rockies hitters are consistently near the top of baseball's offensive charts while their pitchers struggle to lower confidence-shattering and career-threatening ERAs.

Baseball at Coors might not be artistic, but it is exciting. And it comes with crisp mountain air and intimacy, despite the near-capacity crowds that routinely pack the ballpark. The seats are close to the field, views are unobstructed and there are usually fireworks during every game—the bat-on-ball type that keep Coors Field on a Rocky Mountain high.

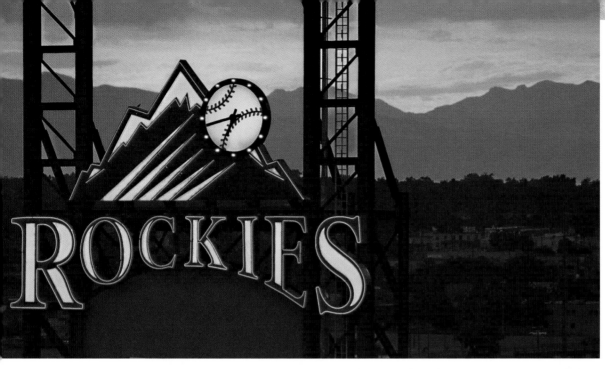

A sunset over the Rockies (above) is as good as it gets, unless you're an aficionado of Mountain Oysters. The purple seats that circle the upper deck (far right) let fans know they are 5,280 feet above sea level.

Comerica
Park

154

They claw, growl, prowl and lurk throughout Comerica Park, fearsome tigers protecting their lair. These aren't just any old tigers—they're the inspirational guardians of one of baseball's grandest new ballparks. The big cats are everywhere, authentic stone sculptures that symbolize the championship hunger of a Tigers franchise hoping to regain its once-ferocious roar.

They also are visual reminders that Detroit baseball, played for 88 years a mile away at the corner of Michigan and Trumbull, has moved light years from the more esoteric and personal kind of game once experienced at Tiger

Comerica Park comes complete with Ferris wheel, carousel and growling tigers on each side of scoreboard

Statues of former Tigers greats keep watch over proceedings from perches in left-center field

Flagpole, like at Tiger Stadium, is in play

Outfielder BOBBY HIGGINSON has been Tigers' most consistent performer since 1996

Fans brave 36-degree temperature and watch Tigers beat Seattle, 5-2, in first game at Comerica Park, April 11, 2000

Center field water spectacular celebrates good plays by the Tigers

Shane Halter becomes fourth player in major league history to play all nine positions in single game—a 12-11 Detroit win on final day of season, Oct. 1, 2000

DAMION EASLEY becomes first Tiger to hit for cycle at Comerica, driving in four runs in 9-4 win over Brewers, June 8, 2001

Dirt track from mound to home plate—a pre-1900s touch

Flying ants swarm stands and send fans scurrying for cover, but Tigers ease their discomfort with 6-5 win over Mariners, Aug. 23, 2000

Tigers are everywhere at Comerica Park, where youngsters get some amusement park fun with their baseball. A carousel (top left) with 30 hand-painted tigers is a must-see attraction, as is a Ferris wheel with baseball-shaped cars (near left).

Stadium. Charming and quaint have given way to big and spectacular in a retro-style facility that takes "entertainment" to a whole different level.

"Comerica redefines what a day at the ballpark means," said longtime Tigers broadcaster Ernie Harwell in pregame remarks at the park's April 11, 2000, opening. Harwell wasn't kidding. This ballpark/amusement park provides an interesting perspective of how far team owners will go to attract fans to their games.

Baseball purists can take heart. Comerica keeps its primary focus on the game while stirring emotions with historical tributes, quirky nuances and a stunning vista of Detroit's downtown skyline. It's easy enough to go to a game and immerse yourself in baseball without succumbing to the family-friendly distractions that lurk just around every corner.

Stainless steel statues of Ty Cobb (left) and other former Tigers greats are primed for action beyond the left-center field fence at Comerica Park.

But for young fans who want more than baseball, this is your place. One area off the main concourse houses a 50-foot-high Ferris wheel with 12 cars shaped like baseballs. For those who prefer round-and-round over up-and-down, there's a carousel with 30 hand-painted tigers and two chariots. Everybody, young and old, can marvel at the high-shooting water spectacular disguised as a horizontal batter's eye in center field—an aquatic fireworks display, choreographed to music, that salutes good plays by the Tigers.

The ornate attention to detail at Comerica is remarkable. The park fits architecturally into the historic Fox theater district (Foxtown), infusing life into one of the country's poorest downtown areas. Tiger claw scratches are carved into the pillars that surround the facility, the Tigers' distinctive old-English "D" appears on 29 special pottery displays and fans are dazzled by seven stone tiger sculptures and 80-foot baseball bats that frame the various gates.

It's also easy to be dazzled by the amusement rides, beer garden, pubs and numerous restaurants and pizza stands that compete for patrons as part of a wide main concourse that never loses contact with the field. But the serious fan will be more intrigued by the Walk of Fame pedestrian museum that details the team's history, decade by decade, with the help of 25-foot bat displays on the main concourse, or the stainless-steel action statues of former Tigers greats Ty Cobb, Hank Greenberg, Charlie Gehringer, Hal Newhouser, Al Kaline and Willie

Sculptures, fountains (above), rides, lifesize statues—no expense was spared in construction of Comerica, which takes entertainment to a whole new level.

Horton that stand in home run territory beyond the left-center field fence.

Everything considered, fans don't discover the real charm of Comerica until they occupy one of its 40,120 seats and examine one of the showcase configurations of baseball. The park is refreshingly open and inviting from the right field foul pole to left-center field, providing an impressive view of downtown Detroit.

The left field view is blocked by what the Tigers call baseball's biggest scoreboard. The 202-by-147-foot structure features a video screen, two matrix boards and a linescore board with a rounded clock top that supports the huge letters,

"T I G E R S." On each side of the clock, two 40-foot-long tigers stand, ever ready to growl and flash their eyes in celebration of a Detroit home run.

Once fans get to the field area, they discover that Comerica, like is predecessor, is both charming and intimate. Most of its seats are in the triple-decked stands (lower level, suites and upper level) that wrap behind home plate from the left field foul pole to just beyond first base and the two decks that extend the rest of the way to the right field foul pole.

Only about 15,000 are in upper-deck territory and outfield seating is minimal, with bleachers offering home run targets in left field below the scoreboard and in right-center and straightaway right, above the bullpens. The sunken field (outsiders can get a glimpse of action from Adams Street) enhances the intimacy and accentuates the skyline's looming presence.

But what really sets Comerica apart is its quirky dimensions. In a baseball age defined by power and home run-friendly ballparks, this was designed as a pitcher's paradise, with a 345-foot foul pole in left, a 395-foot left-center power alley and a 420-foot center field that would necessitate a virtual moonshot to land in the fountain. The right field line is a little more reasonable at 330, but home run heaven this is not.

And Tiger Stadium this is not. That distinctive right field overhang, the roof

Baseball's biggest scoreboard is a "Tiger" extravaganza, complete with big cats (perched on upper corners) that growl and flash their eyes at fascinated fans.

that gave it a band-box feel, the inviting home run dimensions, the shoehorned seats, the view-blocking support pillars, the tiny dugouts—all are gone, part of Detroit's colorful baseball past. The only visual throwbacks are an early century-like dirt track that stretches from the mound to home plate and an on-field flag-pole that stands 38 inches in front of the left-center field fence—much like the one that fronted the center field wall at Tiger Stadium for many years.

Comerica designers worked hard, however, to retain at least a little of that wonderful Tiger Stadium atmosphere. And Harwell, for one, thinks they succeeded. "Now we have the old-fashioned ambience and all the modern conveniences," he said.

Minute Maid

Park

Also known as Enron Field (2000-2002)

Tracks on which bigger-than-life antique locomotive crosses outfield, spewing smoke, blowing whistle and tooting carnival melodies

Craig Biggio hits leadoff home run for third consecutive start and second straight game against Cubs, Aug. 14, 2001

Union Station entrance, site of once-busy Houston train depot

Center fielder LANCE BERKMAN, newest member of Houston's "Killer Bs"

Berkman and Jeff Bagwell combine for 73 homers, 256 RBIs in 2001 . . . Switch-hitting Berkman joins N.L. elite with two-year total of 76 homers, 254 RBIs, 2001-02

Minute Maid Park fits snugly into Houston's downtown landscape, a shocking contrast to the once stately and overwhelming Astrodome. From an "Eighth Wonder of the World" technological palace to a converted train station; from pitching to power, turf to grass, dome to retractable roof, cavernous to intimate—baseball has done a boot-stomping, Texas-size makeover in the Bayou City.

Nowhere has the change from arti-ficial sterility to retro-park charm been more dramatic than in Houston, where the once-proud Astrodome served as the standard for a rash of multi-pur-

Destination of 70th home run by Giants left fielder Barry Bonds—a 454-foot shot off Wilfredo Rodriguez (above) that tied Mark McGwire's single-season record, Oct. 4, 2001

Atlanta wins Game 1 of Division Series when Chipper Jones crashes three-run homer off Astros closer Billy Wagner, breaking 3-3 eighth-inning tie, Oct. 9, 2001

Tal's Hill

An Enron Field first: Jeff Bagwell hits for cycle in 17-11 win over St. Louis, July 18, 2001

Lefty Randy Wolf and Phillies ruin Enron Field grand opening with 4-1 victory over Astros, April 7, 2000

Lefty closer BILLY WAGNER has pushed radar guns to their limit and recorded four 30-plus save seasons since 1998

Minute Maid Park, a former train station, retains that look and feel for Houston fans. The Conoco balcony (right) allows fans to literally become a part of the field.

pose stadiums in the 1960s, '70s and '80s. Minute Maid, the former Enron Field, is a 360-degree about-face in atmosphere and grace, a throwback facility in the image of Baltimore's Camden Yards, Denver's Coors Field and The Ballpark in Arlington.

When Minute Maid opened in April 2000, Astros fans got their first taste of open-air baseball in 35 years. They also experienced the game more intimately on an asymmetrical field covered with natural grass and filled with quirky nooks and crannies. Home runs, hard to come by at the spacious Astrodome, flew out of the new park with shocking abandon and offense became an Astros' tangible

rather than a subjective fan emotion.

The park's intimacy is tied closely to its relationship with historic Union Station, once the railroad hub of Houston and the industry around which the city was built. The restored train depot, renovated and given a baseball facelift, now houses Astros offices as well as various team-related businesses while serving as the primary entrance to the left field side of the ballpark.

The square-shaped complex, located within walking distance of downtown, draws on the natural ambience of Union Station, much like Camden Yards feeds off its old warehouse. But the station gets plenty of help from a brick and con-

The charm of Minute Maid Park is in its views (left) and nuances, one of which affects game action. Tal's Hill (below) has a 30-degree slope and a flagpole that can be an obstacle for center fielders.

crete exterior that blends easily into its city surroundings and a charming clock tower (with carillon) that corners the southeast entrance behind home plate.

Like any ballpark with a retractable roof, Minute Maid has a Jekyll-Hyde personality. When open, the roof's three massive panels stack neatly on top of each other beyond the right field fence, affording fans a larger opening than any other retractable-

MINUTE MAID PARK (2000-)

Also known as Enron Field (2000-2002)

Minute Maid is the classic retro park, a downtown Houston revitalization tool that connects with the city's past through renovation of old Union Station. The former Enron Field plays heavily off the railroad theme, going so far as to entertain fans with a larger-than-life 19th century locomotive replica that celebrates big moments by chugging along the 800 feet of track on the left field roof.

The 29-acre facility features a retractable roof and a natural grass field—and the prospect of open-air baseball after 35 years in the Astrodome. The facility, which took 2½ years to build, is on the northeast end of downtown Houston, bounded by Crawford Street, Congress Avenue, Texas Avenue and Hamilton Street near the George R. Brown Convention Center.

The old Union Station building features a team store, cafe, bakery and lounge on the main floor and team offices on the fourth and fifth. A Roof Deck on the sixth floor allows private groups to enjoy game action from on high (a la Wrigley Field) with a great view of the Houston skyline.

First game: April 7, 2000. Home runs by Ron Gant and Scott Rolen sparked the Phillies to a 4-1 opening day win over the Astros.
- Site of no World Series
- Site of no All-Star Games

roof facility. It doesn't loom overhead like Miller Park in Milwaukee or Bank One Ballpark in Phoenix.

When closed to protect fans from rain or the stifling South Texas heat, the Houston skyline remains visible through the 50,000 square feet of glass built

With the scoreboard flashing from its second-deck perch, right field at Minute Maid Park angles quickly from the line to the bullpen in right-center, a psychological challenge for lefthanded hitters.

into the west wall of the roof. In addition to letting in natural light, the glass allows Crawford Street pedestrians to look in on game action.

Minute Maid offers wide concourses that stay in touch with the action and the park is filled with standing and viewing areas that provide interesting sightlines. Most of the 40,950 seats (a deep green to enhance the retro look) are in three decks that wrap behind home plate from foul pole to foul pole and the double-decked right field stands that extend almost to center field, below a huge, state-of-the-art scoreboard that rekindles memories of the Astrodome's home run spectacular.

The park's most interesting features are in straightaway left and on the play-

ing field itself. A limestone facade, with huge Comiskey Park-like portals to the outside world, forms an eye-catching backdrop beyond the left field fence and provides popular standing-room balconies. One circular balcony, which features an old Conoco gas pump that keeps count of Astros home runs, actually extends over the field, a potential landing point for high fly balls that might normally be caught.

On top of the facade, where the sliding roof connects to the permanent wall, a 50,000-pound, bigger-than-life 1860s-era locomotive chugs across 800 feet of track, whistling and spewing smoke in celebration of key Astros moments. There are plenty because home runs literally jump over the 19-foot-high fence, creating

havoc among fans sitting in the left field Crawford Boxes (a mere 315 feet from home plate at the foul pole) and bouncing off the arched outer facade like pinballs.

Right field is not nearly as friendly, with a 326-foot line that angles quickly to 373 in right center and 435 in dead center. Center fielders have to deal with a 30-degree slope (Tal's Hill) that angles up to a 10-foot fence and an on-field flag-pole—obstacles reminiscent of the terrace at Cincinnati's Crosley Field and the flagpole at Detroit's Tiger Stadium. Other quirky juts and jags make balls richochet unpredictably off the outfield walls.

To call Minute Maid Park cozy is something of an understatement. Fans in both corners are five feet from the line and fans in the right field bleachers can

literally reach out and touch someone—or a ball that might normally remain in play. Foul territory is minimal with front-row fans at first and third base only 43 feet from the action.

In keeping with the retro-park handbook, Minute Maid is filled with obvious and subtle amenities. Restaurants, a variety of food courts and an interactive area for children give it a theme park feel and there's a manual out-of-town scoreboard on the left field wall and an electronic ticker in right that keeps fans apprised of stock quotes.

This is a ballpark for today's dot.com sports fans—a heaping dose of nostalgia spiced with all the conveniences of home.

Pro Player Stadium

Also known as Joe Robbie Stadium (1993-1996)

You can get intimidated by its Teal Monster, lost in its Bermuda Triangle, deflated by its size and overwhelmed by its championship-filled history. Pro Player Stadium doesn't waste any time worrying about frivolous notions like charm and intimacy. This is an imposing concrete-and-steel football edifice that doubles as a diamond in the rough. Young and macho, it already has been the proud championship stage for three Super Bowls and a home-field arena for one of the most unlikely World Series winners in baseball history.

166

Giants' Barry Bonds hits 400th career homer, becomes first member of 400-400 club, Aug. 23, 1998

Where Mark McGwire hit homers 56, 57, 58, 59 over two games en route to record 70-homer season, Sept. 1, 2, 1998

The Teal Monster

First no-hitter in franchise history: Al Leiter beats Rockies 11-0, May 11, 1996

Edgar Renteria's bases-loaded, ninth-inning single gives wild-card Marlins 2-1 Division Series win over Giants in franchise's first postseason game, Sept. 30, 1997 ... 5-year-old Marlins become youngest World Series champs when Renteria delivers Game 7-ending single in 11th inning, Oct. 26

JEFF CONINE: Career leader in many offensive categories

Bobby Bonilla hits two-out, two-strike, bottom-of-the-ninth grand slam to give Marlins dramatic 9-6 win over Rockies, Sept. 16, 1997

Marlins record 8-4 interleague win over Devil Rays in first battle of Florida-based teams at Pro Player Stadium, June 24, 1998

Livan Hernandez strikes out 15 in riveting 2-1 Game 5 NLCS win over Braves, Oct. 12, 1997

Kevin Brown: 17-11, 1.89 ERA in outstanding 1996 season

Luis Castillo's hitting streak ends at 35 in interleague victory over Detroit, June 22, 2002

Strange ending: Braves closer John Rocker commits balk by dropping ball while standing on rubber in bottom of ninth and Danny Bautista scores to give Marlins 3-2 victory, May 8, 2000

The Bermuda Triangle

Alex Fernandez, making comeback from rotator-cuff surgery, posts emotional 98-pitch complete-game win over Rockies and punctuates effort with home run, Aug. 6, 1999

Good start: Expansion Marlins down Dodgers 6-3 in Joe Robbie debut, April 5, 1993

Where Robb Nen blew away hitters for four-plus seasons while compiling 108 saves

GARY SHEFFIELD: hit 42 homers, drove in 120 runs in 1996

Concrete and palm trees dominate the facade at Pro Player Stadium, which successfully blends baseball into a football-first arena.

PRO PLAYER STADIUM (1993-)

Also known as Joe Robbie Stadium (1993-1996)

It has been the home of the Florida Marlins since their expansion debut in 1993, but Pro Player Stadium's roots date back to 1984. That was the year Miami Dolphins owner Joe Robbie announced plans to build a new football facility—with the tentative name of Dolphin Stadium.

In April 1987, before a game had actually been played in the new building, it was officially renamed Joe Robbie Stadium. In August of that year, an NFL exhibition contest christened pro football's new state-of-the-art facility.

It became a multi-purpose facility for the first time in 1988 when a major league exhibition game was played there and a full-time baseball facility in 1993 with the formation of the Marlins. Naming rights were granted to Pro Player, a division of Fruit of the Loom, in 1996.

First game: April 5, 1993. Veteran knuckleballer Charlie Hough pitched the Marlins to a 6-3 victory over the Dodgers.

- Site of one World Series (1997)
- Site of no All-Star Games

Make no mistake: Pro Player is first and foremost a football stadium, opened in 1987 when Joe Robbie constructed a $115-million, fully enclosed, open-air facility for his Miami Dolphins—funded entirely by private money and located on a 160-acre tract midway between Fort Lauderdale and Miami. When Joe Robbie Stadium (formerly Dolphin Stadium) played host to its first regular-season NFL game, baseball was still six years from becoming a South Florida reality. The expansion Marlins eventually turned Miami into a four-sport city, but Pro Player never loses that sense of football, even though it converts into an attractive baseball field—with personality.

It's the size. The stadium's 75,000-plus seats are rocking during football season, mostly empty for baseball, creating a cavernous, hollow sensation enhanced by the blaring sounds of a huge JumboTron board designed to entertain capacity crowds. For several years, the outfield upper-deck seats were covered by a blue tarp during baseball season to compensate, but the effect was minimal.

The best feature of Pro Player is an asymmetrical, natural-grass field that offers enough quirks and surprises to make baseball life interesting. The first thing that captures your eye is a left field barrier that ranges in height from 25 to 30 feet—a so-called Teal Monster that eats up potential home runs. The wall itself is an unremarkable 8 feet, but an uneven out-of-town manual scoreboard tops the fence and extends from just short of the left field corner well into left-center field. A clock sits on top of the scoreboard and seems to pull balls toward it like a magnet.

Just beyond the scoreboard in left-center the fence jogs seriously forward, creating a notch, 434 feet from home plate, called the Bermuda Triangle—a place where balls can disappear and emerge again as triples or inside-the-park home runs. The left field foul pole is 330 feet, straightaway center is 410 and the right field pole is 345, with bleachers covering the entire right field area and the huge video board perched high on the stadium's outer rim. The field's green grass is framed by a sea of orange seats and blue and teal trim, colors that become more vivid with every empty seat.

The normally vacant upper decks at Pro Player were filled to the brim in the 1997 World Series, when the 5-year-old Marlins completed their surprising championship run.

That was not a problem in 1993, when the first-year Marlins drew more than 3 million fans. They were the creation of H. Wayne Huizenga, who purchased 50 percent of Joe Robbie Stadium in 1990 and became the point man for bringing major league baseball to South Florida. This was a state-of-the-art facility that featured more than 200 luxury suites and a breakthrough special level of "club seats" that provided extra amenities for deep-pocketed patrons—the perfect lure for baseball's bottom-line oriented expansion committee.

Huizenga, who would become the facility's sole owner in 1994 and sell naming rights to Pro Player in 1996, made baseball modifications and began building a free agency-enhanced roster that could contend for a championship. In 1997, the 5-year-old Marlins, led by Gary Sheffield, Moises Alou, Kevin Brown, Alex Fernandez, Bobby Bonilla and Alex Fernandez, won a wild-card playoff berth and became the youngest team to win a World Series when Edgar Renteria delivered an 11th-inning single to beat the Indians in Game 7 at

Pro Player Stadium. After the Series, Huizenga conducted a shocking player firesale that gave his depleted roster the look of a hopeless expansion team.

Your first thought upon seeing Pro Player is "expansive"—a monolith surrounded by acres of parking lots and numerous palm trees. Two swirling ramps extend from each corner and lead fans to their seats. Three statues greet you at the main entrance—Robbie, former Dolphins coach Don Shula and the immortal Casey, from *Casey at the Bat* fame.

An outside attraction called Sports Town features interactive games, food stands, bars and souvenir kiosks under huge tents off the stadium's south perimeter, but Pro Player doesn't have the mall culture you get at newer parks. Inside sightlines are set up for football, as is the lighting, which makes the home plate area dark and pitcher-friendly. When you go to Pro Player, be sure to take an umbrella because it probably will rain—16 delays in 1999. If you go to an afternoon game in the summer, prepare to sweat.

After topping 67,000 in each of the four 1997 World Series games, the depleted Marlins have watched attendance slip drastically and the stadium often feels empty and antiseptic. One memorable exception was September 1 and 2, 1998, when Mark McGwire brought his home run-hitting parade to town and the stadium was packed.

McGwire hit four home runs in two games, two of which landed on the big center field backdrop tarp. The lingering memory for a national television audience was of several teenagers diving onto the tarp and scrambling after a Super Bowl-caliber baseball souvenir.

Miller Park

Home run heaven: Dodger Shawn Green goes 6-for-6, hits record-tying four homers, drives in seven runs and sets big-league mark with 19 total bases in 16-3 win over Brewers, May 23, 2002

Where Sammy Sosa deposited series of 500-foot blasts during first round of All-Star home run contest, July 8, 2002

Where Bernie Brewer celebrates Milwaukee home runs

They stood side by side a few miles west of downtown Milwaukee, a technologically enhanced vision of baseball future and a crumbling tribute to baseball past. Nowhere was the transition from old to new more visible than in Brewers country, where fans could follow the brick-by-brick progress of wonderful new Miller Park while enjoying the no-frills, steel-and-concrete simplicity of County Stadium.

Miller Park stands alone now, secure in its mission of transporting Milwaukee into baseball's retro age. All the conveniences of home come with quirky nuances and a retractable

6-foot-8 first baseman RICHIE SEXSON pounded 45 homers and drove in 125 runs during Miller Park's inaugural season

President George W. Bush throws out first pitch and Sexson hits eighth-inning homer in Brewers' 5-4 win over Reds in first game at Miller Park, April 6, 2001

Jamey Wright fires two-hit shutout and Geoff Jenkins hits two home runs, giving him five homers, 12 RBIs and seven hits in two games against Expos, April 28 and 29, 2001

Shortstop Jose Hernandez hits two home runs and ties team record with seven RBIs in 12-4 win over Astros, April 12, 2001

With both teams out of pitchers and no end in sight, 2002 All-Star Game is stopped after 11 innings with American and National leagues locked in 7-7 tie

Jeromy Burnitz called first base home for five-plus Milwaukee seasons while hitting 165 homers, 34 in Miller Park's 2001 debut

BEN SHEETS: Former Olympic star becomes fifth rookie pitcher since 1980 to win 10 games before All-Star break, 2001.

Miller Park's roof can protect fans from the elements or open them to the pleasures of a game in the afternoon sunshine. One familiar face from County Stadium is Bernie Brewer, who enjoys games from his 'Dugout' perch (right) in the left-center field stands.

arched windows that reflect the architecture of the city's abundant warehouses and factories. The simple exterior is enhanced by a home plate-entrance clock tower, statues of Milwaukee Hall of Famers Hank Aaron and Robin Yount and a laid-back, social atmosphere that carries over to the game.

There's nothing simple about the interior of Miller Park. The wide, open concourses, fresh paint and colorful murals depicting the five great industries of Wisconsin provide a startling contrast to the narrow, dingy concrete County Stadium walkways that reeked of hot dogs and stale beer. And visitors can't escape the power of Miller Park's giant roof, which can shelter them from outside elements or open up to the pleasures of sunshine and cool lakefront breezes.

The convertible, fan-shaped roof, the only one of its kind in North America, features seven gigantic panels, five of which pivot on a semi-circular track from a point behind home plate. When open, the movable pieces are stacked on fixed panels atop the grandstands down the left and right field lines—like giant, hovering, mechanical monsters. When closed, paneled windows that surround the

roof to protect some of the game's sturdiest fans from the Lake Michigan-inspired eccentricities of Mother Nature. And they come without sacrificing the distinctive traditions that separate Milwaukee from other less-passionate baseball cities.

Miller Park is, by design, an urban stadium in a suburban setting. While other retro parks like Jacobs Field, Camden Yards and Coors Field are tied closely to the revitalization of struggling downtowns, Miller Park, surrounded by expansive parking lots in an undeveloped area, is tied to the almost obsessive Milwaukee tradition of tailgating. Fans, like college supporters on a football Saturday, show up early for a festive pregame warmup of brats, burgers and beer.

Through the smoky haze that defines baseball in the blue-collar north, visitors to Miller Park discover a hulking brick-and-limestone stadium with huge

stadium exterior let in natural daylight.

On a perfect summer day or night, the roof and windowed panels beyond the center field fence will be open, Bernie Brewer will be celebrating Milwaukee home runs from his "Dugout" perch and slide in left-center field and fans will revel in the traditional delights of sixth-inning Sausage Races and seventh-inning renditions of "Take Me Out to the Ballgame" and "Roll Out the Barrel." When Miller Park's 41,900 seats are filled, things do get crazy.

Most of the seats are located in four levels that rise steeply behind home plate and extend from foul pole to foul pole. Fair-territory bleachers stretch from both lines to left-center and right-center field and the huge "Miller Time" scoreboard rises prominently in straightaway center, a technological masterpiece surrounded by an airy, open concourse that allows wandering fans a

The dingy, crowded days of County Stadium are gone, but not the down-home fun of a Brewers game—complete with the popular sixth-inning Sausage Race (left).

different game perspective.

The natural grass field was designed with input from Yount. The lines (344 feet and 345) are nearly symmetrical and the power alleys (371, 374) are 20 feet closer than they were at County Stadium. The only outfield oddity is a straightaway center field indention that measures 400 feet in front of an 8-foot wall. Like most of the retro ballparks, foul territory at Miller Park is minimal and front-row fans must resist the urge to reach out and touch someone.

Such urges can be resolved in different ways at a ballpark that gives fans much more than a baseball game.

MILLER PARK (2001-)

Located a long line drive from the former site of County Stadium, Miller Park stands as a monument to perseverance. It took almost five years to build, opened a year later than originally scheduled and withstood criticism over its $400 million price tag.

The facility was scheduled to open the 2000 baseball season, but three workers died in a construction accident that did considerable damage to the first base side and pushed Miller Park's debut back to 2001. When completed, it stood 330 feet at its highest point and was more than three times taller than 49-year-old County Stadium.

Miller Park features a distinctive fan-shaped retractable roof that covers 1.2 million square feet on a 25-acre tract and a state-of-the-art scoreboard with a color replay screen that measures 48-by-37 feet and a 76-by-32-foot matrix board. The stadium, which sits in an undeveloped area surrounded by tailgate-friendly parking lots, operates under a naming-rights agreement with locally-based Miller Brewing Company.

First game: April 6, 2001. Richie Sexson's eighth-inning home run gave the Brewers a 5-4 victory over Cincinnati.
- Site of no World Series
- Site of one All-Star Game (2002)

Suites, clubs, restaurants and an interactive area for children are spread throughout the 25-acre facility and the sight of the roof opening or closing still draws oohs and aahs from curious fans. When Miller Park opened in April 2001, the crowd would remain after the game to watch the roof in action—to the music of Johann Strauss.

Mechanical glitches have forced the Brewers to stop showcasing their architectural innovation, but the games always go on at Miller Park—come rain, shine, sleet or that dreaded spring snow. Games and, of course, tailgating. It's still Milwaukee-style baseball, but it now has a distinct retro flair.

Bank One
Ballpark

Where Mark McGwire's 510-foot batting practice home run bounced through open window in 1999

Bank One Ballpark does not exactly blend into its Phoenix surroundings. It doesn't even try. BOB creates its own skyline, a monstrous entertainment oasis located strategically in the Valley of the Sun. Inside this 21.9-acre facility exists a veritable Disneyland of baseball where you can go to play, swim, dream, watch, browse, shop, eat, drink and be merry—free from life's worries and the blistering Arizona heat.

Make no mistake: Bank One is not a dome. It sometimes looks and feels like a dome, but that slatted white top is really a retractable roof, a technological cap that can be put on and removed in a five-minute blur. What Bank One lacks in aesthetic

RANDY JOHNSON:
Four straight Cy Youngs, three ERA titles and 81-27 record from 1999-2002

National television audience watches Andy Benes and Diamondbacks end franchise-opening five-game losing streak with 3-2 victory over Giants, April 5, 1998

Johnson strikes out 364 batters—fourth-best total all-time—in 1999 ... ties nine-inning strikeout record with 20 against Reds, May 8, 2001

174

Kelly Stinnett (right) hits game-tying two-run homer in 16th and Dante Powell (left) singles home winning run in 7-6 win over Dodgers — a 5-hour, 14-minute marathon, April 13, 1999

Where Matt Williams exploded for 35 homers, 142 RBIs while leading Diamondbacks to first West Division title in 1999

THE ARIZONA REPUBLIC

Cardinals righthander Jose Jimenez not only outduels Johnson, he pitches no-hitter and posts 1-0 win with only run scoring in ninth inning, June 25, 1999

Johnson, Curt Schilling combine for 43 wins in 2001 ... 47 in 2002

Hard-hitting Rockies overpower expansion Diamondbacks 9-2 in first game at new ballpark, March 31, 1998

Where Cubs first baseman Mark Grace made a 1998 splash, literally, when he became first player to hit home run into swimming pool

One of two parks with dirt track from pitching mound to home plate

That championship feeling: Gonzalez's ninth-inning single off Yankees ace Mariano Rivera gives 4-year-old Diamondbacks stunning 3-2 win in Game 7 of World Series, Nov. 4, 2001

LUIS GONZALEZ: 57 homers, 142 RBIs in magical 2001 season

merit, it makes up for with utilitarian practicality. Every Diamondbacks fan understands that without that roof, summer baseball would not exist in Arizona.

Like its retractable-roof predecessor in Toronto, Bank One is an entertainment complex with baseball as its centerpiece. But unlike SkyDome, Bank One is sensitive to the detail and nuances that give the stadium a baseball personality beyond its bells and whistles. It's one of the few air-conditioned retractable-roof sports facilities in the world with a natural grass playing surface and you can't go there without getting a heavy dose of baseball history, no matter where you sit, walk or look.

Bank One can overpower you. It's huge, big enough to fit the nearby America West Arena (home of the NBA's Suns and NHL's Coyotes) inside its 1.3 million square feet—eight times. A traditional red-brick facade combines with green structural steel to give

Bank One Ballpark is a huge entertainment complex that creates its own skyline.

the building design elements in keeping with its warehouse surroundings and outside walkways buzz with activity before and after games, highlighted by the Leinenkugel's Ballyard Brewery in the plaza along Fourth Street.

The roof dominates the inside, whether open or shut. Most games are played with roof closed after the first week of May because of stifling heat, but the top remains open most days so sunshine can feed the natural turf. Only about three hours is needed to cool the facility before games and fans often stay after the final out to watch the roof silently slide open, revealing a whole new universe beyond.

With roof in place, its steel girders give you the feel of a giant airplane hangar. And your first panoramic view reveals an advertising blitz that almost knocks you over—there's nothing subliminal about Bank One's ties to its many sponsors. But other visual effects help ease that pain and baseball takes care of the rest.

Your eyes are drawn quickly to a giant center field scoreboard with one of baseball's most active JumboTrons. On each side of the board are massive square panels

BANK ONE BALLPARK (1998-)

With its perpetually clear blue skies and warm temperatures, Arizona has long been an ideal baseball destination, especially for spring training and fall instruction. But when it came to bona fide major league baseball, the 162-game, summer-long variety that was eventually committed to Phoenix in 1995, stadium designers and planners had to overcome a major obstacle—the searing desert sun.

To beat the heat, Phoenix opened its state-of-the-art retractable-roof facility in 1998—the first in the world to combine air-conditioning with a natural grass playing surface. Bank One, known to Diamondbacks fans as The BOB, has a cooling system that can drop the temperature 30 degrees in three hours and a sliding roof that opens and closes in five minutes.

Bank One, an amenity-filled entertainment center, is the only ballpark with a swimming pool, a dip-and-watch area beyond the right-center field wall that replicates "an upscale Arizona backyard." Another Bank One distinction is the strip of dirt that runs from the pitcher's mound to home plate, a pre-20th century design element since copied by Comerica Park in Detroit.

First game: March 31, 1998. Arizona's first franchise hit, RBI and home run came on a blow by Travis Lee, but the D-backs lost to Colorado, 9-2.

■ Site of one World Series (2001)
■ Site of no All-Star Games

that open and close—advertisements one minute, open-air windows the next. It was through one of these panels that Mark McGwire once bounced a prolific batting practice blast estimated at 510 feet. Additional scoreboards are perched high above the stands down both lines and fans are treated to running pitch counts and Randy Johnson strikeout totals. The most distinctive field feature is a dirt track from the mound to home plate, reminiscent of pre-20th century baseball.

Most of the 49,075 seats are located in foul territory, forcing a five-level grandstand to rise steeply into the baseball stratosphere. The trick at Bank One is securing seats in one of the three lower levels between first and third base, where you actually get a cozy-ballpark feel. But with such hitters as Matt Williams and Luis Gonzalez taking advantage of the second-highest elevation (approximately 1,100 feet) in baseball, you're bound to get plenty of action no matter where you sit.

A glove might be in order in bleacher sections located behind the left and right field fences. The bleachers wrap around unusual bullpens that angle behind the foul poles toward the main lower-deck grandstand, meaning balls hit into them can be either home runs or long fouls. The field is oddly asymmetrical—330 feet to left, 407 to center and 334 to right, with the deepest points in right-center and left-center (413) where 7 1/2-foot left and right field fences angle away from a 25-foot center field barrier.

One of Bank One's charms is the variety of ways in which baseball can be viewed. The most novel is from a swimming pool/hot tub area that can be rented for parties beyond the right-center field wall—an inviting 415-foot home run splash from home plate. Others include a tiered picnic area behind the center field wall, beer gardens that overlook the field, a restaurant down the left field line, a stadium club down the right field line and from the main concourse, which circles the lower deck without losing sight of the action.

That concourse offers a variety of shops, concessions and even a playground—as well as a progressive dose of baseball history. The Cox Clubhouse is like a mini-Hall of Fame with displays on loan from Cooperstown and as you circle the park you're besieged by interesting photographs, glass-encased memorabilia, a graphic sports timeline and videos—monitors everywhere offering glimpses of baseball's past. Fans are greeted at the main entrance by a terra cotta rotunda floor display honoring the state of Arizona.

The Bank One package was enough to lure 3.6 million fans to

games in the Diamondbacks' 1998 debut season and more than 3 million in 1999—when the free agency-built team rose from the expansion ashes to claim its first National League West Division title. Two years later, Bank One Ballpark occupied baseball's center stage when the 4-year-old Diamondbacks earned championship distinction by defeating the New York Yankees in a seven-game World Series.

The interior is dominated by the roof (below), but one of Bank One's special features is the swimming pool (right) that allows fans to enjoy a game in real comfort.

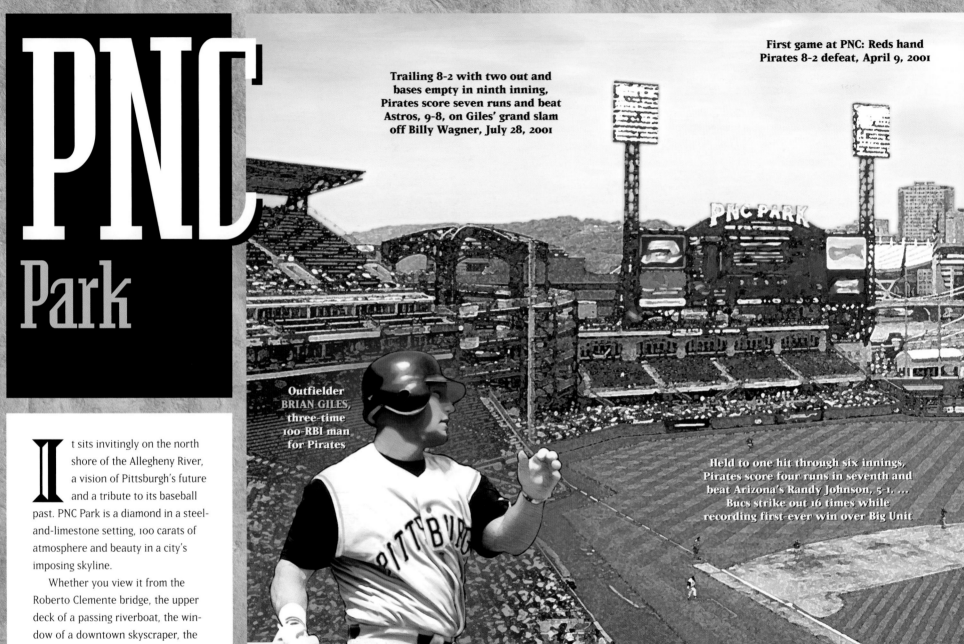

PNC
Park

First game at PNC: Reds hand Pirates 8-2 defeat, April 9, 2001

Trailing 8-2 with two out and bases empty in ninth inning, Pirates score seven runs and beat Astros, 9-8, on Giles' grand slam off Billy Wagner, July 28, 2001

Outfielder BRIAN GILES, three-time 100-RBI man for Pirates

Held to one hit through six innings, Pirates score four runs in seventh and beat Arizona's Randy Johnson, 5-1. ... Bucs strike out 16 times while recording first-ever win over Big Unit

It sits invitingly on the north shore of the Allegheny River, a vision of Pittsburgh's future and a tribute to its baseball past. PNC Park is a diamond in a steel-and-limestone setting, 100 carats of atmosphere and beauty in a city's imposing skyline.

Whether you view it from the Roberto Clemente bridge, the upper deck of a passing riverboat, the window of a downtown skyscraper, the walkway that separates it from the Allegheny or any of its 38,365 up-close-and-personal seats, PNC is an architectural and aesthetic work of art. Few major league ballparks can match the retro blend of grace, ambi-

Roberto Clemente Bridge allows fans to walk from downtown Pittsburgh to PNC

Out-of-town scoreboard wall is 21 feet high—a tribute to Hall of Fame right fielder Roberto Clemente, No. 21

Allegheny River is inviting target for lefthanded sluggers

Astros' Daryle Ward becomes first home run hitter to reach Allegheny River with 479-foot grand slam, July 6, 2002

Where Todd Ritchie, two outs away from no-hitter, gave up single to Kansas City's Luis Alicea in 1-0 Pirates victory, July 13, 2001

Four-time .300 hitter JASON KENDALL has handled Pittsburgh's catching duties since 1996

A Coast Guard station sits idly on the Allegheny River at the base of the Roberto Clemente bridge, one of many nuances that add to the atmosphere outside PNC Park.

ence and nostalgia that provides a stark contrast to Pittsburgh's "Steel City" reputation.

PNC is nothing if not sentimental. Its picturesque surroundings trigger thoughts of Three Rivers Stadium, which was located about a half mile to the west, near the scenic confluence of the Allegheny, Monongahela and Ohio rivers, where Heinz Field (home of the Steelers) now sits. Its striking interior rekindles memories of old Forbes Field, a charming Schenley Park facility the Pirates called home for more than six decades.

But whereas Forbes was a worn-down relic by its close in 1970 and bowl-shaped, symmetrical, multi-purpose Three Rivers provided a sterile baseball atmosphere until its final game in 2000, PNC combines the best of both worlds. River traffic chugs back and forth beyond the park's wide-open outfield, downtown buildings provide an inspiring backdrop and fans scurry back and forth across the bright-yellow Clemente bridge, which becomes a pedestrian walkway on game days and connects the state-of-the-art facility to downtown Pittsburgh.

The Three Rivers connection is apparent outside the impressive stone-and-steel facility, which is nestled snugly into the city's river-shaped contours. A riverboat drops off passengers near the right field entrance, strollers and joggers pass on the busy river walkway and banners, hanging from the facade, honor former Pirates players. Larger-than-life statues of Willie Stargell and Clemente guard the "Left Field" and "Center Field" gates while Honus Wagner, a former fan attraction at both Forbes and Three Rivers, stands sentry from his pedestal at the

The home plate entrance is guarded by an oversized statue of Honus Wagner, a familiar figure for fans who attended games at Three Rivers Stadium and Forbes Field, PNC's ballpark predecessors.

Sightlines are outstanding, no matter where you sit at PNC, and Roberto Clemente tributes are everywhere, including a statue (right) outside the center field entrance.

PNC PARK (2001-)

The Pirates constructed PNC Park in the image of old Forbes Field, giving their fans a charming, intimate baseball-only facility that adds life to the city's downtown area. PNC, located on the north shore of the Allegheny River in the shadow of a spectacular Pittsburgh skyline, is a retro-park masterpiece with enough visual effects, quirky nuances and modern conveniences to match up favorably with its retro predecessors at Baltimore and Cleveland.

Located about a half mile from the former site of Three Rivers Stadium and the confluence of the Allegheny, Monongahela and Ohio rivers, PNC has the second-smallest capacity in baseball and near-perfect sight lines, whether watching game action or lively river traffic. Also of interest beyond the center field fence is the Roberto Clemente bridge, which links the ballpark and downtown for a seemingly never-ending stream of pedestrians.

PNC, with its open concourses, numerous food courts and yellow-and-black design, is a major departure from Three Rivers Stadium, one of the original cookie-cutter, multi-purpose facilities that served as Pirates home from 1970-2000. The double-decked facility, built in two years, was named after PNC Bank Corp.

First game: April 9, 2001. The Pirates lost their PNC opener to Chris Reitsma and the Cincinnati Reds, 8-2.
- ■ Site of no World Series
- ■ Site of no All-Star Games

"Home Plate" rotunda.

PNC's inside evokes memories of Forbes Field, from its intimacy and openness to its seven toothbrush-shaped light towers. As the first two-decked facility to be built since Milwaukee's County Stadium in 1953, it has an old ballpark charm and a new ballpark feel. A strong sense of deja vu is countered by seats that angle toward home plate, girders that match Pittsburgh's always prominent bridgework and limited foul territory that allows front-row fans within 42 feet of game action at first and third base.

Whether sitting in the lower or upper deck (a mere 88 feet from the field at its highest level), you quickly become captivated by the granddaddy of ballpark vistas. At night from the double-deck stands that wrap almost from foul pole to foul pole, fans look directly into a well-lighted city skyline that reflects spectacularly off the river below and three yellow spans that cross the river to the southeast.

Everything at PNC comes with a yellow-and-black tint and a choreographed flair. The perfectly manicured grass field is complemented by outfield walls that curve and jag at strategic points, giving the park a personality missing from Three Rivers Stadium. The 6-foot left field wall (only 325 at the yellow foul pole) curves quickly toward a 410-foot left-center field jut, the deepest point of the outfield,

The Pittsburgh skyline, with the yellow Roberto Clemente bridge crossing the Allegheny River, forms a stately and scenic backdrop for PNC Park.

and the right-center field alley measures 375 feet where the fence quickly rises. The entire right field wall, which is 21 feet high in honor of Clemente's uniform number, is a fan-friendly out-of-town scoreboard that extends to the foul pole, 320 feet from home plate.

But it's not the main scoreboard. That 47-by-187-foot monster, which rises above a left field bleacher section and a 10,000-square foot restaurant, is sandwiched by two light towers. Its video board, topped by a huge "PNC Park" sign, is put to good use by the Pirates, who entertain fans with various animated treats, including a pregame warmup that features pirates, ships and cannon blasts that sink overmatched opponents in the shadow of Pittsburgh's skyline.

Bullpens are elevated behind screened panels, just to the left-center field side of the green batter's eye, and a picnic area and walkway accord views of the river behind the right field stands. Those seats provide an inviting home run target for lefthanded sluggers, who can make a much bigger splash with a 444-foot shot into the Allegheny.

PNC's charm is subtle, as are the amenities that make it special. Luxury suites are tucked cleverly below the second deck and the press box is perched atop the stadium's rim, stretching from dugout to dugout. Advertising is subtle; the concourse is open and free from congestion. Fans can explore the many food venues (the "Tastes of Pittsburgh"), shops, arcades and museums, both inside and out, without a sense of urgency.

This is a ballpark that encourages exploration and fans experience the game in different ways. One of the best vantage points is from a spiral up-ramp that leads to different levels of the park, just inside the left field line. At four different spots, as ramp walkers pass the field, they can stop, lean against the rail and watch the game—a wonderful view that never fails to fascinate.

Such fascination is hard to control for Pittsburgh fans, who find PNC Park a prodigious home run or two beyond Three Rivers Stadium in atmosphere and panache. Those are feel-good qualities for a blue-collar city with a no-nonsense loyalty to hard-nosed, old-fashioned baseball.

Pacific Bell
Park

Giant glove and Coca-Cola bottle are signature features in left field stands

Giant glove and Coca-Cola bottle are signature features in left field stands

San Francisco fans have dubbed it the "anti-Candlestick" and visitors marvel at its stunning beauty and Camelot-like charm. When the ill wind blows off the Bay, it respectfully bypasses Pacific Bell Park, where long-suffering Giants fans now witness their baseball in unprecedented comfort. Memories notwithstanding, the tradeoff from cavernous Candlestick Park to intimate Pac Bell; from multi-purpose to retro; from the perfect storm to refreshing calm has met with unanimous approval.

For pure viewing pleasure, no ballpark combines function and aesthetics

Scenic Pacific Bell Park opens with 6-5 loss, thanks to three-homer explosion by Dodgers infielder Kevin Elster, April 11, 2000

Office of 10-year Giants manager Dusty Baker, who led team to major league-best 97-65 record and West Division title in first season at new ballpark

Kent enjoyed six straight 100-RBI seasons for Giants from 1997-2002, three at Pac Bell

Second baseman JEFF KENT earned 2000 MVP with .334 average, 33 homers, 125 RBIs

Site of 2002 World Series: Wild-card Giants lose seven-game all-California thriller to Angels

Super closer Robb Nen recorded N.L.-leading 45 saves in 2001, his third of four 40-or-more-save seasons with Giants

Pinch-hitter J.T. Snow's shocking three-run, ninth-inning homer off Armando Benitez ties Game 2 of 2000 Division Series, but Mets go on to win game in 10 innings and series in four games

Bonds connects off Dodgers righthander Terry Adams for 500th career homer—a two-run, eighth-inning game-winner into McCovey's Cove, April 17, 2001

McCovey's Cove, where souvenir-hunters chased down nine "splash hits" by Bonds in 2001

Bonds hits 600th career homer off Pirates' Kip Wells, joining Hank Aaron, Babe Ruth and Willie Mays in exclusive club, August 9, 2002

Areas where Bonds deposited record-shattering home runs 71 and 72 off Chan Ho Park and 73 off Dennis Springer in season-closing weekend series against Dodgers, Oct. 5 and 7, 2001

Portals provide windows to outside world and allow fans without tickets to see game action

Where Livan Hernandez outpitched Mets lefty Mike Hampton in opener of Division Series, a 5-1 Giants win, Oct. 4, 2000

Where Bonds put together one of most devastating offensive seasons in history: 73 homers, 177 walks and .863 slugging percentage were major league records; also scored 129 runs and had 137 RBIs, .515 on-base percentage and 107 extra-base hits

BARRY BONDS: Baseball's only five-time MVP and single-season home run champion

From palm trees at the main entrance to boats on the bay, Pacific Bell Park is a scenic wonderland. Fans entering its gates get a baseball experience unlike that in any other major league facility.

like Pac Bell, which is nestled snugly into the South Beach waterfront district, within walking distance of downtown San Francisco. It's trendy, like the China Basin area in which it is located, and it charms visitors with multiple personalities—from its quirky playing field and stunning views to its fan-friendly activities and diversions.

This is home of the "Splash Hit," a home run that clears the right field walkway and lands in aptly named McCovey's Cove. It also is the place to go for garlic fries, clam chowder, Doggie Diner hot dogs and sweeping vistas of the Lefty O'Doul and Bay bridges, downtown San

Francisco and Oakland and boats on the distant horizon. There's an interactive baseball experience for everyone here, including the fans who show up to watch a few innings for free.

Pac Bell's primary focus is the Cove, which bristles in the sun beyond the outer right field wall. The entire home run area in right, three rows of elevated seats (25 feet above the field) that front an extended walkway, offers an extraordinary view of both the field and water and attracts thousands of curious spectators during the course of a game. A lower walkway outside the stadium attracts "hang out" fans who can watch the action without charge on three-inning rotations through five chain-link portals (25 fans per) in the outfield wall—a modern-day "Knothole Gang."

For a typical weekend game, McCovey's Cove is sure to be filled with souvenir hunters—fans on surfboards or in canoes, kayaks, row boats, sailboats and yachts. Radios are standard equipment to supplement the sounds of a game that cannot be seen. Motors are not allowed and no boat can anchor, which some-

Portals at the base of the right field wall offer windows into Pac Bell (above) for non-paying fans. Other signature features include McCovey's Cove (above right) and the giant bottle and baseball mitt (below right) atop the left field bleachers.

times turns the crowded Cove into a bumper boat attraction for walkway fans who spend much of the game with their back to the field.

This might be the only ballpark where fans outside the stadium actually contribute to the ambience within. A Barry Bonds blast into the Cove is sure to set off a wild, wet scramble that is more fun, and often more memorable, than the most elaborate home run fireworks celebrations at other parks.

Most of Pac Bell's "fireworks" will be witnessed from one of the three foul-territory decks that stretch from pole to pole and account for most of the park's 41,467 seats. Fans never feel out of touch with the action, especially those who battle outfielders for home run balls in both corners, and upper-deck patrons can take consolation in the view. They also get a more sweeping sense of the field's architectural oddities.

They see an unusually expansive right field that tempts lefthanded batters with a 309-foot foul pole, the shortest in the major leagues, and frustrates them with a high fence that angles sharply toward a right-center field jag. Straight-

PACIFIC BELL PARK (2000-)

From the cold, windy, unpredictable whims of Candlestick Park to the picturesque, quirky nuances of Pacific Bell, the Giants have come a long way, baby. The 41,467-seat masterpiece, located in the China Basin area along San Francisco Bay, has become the newest model for retro-park magic and one of the favorite places for home run souvenir hunters.

Built on a modest 13-acre site, Pac Bell is the first privately financed ballpark since Dodger Stadium was completed in 1962. The $357 million facility, built in 2½ years, was positioned to incorporate the natural beauty of the Bay Bridge, the distant San Francisco and Oakland skylines and, of course, the water into its baseball design. Lefthanded hitters can take aim at McCovey's Cove, the water beyond the outer right field wall where fans gather in boats to chase down "splash hits."

Pac Bell, which is accessible by every kind of public transportation imaginable, has an unusual configuration—the shortest right field line (309 feet) in either league with a wall that angles out quickly to 421 feet in right-center.

First game: April 11, 2000. Three home runs by shortstop Kevin Elster was enough to ruin Pac Bell's big-league debut—a 6-5 Dodgers win over the Giants.

■ Site of one World Series
■ Site of no All-Star Games

Willie Mays Plaza, with its 9-foot statue of the Say Hey Kid (left), attracts attention outside Pac Bell. Once inside, fans enjoy sweeping views, including the massive scoreboard that rises over the Bay in left-center field (right).

away right is 365 feet and the jag, marking the deepest point of the field at 421, connects to an 8-foot wall that wraps to the left field line. Dead center field is 399 feet; the left field pole is 339.

Fans in search of a more conventional home run souvenir buy tickets in bleachers that stretch from the left field foul pole to the right-center field jag—with two sections of seats on the right field side of a batter's eye. Rising behind the batter's eye is a multi-functional scoreboard, one of three visual obstacles in an otherwise open outfield.

Two of Pac Bell's signature features stand side-by-side at the top of the left field bleachers. An 80-foot neon-colored Coca-Cola bottle houses four giant slides, an arcade and a mini-Pac Bell field that invites children to hit wiffle balls and run the bases. Next to the bottle is a 27-foot, 20,000-pound steel-and-fiberglass baseball mitt.

This is a ballpark that encourages wanderlust. Most fans arrive by mass transit systems—ferry, bus, streetcar, train, BART—and are greeted by a compact, 13-

Pac Bell entices fans crossing McCovey's Cove (left) beyond the right field wall. A replica San Francisco cable car (below) is available for inspection inside the park beyond the right-center field fence.

acre facility that brings the waterfront area to life. The stadium's brick architecture mimics the older warehouses and industrial buildings of the district and the main entrance, Willie Mays Plaza, is shaded by 24 palm trees and guarded by a 9-foot bronze statue of the Say Hey Kid.

Once inside, it's possible to stroll the open concourses, buy food and check out the views without ever sitting down—or losing sight of the field. It's also possible to walk behind the scoreboard, lean over the outfield wall and check out an official San Francisco cable car that sits just beyond the right-center field fence.

Pac Bell, borrowing from the blueprints of Baltimore's Camden Yards, Cleveland's Jacobs Field and Denver's Coors Field, has lifted the retro ballpark to a new level. It pays tribute to the city's baseball roots while giving older fans charm and atmosphere; it is hip, interactive and sleek, a turn-on for young Giants followers.

It is not Candlestick. Balls hit above the stadium rim can still turn into a defensive adventure and night games can occasionally get uncomfortably chilly, but parkas are strictly optional and "San Francisco-style baseball" has taken on a whole new meaning.

Safeco
Field

On a clear summer afternoon, it basks radiantly in the sunshine—a warm, fuzzy glow that used to bounce indifferently off the roof of the Kingdome, its not-so-stately predecessor. On those inevitably damp and rainy days, it shields Seattle fans with a 22-million-pound, steel-paneled umbrella.

Safeco Field is the best of many worlds. It offers the charm of Sick's Stadium, the tiny baseball-only facility that served as home to Seattle's first major league team in 1969, and it provides a utilitarian relief from the elements, the most endearing feature of the otherwise-bland and multi-purpose

Outfielder Mike Cameron hits 19th-inning home run to beat Boston, 5-4, and end longest home game in Mariners history, Aug. 1, 2000

Manager Lou Piniella: architect of franchise's first three West Division titles ('95, '97, 2001) and four playoff appearances

Team leader and master DH EDGAR MARTINEZ: six 100-RBI seasons, two batting titles in Seattle career that started in 1987

Where Bret Boone set two single-season records for A.L. second basemen in 2001—37 homers, league-leading 141 RBIs

Carlos Guillen's squeeze bunt scores Rickey Henderson in bottom of ninth, giving wild-card Mariners 2-1 win over Chicago and three-game Division Series sweep, Oct. 6, 2000

Safeco Field opens with whimper—Mariners lose to Padres, 3-2, July 15, 1999

Starting rotation of Jamie Moyer, Freddy Garcia, Aaron Sele and Paul Abbott combine for 70 wins in spectacular 2001 campaign

Yankees win first two games of 2001 ALCS at Safeco en route to five-game victory that denies Mariners first World Series appearance

Safeco is popular vacation spot for Japanese fans, who cheer on Ichiro and closer Kazuhiro Sasaki, A.L.'s 2000 Rookie of Year

Yankees ace Roger Clemens strikes out 15 Mariners and allows one hit, Al Martin's seventh-inning double, in 5-0 Game 4 win in ALCS, Oct. 14, 2000

Mariners gain temporary tie for first on second-to-last day of season when shortstop Alex Rodriguez hits two homers, drives in seven runs in 21-9 win over Angels, Sept. 30, 2000

Mariners, after 3-1 win over Red Sox, own 26-10 record and 142-56 two-year mark, May 11, 2002

Five pitchers combine on two-hitter and Bret Boone homers in 1-0 victory that gives amazing Mariners major league record-tying 116th win, Oct. 6, 2001

Ichiro, first Japanese position player in major league history, wins over Seattle fans by leading A.L. in average (.350), hits (242) and stolen bases (56) in 2001, becoming second rookie batting champ

ICHIRO SUZUKI: Speedy right fielder wins 2001 Rookie of Year and MVP awards, leads Mariners to record-tying 116 wins in brilliant first season

The open roof gives Safeco Field an ambience the Kingdome could never provide—outdoor baseball, complete with sunshine, fresh air and the retro-classic ballpark feel.

Kingdome. But Safeco's real personality is defined by the hip and trendy veneer it adds to the Pacific Northwest's most progressive city.

Safeco Field is a classic retro park, straight off the Camden Yards blueprint and sprinkled liberally with visual nuances from such Camden successors as The Ballpark in Arlington and Coors Field. The brick facade that greets visitors along First Avenue South evokes more venerable memories of Brooklyn's Ebbets Field and Philadelphia's Shibe Park, but there's nothing old or stodgy about the park's glitzy atmosphere.

Longtime Mariners fans marvel at the major differences between Safeco and the Kingdome—fresh air instead of enclosed sterility; natural grass instead of artificial turf; sunshine instead of artificial lighting; natural playing conditions instead of a controlled climate. When the shiny new facility opened after the 1999 All-Star break, it was a few Ken Griffey home runs away from the Kingdome physically, but a few thousand Mark McGwire moonshots away in spirit.

From the moment you pass under the swirling 1,000-bat sculpture that dominates the main-entrance stairway, you become overpowered by an urge to look up. It doesn't go away when you reach a green, perfectly manicured field that rests peacefully in the shadow of a Darth Vader-like roof. When open, the three-paneled cover lurks menacingly over the right field stands, ready to spring into action at the flick of a switch. When closed, it provides protection at a cost—you lose the sweeping views of the downtown Seattle skyline and nearby Puget Sound.

The 2001 All-Star Game brought pageantry to Safeco Field, which became a beehive of activity (right) for fans, vendors and park officials. The left field "Safeco Field" sign (left) serves as a window to downtown Seattle.

There's no way to avoid the looming presence of Safeco's roof. It's an engineering innovation designed to cover, but not totally enclose the field, preserving the open-air environment missing from the Kingdome. The roof, when closed, covers almost nine acres and contains enough steel to build a 55-story skyscraper. It takes 10 to 20 minutes to open or close depending on weather conditions, and fans who enjoy an open-air game often remain afterward to watch the roof slide shut.

When you escape the roof's hypnotic spell, you're treated to a visual and audio epiphany. The downtown skyline is spectacular, but no more so than nearby Elliott Bay or distant Mount Ranier. The field itself, with slightly irregular dimensions, nestles comfortably into its scenic surroundings. Three decks wrap around home plate, from the left field foul line to right-center

field, and bleacher sections in left and center offer fans a Wrigley Field-like experience.

The left field seats, which overlook the bullpens, are topped by one of the park's signature features—a massive Safeco Field sign attached to a four-pronged light standard. An 8-foot wall circles the outfield (331 feet down the left field line; 327 in right) and sound echoes throughout the triple-decked facility—the traditional whaps of ball hitting bat or glove as well as the rumbling and whistles of trains passing close beyond the right field stands.

It didn't take long for fans to discover that mobility gives Safeco a special charisma. The park is filled with charming, unexpected nooks and crannies where people can stand briefly to watch the game before moving on to a different perspective. A wide concourse circles the 47,116-seat facility and allows pedestrians

A bird's-eye view from the left field corner reveals a picturesque Safeco Field that lifts Mariners baseball to a new level, especially when the roof is open.

to watch game action whether walking or standing in line to buy their garlic fries.

Players such as Griffey (before his early 2000 trade to Cincinnati), Alex Rodriguez (before his free-agent departure to Texas), Jay Buhner and Edgar Martinez quickly discovered that the ball, suddenly affected by wind, damp air and other quirks of nature, doesn't carry as well as it did in the Kingdome, which featured similar dimensions. But the grass field is kinder to their knees, the ambience is greatly improved and everything is state-of-the-art, starting with what the Mariners bill as one of the most comprehensive scoreboard systems in baseball.

SAFECO FIELD (1999-)

The move from Seattle's oft-maligned Kingdome to sparkling new Safeco Field was, literally, a breath of fresh air. Mariners fans, no longer forced to watch baseball in the artificial confines of an enclosed downtown facility, could bask in the double wonders of top-notch baseball and sweeping views of the Seattle skyline and Puget Sound.

Safeco protects fans from the inclement Seattle weather with a retractable roof that covers the nine-acre playing area but does not enclose it, maintaining that open-air feel. The stadium, located south of the Kingdome site within the boundaries of First Avenue South, South Atlantic Street, Third Avenue South and Royal Brougham Way, seats 47,116 and offers numerous fan amenities.

Two of the favorites are Lookout Landing, an upper-deck area near the left field corner that provides incredible views of both the field and surrounding landmarks, and The Bullpen Market, which offers interactive games and other activities. Named after the Seattle-base insurance company, Safeco Field required almost 2½ years to build and opened after the 1999 All-Star break.

First game: July 15, 1999. The Padres scored a pair of ninth-inning runs off closer Jose Mesa and ruined Safeco's debut with a 3-2 win over the Mariners.

■ Site of no World Series
■ Site of one All-Star Game (2001)

Safeco's First Avenue South main entrance evokes memories of the brick facade that greeted visitors at Brooklyn's Ebbets Field.

The main 56-foot-high scoreboard towers over the center field bleachers and batter's eye, offering information and replays on its huge video and matrix boards. An old-fashioned hand-operated scoreboard and out-of-town board attract attention in left field and play-by-play boards operate in foul territory down the left and right field lines. Other visual landmarks are the Bullpen Market, Hit It Here Cafe, Bullpen Pub and displays from 11 regional artists, including a large bronze catcher's mitt sculpture that sits outside the "Left Field" gate.

Also state-of-the-art is a Mariners team that rose to unprecedented heights in 2001 by winning 116 games and the franchise's third West Division title—without Griffey and Rodriguez. As a result, more than 7 million fans had watched baseball at Safeco by its two-year anniversary and the ballpark had become a "home away from home" for Japanese fans, who flocked to Seattle to watch favorite sons Ichiro Suzuki and Kazuhiro Sasaki perform their baseball magic.

Adding to Safeco's atmosphere is one staple from the Kingdome—a peanut-slinging vendor named Rick Kaminski, whose accuracy often is better than the pitchers on the mound.

Tropicana Field

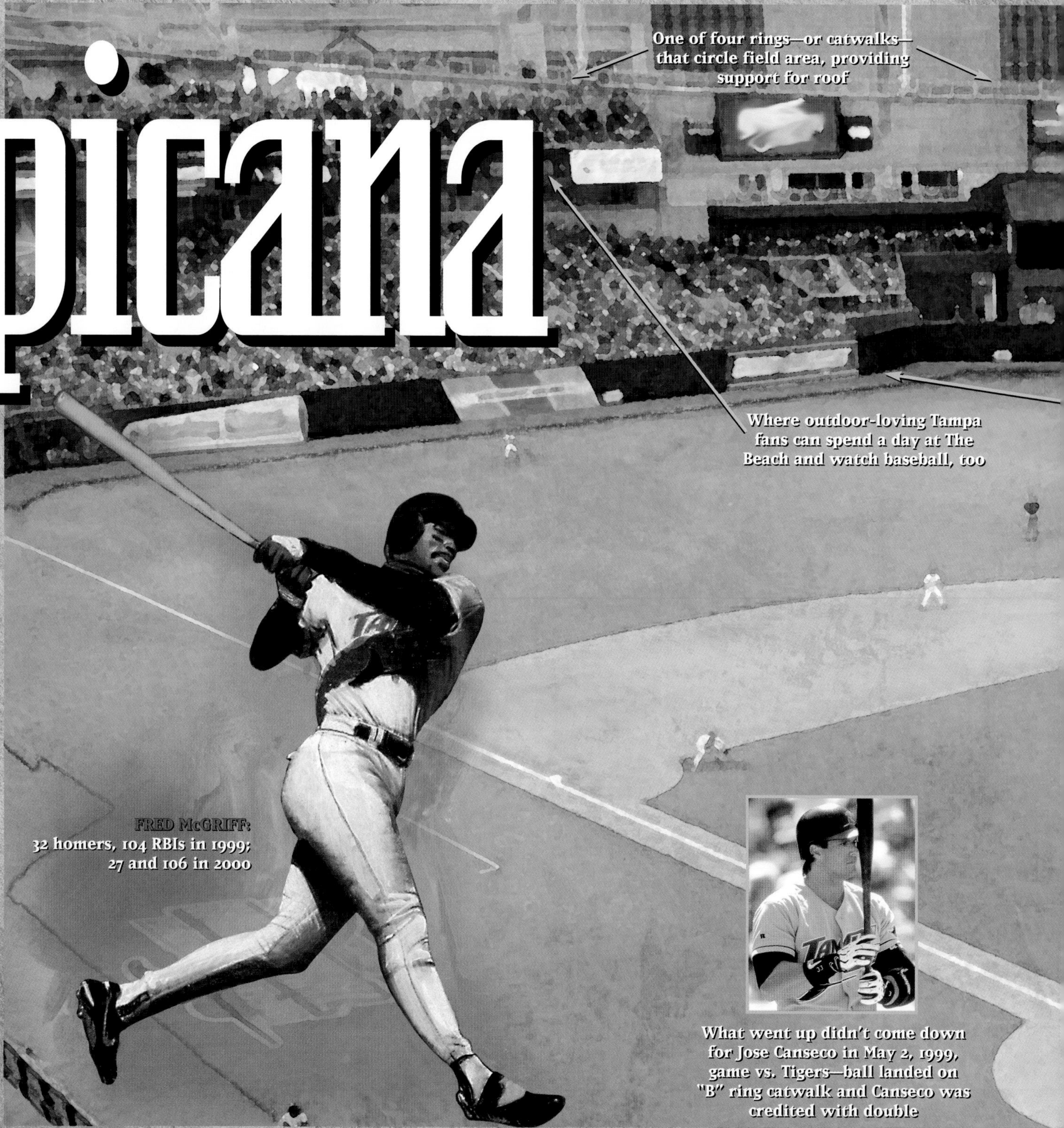

One of four rings—or catwalks—that circle field area, providing support for roof

Where outdoor-loving Tampa fans can spend a day at The Beach and watch baseball, too

It's the self-billed "Ballpark of the 21st Century," a technologically enhanced playground with a distinctive surf-and-sand personality. Tropicana Field is downright proud of the cutting-edge amenities and entertainment options it serves up with its baseball. Where else can you combine pitch counts and batting averages with a beach, a shopping mall, a cigar bar, a bank, a travel agency, a climbing wall and more food groups than you ever knew existed?

The Devil Rays boast that their stadium has "nearly 290 points of sale" around its wide, visitor-friendly concourses. It also has one of the

FRED McGRIFF:
32 homers, 104 RBIs in 1999;
27 and 106 in 2000

What went up didn't come down for Jose Canseco in May 2, 1999, game vs. Tigers—ball landed on "B" ring catwalk and Canseco was credited with double

196

Where Jose Canseco hit his franchise-record 34th home run onto the roof of the Batter's Eye Restaurant, Sept. 28, 1999

McGriff drives in four runs and Rolando Arrojo (left) pitches six innings as Devil Rays record franchise's first win with 11-8 decision over Tigers, April 1, 1998

Jogs in left-center, right-center field fences create erratic bounces

Two-run, 14th-inning home run by light-hitting Kevin Stocker gives first-year Devil Rays 6-5 win over Indians and two-game series sweep, May 12, 1998

Leadoff man Gerald Williams charges Boston pitcher Pedro Martinez in first inning, triggering brawl ... Martinez goes on to fire one-hitter in 8-0 Red Sox win, Aug. 29, 2000

WADE BOGGS: Veteran third baseman brought Hall of Fame air to Devil Rays' franchise-beginning lineup

Boggs becomes baseball's 23rd 3,000-hit player, and first to reach milestone with home run, off Indians lefty Chris Haney, Aug. 7, 1999

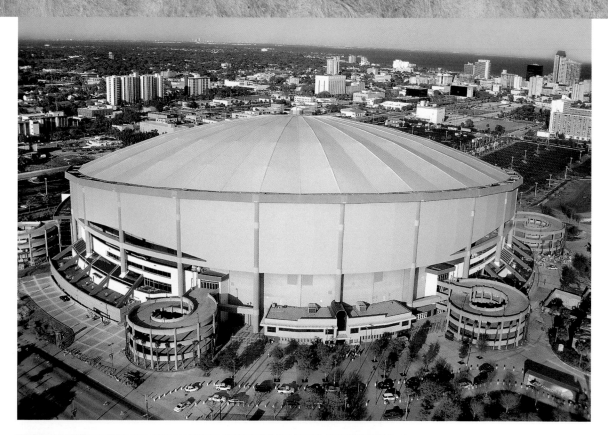

oddest-looking domes ever construct-ed—a Teflon-coated fiberglass cap that slants at a 6.5-degree angle. That slant makes Tropicana, the world's largest cable-supported dome, look like a tilting spaceship ready to shoot into the stratosphere. If it does, nobody inside will ever be bored.

Come early, stay late because there is never a dearth of things to see or do. Your Tropicana experience begins spectacularly with a walk toward the main entrance along a 900-foot, tropical-theme ceramic mosaic walkway—1,849,091 brightly colored tiles depicting the sun, sea and beach. The walk is enhanced by a sound system delivering play-by-play of great baseball moments and Devil Rays games as well as music and theatrical lighting.

The main entrance, an elaborate and ornate eight-story rotunda patterned after the one that greeted visitors for almost a half century at Brooklyn's Ebbets Field, is merely an appetizer for what lies beyond. You step out of the rotunda onto Center Field Street—a bustling retail area featuring the Batter's Eye Restaurant, Cuesta-Rey Cigar Bar, the Budweiser Brew House and an assortment of other shops and business establishments. The Taste of Tampa Bay food court offers samplings of the area's most popular cuisine.

The barrage of food, shops, gimmicks and conveniences never stops as you circle the concourses—or even after you step into the field area. High over the left field fence, covering most of the second deck, is The Beach—a 1,339-seat section featuring palm trees, pina coladas, ushers in Hawaiian shirts, a spa, a restaurant and drinks at the Tiki Bar. The hitter's backdrop in center field is the backside of the Batter's Eye Restaurant, with diners hidden by tinted windows that allow them to view action while they eat. Special seats behind the plate come armed with touch video screens that allow you to sample views and replays from various camera angles.

Catwalks, fence jogs and a center field restaurant make Tropicana interesting, as does a slanted dome (top photo) that gives it a spaceship-like look.

And then there's baseball, which supposedly is the facility's major attraction—if not its only focus. When you get past all the distractions, this really is not a bad place to watch a game. Seats are close (only 50 feet from plate to backstop), you're out of the Florida heat and rain and the field is well lit, brighter than any other roof-covered park. And it has some funny little quirks that make baseball life interesting.

The artificial surface is soft and fast and balls shoot the gaps quickly and are prone to strange bounces, thanks to a sharp backward angle in the left-center field fence—a dropoff to the park's deepest point at 410 feet—and a lesser angle in right-center (404). The lines are an inviting 315 (left) and 322 (right) and the basepaths are all dirt, a departure from the base-cutout design employed by most other domed stadiums. Bullpens, once located in home run territory beyond the left and right field fences, now are located in foul territory down both lines.

But the granddaddy of quirks is a product of the cable design—four rings, or catwalks, that circle the roof and help keep it in place. Two of the rings are high and well out of play. Two others are reachable with batted balls and can affect the game. The lowest is a potential foul ball obstacle, the second actually crosses fair territory in the outfield. Catwalks, used only for maintenance purposes, have been hit a handful of times and one Jose Canseco drive actually landed on the second catwalk and never came

Tropicana was in a festive mood when the Devil Rays and Red Sox prepared for battle in the 1999 home opener.

TROPICANA FIELD (1998-)

Also known as Florida Suncoast Dome (1990-93) and ThunderDome (1993-96)

Opened in 1990 as the Florida Suncoast Dome, it stood for eight years before the Tampa/St. Petersburg area became a home for major league baseball. The former arena of the NHL's Tampa Bay Lightning (1993-96) was closed for 17 months and reconfigured for baseball.

Of the domed facilities in use today, it's the only one that features all-dirt basepaths on a turf field, instead of the typical dirt cutouts around the bases. Another distinction is the Devil Rays' practice of lighting the dome orange (Tropicana orange) after each victory.

First game: March 31, 1998. An opening day sellout crowd watched the Tigers ruin the Devil Rays' debut, 11-6.

■ Site of no World Series
■ Site of no All-Star Games

down, resulting in a double.

Such an occurrence probably was never envisioned when the 1.1-million-square-foot facility, built for baseball, opened in 1990 as the Florida Suncoast Dome—not as you would expect in trendy, progressive Tampa, but in nearby St. Petersburg, a quiet haven. The translucent roof, which is lighted orange after a Devil Rays home victory, was slanted to decrease construction costs and the amount of air that requires climate control. The apex of the dome, which sits 6 feet above sea level, measures 225 feet above second base and declines to 85 feet at the center field wall.

Tampa/St. Petersburg officials hoped the facility would attract a major league team, but that didn't happen through its first eight years. Various sports events were staged there and the NHL's Tampa Bay Lightning played their home games there for three years (1993-96, when it was called ThunderDome), but baseball didn't arrive until 1998 in the form of an expansion team that would win only 63 games and draw 2.5-million fans.

The Devil Rays have struggled to get beyond that expansion-team look and attendance has dropped off as the losses have continued to pile up, keeping baseball from claiming a bigger piece of Tropicana's multi-attraction pie. But one thing is unlikely to change inside the coral-gray structure with green-tinted glass: Win or lose, the game will always share the spotlight, but it never will own it.

Gone, But Not Forgotten

S ome have been gone for decades—League Park, Braves Field, the Polo Grounds, Ebbets Field, Crosley, Shibe, Forbes; others have just departed—Tiger Stadium, Candlestick, the Astrodome, the Kingdome and Three Rivers.

Nearly all were classics, places of the heart and longtime stages for baseball magic. But some are immortalized only by a few remnants scattered about, marking their place in the game's long history, while others have been razed without much thought given to permanence.

No matter. Their permanence is in the memories that baseball fans continue to cherish. They might be gone, but they're not forgotten.

Arlington Stadium

Also known as Turnpike Stadium (1965-1971)

Where 18-year-old Texas high school pitching sensation David Clyde won his major league debut, June 27, 1973

Arlington Stadium never played host to a postseason game in its 22-year existence

Rangers surrendered A.L.-record 13 runs in ninth inning, Sept. 14, 1978

Where 46-year-old Ryan pummeled Chicago's Robin Ventura, who charged mound after being hit by pitch, Aug. 4, 1993

Toby Harrah: Texas' palindromic infield fixture from 1972-78

Catcher JIM SUNDBERG won six Gold Gloves from 1974-83

For 22 years, it was the hottest sports ticket in town—literally. Baseball was served at Arlington Stadium with a complementary sauna and a guaranteed tan. You had to appreciate the open friendliness and down-home simplicity of the best little ballhouse in North Texas, but you also had to curse its refusal to hide from the oppressive summer heat.

Unlike Houston's air-conditioned Astrodome, Arlington Stadium was not a venue for the faint of heart. It was uncovered and vulnerable, an erector-set facility that dared to challenge the scorching Texas sun. If the 100-plus-degree heat didn't get you, the inelegant teams that competed there would. It wasn't easy to be a Rangers

Rangers become third team in 55 years to produce three 200-hit men in same season—Rafael Palmeiro (203), Ruben Sierra (203), Julio Franco (201) in 1991

A perfect ending: California's Mike Witt retires all 27 Rangers he faces in season-closing 1-0 victory, Sept. 30, 1984

Fergie Jenkins earned 1974 Comeback Player of the Year honors during his 25-12, 225-strikeout, 2.83-ERA season

Training ground for Juan Gonzalez (right) and Ivan Rodriguez (left), the next generation Rangers

Ryan makes Rickey Henderson 5,000th career strikeout victim, Aug. 22, 1989 . . . On May 1, 1991, at age 44, Ryan celebrates "Arlington Appreciation Night" by beating Blue Jays with seventh no-hitter

Where big Frank Howard thrilled Texas fans with long first-inning homer in Rangers' first game at Arlington Stadium, April 21, 1972

Bill Stein sets A.L. record with seventh straight pinch hit, May 25, 1981

Dave Nelson steals show on Aug. 30, 1974, when he swipes second, third and home in one inning

NOLAN RYAN: The Rangers' first Hall of Famer completed his 27-year career here

Jeff Burroughs: 25 homers, 118 RBIs, .301 average in MVP 1974 season

Buddy Bell becomes first A.L. player to collect 200 hits without batting .300, 1979

Yankees first baseman Don Mattingly homers in his record-tying eighth straight game, July 18, 1987

Larry Parrish belts third grand slam in one week, July 10, 1982

fan, but it was hard not to like Arlington Stadium.

Located in an entertainment strip of suburban Arlington next to the Six Flags amusement park, it was a former minor league facility that attempted to introduce two divergent Texas cities to major league society. A few miles to the east was Dallas, cosmopolitan and glitzy—fans armed with cell phones and beepers. A few miles to the west was Fort Worth, blue collar and basic—fans who took life seriously. This was a baseball melting pot, a no-frills stadium with a simple charm behind its plain, patchwork exterior.

Much of that charm was a byproduct of Arlington's humble roots. It opened in 1965 as Turnpike Stadium, the 10,600-seat home of the Class AA Texas League's Spurs on the Dallas-Fort Worth Turnpike. It was constructed with an eye toward expansion, the first of which took place in 1970 and raised seating capacity to 21,000. When the former Senators were moved from Washington to Arlington before the 1972 season, emergency construction lifted capacity to 35,694 and gave the stadium the basic look it would retain throughout its history.

The renamed Arlington Stadium was a basic single-deck structure with a make-it-up-as-we-go architectural design. Set in a natural bowl that dropped the playing surface 40 feet below street level, it featured a leveled grandstand behind home plate, high-rising seats down both lines and fair-territory bleachers that extended from foul pole to foul pole. A special "plaza" deck, built atop the stands behind the plate in 1978, raised capacity to 41,284 and captured the essence of a

makeshift construction that resulted in peculiar nooks and crannies as well as unexpected open-air windows to the outside world.

If Arlington wasn't the most sightline-friendly ballpark in the majors, it had to be close. It also was the hottest, with little shade to compensate. More than a third of its seats were in the expansive outfield bleachers—sun-blistered aluminum benches that dispensed their heat to general admission fans. From mid-May to September 1, the Rangers were forced to play all their games at night, with temperatures seldom getting out of the 90s.

The left field bleachers were topped by a distinctive 200-by-60-foot scoreboard, a piece of which was shaped like the state of Texas. The field, with lush green grass that somehow withstood daily assaults from the sun, featured hitter-friendly 330-400-330 symmetrical dimensions, but swirling winds blowing over the center field fence made life easy for pitchers.

That changed after the 1983 season, when the Rangers removed the scoreboard and topped the outfield rim with a 30-foot wall that stretched from foul pole to foul pole. Not only did the barrier block the winds and make life tougher for pitchers, it gave the park a whole new personality. Five state-of-the-art video and scoreboards were spaced along the wall, separated by huge advertising billboards. On one, the Marlboro Man gazed down with apparent disinterest from his right-center field perch.

That disinterest might have stemmed from Rangers teams that only occasionally contended for division

---

ARLINGTON STADIUM (1972-1993)

Also known as Turnpike Stadium (1965-1971)

Dedicated on April 23, 1965, 10,600-seat Turnpike Stadium (a nod to its location on the Dallas-Fort Worth Turnpike, which today is Interstate 30) provided the nucleus of the Texas Rangers' first home on land just northwest of the team's current home, The Ballpark in Arlington.

After American League owners voted in September 1971 to allow the transfer of the Washington Senators to Texas, an expanse of bleacher and outfield seats running from foul line to foul line was added in order to meet A.L. seating requirements, taking capacity from an already expanded 20,000 to 35,694.

The rechristened Arlington Stadium featured a 200-by-60-foot scoreboard that rose up over the left field stands and included a 60-by-60-foot image in the shape of Texas—easily the park's most distinctive visual. One of the stadium's most memorable moments corresponded with its first sellout—June 27, 1973, when Texas high school sensation David Clyde made his major league debut and pitched five innings against the Twins, getting credit for a 4-3 victory.

But Clyde was not the native Texan who made the biggest impact on Arlington Stadium and the Rangers franchise. Just stand outside The Ballpark in Arlington, look around and you will be overpowered by images and references to Nolan Ryan. And if you look northwest from Nolan Ryan Expressway, you can almost see a ghost of the old stadium and hear fans stomping their feet on the metal outfield bleachers as the future Hall of Famer, at age 44, pitches his seventh no-hitter (May 1, 1991) against the Blue Jays.

First game: April 21, 1972. The Rangers, with their scheduled April 6 home opener canceled by a players' strike, defeated the California Angels, 7-6, before 20,105 as Dick Bosman got the victory and Frank Howard hit a first-inning home run. Managed by Ted Williams, the Rangers won their first four home games before suffering an Arlington Stadium loss.

Final game: October 3, 1993. Gary Gaetti's two-run homer off Tom Henke paced the Royals to a 4-1 victory. Juan Gonzalez made the last out for the Rangers, who finished 906-844 (.518) in 22 seasons at Arlington Stadium.

- ■ Site of no World Series
- ■ Site of no All-Star Games

titles in the stadium's life-span. Players like Toby Har-rah, Buddy Bell, Jeff Bur-roughs, Richie Zisk and Fer-guson Jenkins were fan favorites, but the Rangers always competed in the massive shadow of Texas' first sports love—almighty football. From August through the remainder of the season, a Dallas Cow-boys score relayed by the public address announcer generated bigger cheers than anything on the base-ball field.

That changed in 1989, when the Rangers acquired aging Nolan Ryan, a tried-and-true Texan who be-

Arlington Stadium was packed (right) when the Rangers staged a special day for favorite son, Nolan Ryan, in September 1993. The Texas state flag greeted visitors at the facility's main entrance (above).

came the most popular player in franchise history. Arlington Stadium, seldom packed, was filled to capacity every time he pitched—and the atmosphere was electric. The P.A. announcer would implore fans in the outfield bleachers to "scooch together" and a huge Ryan photograph greeted visitors, right alongside the Texas flag, at the main entrance.

Sights and sounds were important to Arlington fans. They still remember the right field temperature board, the sound of roller coasters and other rides from nearby Six Flags, superfan Zonk behind the first base dugout, Lone Ranger clips on the video board and Dot Races—an Arlington invention, according to some Texans. But nothing stirred emotions more than the first musical notes of "Cot-ton-Eyed Joe," a stadium staple during the seventh-inning stretch.

Sun beaten and worn beyond its years, Arlington Stadium gave way to a mod-ern new facility after the 1993 season. Ironically, the Rangers won their first divi-sion championship and brought postseason play to North Texas only three years later.

Fulton County Stadium

Also known as
Atlanta Stadium (1966-1975)

They called it "The Launching Pad," a place where teams could go to inflate their home run and victory totals. But Fulton County Stadium was so much more than a ballpark stereotype. It was Atlanta's ticket into the big leagues, baseball's doorway to the deep South and the stage on which Hank Aaron achieved baseball immortality. Round, symmetrical, multi-purpose and plain in many ways, Fulton County Stadium also was a venue of special significance and history.

You sometimes struggled to get that sense of significance over the

Francisco Cabrera's two-out, ninth-inning pinch single beats Pittsburgh and gives Braves their second straight pennant, Oct. 14, 1992

Braves set modern record by winning first 13 games in 1982 en route to West Division crown

Aaron's 715th

Where Chief Noc-A-Homa pitched his tepee

Braves clinch third straight West Division title with final-day victory, Oct. 3, 1993

PHIL NIEKRO: Knucksie won 268 games for Braves and threw Atlanta's first no-hitter, Aug. 5, 1973

Bob Horner hits four homers on July 6, 1986, but Braves still lose to Expos

Braves pitchers Larry McWilliams and Gene Garber stop
Pete Rose's 44-game hitting streak, Aug. 1, 1978

Tom Glavine, Mark
Wohlers stop Indians on
Game 6 one-hitter, Oct. 28,
1995—Braves' first World
Series crown since 1957

San Diego's Nate Colbert clubs five
homers and drives in 13 runs in
doubleheader, Aug. 1, 1972

Cy Young heaven: Braves (left to
right) Tom Glavine (1), John Smoltz
(1) and Greg Maddux (3) dominate
over 6-year span, 1991-96

Pirates' slugger Willie Stargell spoils Braves' Atlanta
debut with 13th-inning homer, April 12, 1966

Launching pad for many milestone home runs: Aaron's 500th . . .
July 14, 1968; 600th . . . April 27, 1971; 700th . . . July 21, 1973; 715th
. . . April 8, 1974; Willie McCovey's 500th . . . June 30, 1978

The Braves' 40-homer 1973 triumvirate:
Dave Johnson 43, Darrell Evans 41, Aaron 40

Aaron thrills Atlanta
Stadium crowd with homer
in N.L.'s 10-inning All-Star
win, July 25, 1972

Where 46-year-old
Hoyt Wilhelm pitched
in 1,000th career
game, May 10, 1970

Dale Murphy hits two
homers, drives in six in
sixth inning of 10-1 win
over Giants, July 27, 1989

Center fielder Dale Murphy:
Consecutive MVPs in '82, '83

HANK AARON:
Baseball's all-time
home run king

years because of the Braves' consistent losing and some bizarre promotions designed to attract fans to the 52,710-seat facility. But you never lost the sense of history, enhanced by the stadium's location a mile south of midtown Atlanta, in the shadow of Georgia's state Capitol building. By itself, the white, bowl-like structure was nondescript. In the bright Georgia sunshine, it glowed majestically against Atlanta's modern skyline.

It was all a matter of perspective. And there were many ways of looking at Fulton County Stadium.

You could circle the stadium's exterior and experience the sights and sounds of the open-backed concourses and runways, stopping periodically to admire statues of Aaron in home run form, Phil Niekro floating a knuckleball homeward and Atlanta-born Ty Cobb, the Georgia Peach, sliding spikes-first into baseball history. Or you could step inside and experience the explosion of color, starting with the green grass field and the rich, red, eye-popping Georgia dirt.

The color rose around you, courtesy of multi-tinted seats in triple-tiered stands that circled the field. The lower level gave way to a narrow press and club level and an expansive upper tier that climbed precipitously to a white-rim overhang. Horizontal light standards balanced perilously from the rim, threatening to drop on unwary patrons below, and a multi-paneled scoreboard provided need-to-know information from the rim in straightaway center. A giant Calliope added a strange backdrop to the atmosphere of the ballpark.

The field was symmetrically perfect with lots of foul territory down both lines. Pop fouls into the stands at other parks were easy outs here. It didn't take long to figure out this was a hitter's park, and the home run was the weapon of choice.

"It was a fun place to play," recalled former center fielder Dale Murphy, the National League's MVP in 1982 and '83. "The ball carried great. Good light, could always see the ball. It's always been a great place to hit."

The home run-haven reputation was enhanced by the city's elevation—1,057 feet above sea level, the major leagues' highest until Colorado began play. Balls shot out of the park and the Braves celebrated their home runs with a war dance by Chief Noc-A-Homa, who maintained his tepee for many years in the left or center field stands. The Braves built a power lineup around Aaron, who would take the art of home run hitting into uncharted territory.

It was hard to sit anywhere in the park without thinking about Atlanta's No. 44, baseball's all-time home run king. His presence overshadowed the team's meager accomplishments for many years; his aura hung over the place like a thick cloud after retirement. A "715" circle just over the left field wall marked the spot of Aaron's record-breaking homer on the night of April 8, 1974—a shot into what was then the Braves' bullpen. It was not only the most momentous moment in Fulton County Stadium history, it was one of the great moments in baseball's glorious past.

FULTON COUNTY STADIUM (1966-1996)

Also known as Atlanta Stadium (1966-1975)

The story of Atlanta Stadium, as it was known until 1976, began in 1961, when Ivan Allen Jr., in a campaign for mayor, said he would build a modern sports stadium. After he was elected, he embarked on the challenge of finding a team to play in his prospective park—the necessary prerequisite to acquiring land and money.

Allen's first target was Charles O. Finley's Kansas City Athletics, who were forced by league orders (temporarily, at least) to stay put. Then he turned to the Milwaukee Braves, who assured him in the spring of 1964 they were interested in making the move, giving him the needed impetus to break ground on a new stadium.

It wasn't until the fall of '64 that the Braves announced their official plans to move to Atlanta and it wasn't until 1966 that the team began play there. In the interim, Atlanta Stadium served as home of the Atlanta Crackers, a Braves farm team.

The former stadium site is now a parking lot that sits in the shadow of Atlanta's new baseball facility, Turner Field.

First game: April 12, 1966. Pittsburgh's Matty Alou was the game's first batter and Felipe Alou batted first for the Braves. (In the final game at the stadium in 1996, Montreal's Moises Alou was the stadium's final regular-season batter.) Pittsburgh won the opener 3-2 in 13 innings on a Willie Stargell home run.

Final game: October 24, 1996. In the fifth game of the World Series, the Yankees shut down the Braves—and the stadium—with a 1-0 victory.

■ Site of four World Series (1991, '92, '95 and '96)
■ Site of one All-Star Game (1972)

But Aaron's accomplishments often were offset by the erratic play of Braves teams that posted non-winning records in 18 of their first 25 Atlanta seasons and the questionable antics of a fan-hungry owner. After the early excitement of major league baseball, the stadium often took on a ghost-town atmosphere with fewer than 2,000 fans once turning out to watch Nolan Ryan pitch.

In retrospect, the stadium really was nothing more than a means to get Atlanta to its 1990s end—a job it performed admirably. It was a symbol of hope in 1965 when it opened its gates to the International League's Atlanta Crackers as a prelude to stunning announcements that the Braves would move operations from Milwaukee to Atlanta and the NFL would award the city an expansion franchise (the Falcons) for the 1966 season.

By the time Ted Turner took control of the team in 1976, attendance had dwindled so much that he instigated a line of crazy promotions — "Wedlock and Headlock Night," fans racing on ostriches, a local disc jockey diving into a huge ice cream sundae and even a wet T-shirt contest. But all Turner had to show for his efforts through the 1980s were two division titles and consistently-low attendance figures.

Fulton County Stadium was a multi-purpose facility that ushered Braves baseball into a new era of prosperity. It gave way to Turner Field, which in 1996 could be seen under construction right across the street (below).

Everything changed in 1990, thanks to the efforts of new general manager John Schuerholz and new manager Bobby Cox, who transformed the Braves into the "team of the '90s." One of the first things they did was rip up the turf, long considered the worst in baseball, resurface the field and hire a crack groundskeeping crew. Other amenities were added, as was an outstanding pitching staff featuring Greg Maddux, Tom Glavine, John Smoltz and Steve Avery and a lineup with Fred McGriff, David Justice, Chipper Jones and Javy Lopez. The Braves began collecting division titles, N.L. pennants and a 1995 World Series championship—their first since 1957.

When Fulton County Stadium played host to its final major league season in 1996, it was more alive, fans were chanting and performing tomahawk chops and baseball life was suddenly good for Turner and actress wife Jane Fonda, who were visible ballpark regulars in their box near the first base dugout.

Ironically, when the Braves moved across the parking lot to Turner Field in 1997, they said goodbye to a baseball facility that was much better than the one that had put Atlanta on the major league map 31 years earlier.

HANK AARON
HOME RUN
715
April 8, 1974

The view from under the stadium's overhang was steep and spectacular (right). Sights at Fulton County ranged from superfans (below) to a circle beyond the left field fence marking Aaron's record home run.

A disappointed fan raises his tomahawks in salute to Fulton County Stadium after a Game 5 loss to the Yankees in the 1996 World Series—the park's grand finale.

Memorial
Stadium

Ripken country: Cal Jr.(right) and Billy (center) become double-play partners for manager Cal Sr., July 11, 1987

Cal Ripken Jr.: MVP in 1983, '91

Like a Dave McNally fastball, Memorial Stadium kind of snuck up on you. At first glance, it wasn't impressive architecturally, it didn't assault your emotions and it didn't fill you with anticipation. But, oh, that perfectly manicured, emerald-green grass field!

This wasn't heaven; it was Baltimore. Memorial Stadium, broken down to its most common denominator, was about as close as baseball could get to the pastoral Field of Dreams portrayed so eloquently on the movie screens. It was impossible to resist its grass, the foul pole-to-foul pole openness of its outfield and the stately green trees that did double sentry over the back of the field and the residential neighborhood beyond.

Frustrated O's open 1988 season 0-21

Brooks Robinson frustrates Reds by making numerous spectacular plays throughout 1970 World Series . . . Pitcher Dave McNally rocks Cincinnati with grand slam in Game 3

Senators' Tom Cheney strikes out 21 Orioles in 16-inning game, Sept. 12, 1962

Four 20-game winners in 1971: Jim Palmer, Dave McNally, Pat Dobson and Mike Cuellar

BROOKS ROBINSON: Caretaker of A.L. third base Gold Glove for 16 years

Orioles lose 1983 Series opener 2-1 when Scott McGregor serves up eighth-inning homer to Phillies' Garry Maddox after waiting for completion of TV interview with President Ronald Reagan

Six Cy Youngs in 12-year span: Mike Cuellar 1969; Jim Palmer (right) 1973, '75, '76; Mike Flanagan 1979; Steve Stone 1980

Mike Cuellar stops New York on six hits in Game 1 of World Series—the O's last win vs. the Miracle Mets, Oct. 11, 1969

Target for fan favorite Boog Powell, who pounded 303 Oriole homers

Frank Robinson's homer wins fourth and final game of 1966 World Series 1-0

Indians slugger Rocky Colavito hits four consecutive home runs vs. Orioles, June 10, 1959

Steve Barber, Stu Miller combine for no-hitter, but Tigers score twice in ninth on walks, wild pitch and error for 2-1 win, April 30, 1967

Sammy Stewart sets big-league debut record by striking out seven straight batters, Sept. 1, 1978

Frank Robinson hits homer No. 500, Sept. 13, 1971 . . . Baltimore-born Tigers star Al Kaline doubles for 3,000th hit, Sept. 24, 1974

Where Orioles lefty Billy O'Dell retired final nine hitters he faced in All-Star Game, preserving 4-3 A.L. win, July 8, 1958

Feisty Earl Weaver (left) managed Orioles to four pennants and one Series championship in 17 years . . . Jim Palmer won 268 games over 19-year career

FRANK ROBINSON: 1966 MVP and Triple Crown winner

That's what Memorial was all about—baseball for the senses. You went there for the smells, the sounds and the visual simplicity of the game as it was meant to be played. The memories were a bonus, locked into the essence of the ballpark like a soul is to the body.

How could you look at the venerable ground around third base and not see Brooks Robinson diving left, then right, throwing from his knees or from beyond the foul line? That was the mound of Jim Palmer, Mike Cuellar, Mike Flanagan and Steve Stone, Cy Young winners all, and the home plate dirt kicked, tossed and spit upon by the always-feisty Earl Weaver. First base belonged to Eddie Murray, shortstop to Mark Belanger and Cal Ripken, center field to Paul Blair. Frank Robinson was to the left field bleachers what Boog Powell was to the bleachers in right.

Memorial Stadium's considerable aura was well concealed by a plain, reddish-brown and tan brick facade that surrounded a horseshoe-shaped facility. It looked like a big museum set awkwardly in the midst of family neighborhoods just north of downtown Baltimore. Only a careful inspection and towering light standards revealed its true identity as a ballpark.

Still, your first greeting stirred somber emotion rather than excitement—an inscription etched into the concrete facade above the main entrance that read: "Time Can Never Dim the Honor of Their Deeds," a tribute to Baltimore veterans who died in both World Wars and the Korean War. Your baseball senses began perking up on the walk from the gate through easy-to-negotiate corridors lined with concessionaires hawking their wares.

The inside was a revelation. You just never expected the rush of green, white and brown, no matter how many games you attended there. Only after you had settled into the intimacy of the park did you realize you had been duped—this was really a good-sized facility (53,371 capacity when it closed to baseball), big enough to double as home of the NFL's Colts for 30 years, with a three-level grandstand that rose steeply from foul pole-to-foul pole behind home plate.

Enhancing the open feel was an upper deck without a roof—baseball's first open-air topside when the stadium was opened to major league baseball and the relocated St. Louis Browns in 1954. The grandstands gave way to single-deck bleachers that extended at an angle into left-center and right-center field before giving way to a scoreboard (left-center), video board (right-center) and the tree-surrounded (dead center) flagpole.

Because of the field's unusual shape (two crescents that came together at points behind home plate and in center field), you never got a sense of the park's symmetry. Dimensions changed drastically over the years as Memorial Stadium, a rebuilt version of old Municipal Stadium at the same site, became more comfortable with its baseball ties. Memorial's 1954 debut season was played with a green concrete wall that curved sharply away from the 309-foot foul poles toward a makeshift wire fence in center that was a distant 450 feet from home plate.

"To play that outfield right, you needed five outfielders," said former Oriole Gil Coan.

That changed when an inner fence was constructed from right field to left, leaving the foul poles intact but gradually reducing center field to a more reachable 405 feet. To its final day, fans in the corners were right on top of the field and balls hitting the angled corner walls bounced sharply toward center instead of back to the infield.

Memorial Stadium, while retaining an "old" feel, was not averse to modern tastes and technology. The scoreboard and video board were state-of-the-art, the sound system was outstanding and the food of choice, crab cakes, ranked high among ballpark delicacies. Baseball also was state-of-the-art, thanks to pitching-loaded Orioles teams that finished an incredible 612 games over .500 in a 24-year stretch from 1960 to '83 while winning six American League pennants and three World Series.

MEMORIAL STADIUM (1954-1991)

It was a football stadium—known as Venable Stadium, Metropolitan Stadium and Babe Ruth Stadium—before major league baseball arrived in 1954. Major renovations began in 1949 and continued until just before the '54 season, when the St. Louis Browns sealed their relocation to Baltimore.

The facility's name was an honorable tribute to Baltimore veterans who had died in both World Wars and the Korean War. The reddish brown and tan-bricked stadium stood like an out-of-place museum on East 33rd Street, in a family neighborhood just north of the downtown area.

First game: April 15, 1954. Vice President Richard M. Nixon threw out the first pitch and major league baseball returned to Baltimore with a 3-1 Orioles win over the White Sox.

Final game: October 6, 1991. A 7-1 Tigers win took a backseat to postgame festivities in which almost 100 former Orioles took the field and said tearful goodbyes to the stadium.

■ Site of six World Series (1966, '69, '70, '71 '79, '83)
■ Site of one All-Star Game (1958)

Opening day at Memorial in 1960 provided a good view of the 309-foot right field corner with fans right on top of the action.

Memorial featured an unusual shape, a scoreboard topped by the 'Gunther Beer' sign and a distant center field fence when it opened for major league play in 1954.

Memorial Stadium's tan-brick facade gave the facility a museum look. Greeting visitors was a giant inscription over the building's main entrance that paid tribute to veterans who died in both World Wars and the Korean War.

Robinson's 450-foot home run off Luis Tiant made history as the only ball to leave Memorial Stadium.

Memorial-style baseball also was about bugle-induced "Charge!" calls, ushers dressed in orange jackets, Wild Bill Hagy standing on the dugout, inciting the crowd by contorting his body to spell out "Orioles," tomato vines climbing the wall up the third base line and the national anthem, during which fans screamed out "O" when the song reached its "O say does that star spangled banner yet wave" crescendo.

Memorial Stadium reached its crescendo in 1991, after 38 seasons, when the Orioles moved to a beautiful new ballpark facility in a downtown Baltimore area near the Inner Harbor. The team might be gone, but the memories will hang forever over the East 33rd Street site—like a towering fly ball in the blue sky of a crisp summer afternoon at Baltimore's first real ballpark.

Over the years, Memorial Stadium became known as a homey stadium with a ballpark feel. That perception was enhanced by signature sights and traditions that gave it a distinctive flavor.

A "Gunther" beer scoreboard sign was a fixture for many years, as was the "HERE" flag that flew above the left field bleachers, marking the spot where, in 1966, Frank

Braves
Field

Braves finish 38-115, 61½ games
behind Cubs in futile
1935 season

Bob Elliott hits
three-run homer,
Braves beat Giants
3-2 and clinch first
N.L. pennant since
1914, Sept. 26, 1948

Shortstop Rabbit
Maranville (right)
made his belt-
buckle catches here
. . . Casey Stengel
clowned his way
through six
managerial seasons

JOHNNY SAIN:
Four-time 20-game winner
led Braves to 1948 pennant

Red Sox lefty Babe Ruth
wins 14-inning pitching
duel vs. Brooklyn in Game
2 of 1916 World Series

Red Sox used more spacious Braves
Field as home base during 1915 and
1916 World Series

Paul Waner collects hit
No. 3,000, June 19, 1942

I t was a curious antique, a
dead ball-era survivor that
never quite made the
transition to modern
baseball. Braves Field was a huge,
luxurious palace when it opened in
1915, an outdated, oft-renovated
dinosaur when it closed 38 years
later. From beginning to end, it
was a house of pain for fans and
players of the National League
Braves.

Braves Field was a victim of bad
timing and ownership without
vision. The last of the early-
century steel-and-concrete
ballparks opened the season after

Tommy Holmes
hit in 37 straight
games in 1945

218

1948 slogan: "Spahn (left) and Sain (right) and two days of rain"

Braves, Dodgers play to 2-2 tie in 23-inning game called by darkness, June 27, 1939

Jim Tobin hits three homers and pitches Braves to 6-5 win over Cubs, May 13, 1942 . . . no-hits Dodgers, ices 2-0 win with home run, April 27, 1944

Braves' Joe Oeschger and Brooklyn's Leon Cadore wage Herculean pitching battle that ends in 1-1 tie after major league-record 26 innings, May 1, 1920

Thirtysomething rookies Jim Turner and Lou Fette post their 20th wins on consecutive days, Oct. 2, 3, 1937

Where Augie Galan's disputed homer hit old foul pole during N.L.'s first All-Star Game win in 1936

Umpire rules Phil Masi safe on controversial pickoff play, helping Sain outduel Bob Feller 1-0 in Game 1 of 1948 World Series

Jury Box was home for about 2,000 bleacherites

Where Ernie Padgett turned baseball's fourth unassisted triple play, Oct. 6, 1923

Catcher Hank Gowdy left team to enlist as first major leaguer in World War I

Dodgers clinch 1952 N.L. pennant in final game at Braves Field

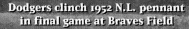

Where Dutch Leonard and Ernie Shore pitched Red Sox to consecutive 2-1 wins in Games 3 and 4 of 1915 Series

WALLY BERGER hit rookie-record 38 homers in 1930, 199 in eight seasons with Braves

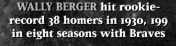

Lester Bell hits three homers into special section of seats in front of left field fence, just misses fourth, June 2, 1928

the Miracle Braves had captured the hearts of Boston fans with their mad rush to a World Series championship and a few years before Babe Ruth would change the course of baseball with his booming bat. Most of Braves Field's existence was spent in a losing funk while the American League's Red Sox thrived at Fenway Park, only a few blocks away.

Braves Field, in deference to owner James Gaffney's love of inside-the-park home runs, spent the first third of its existence promoting nineteenth-century baseball while the rest of the nation was stricken with home run fever. Early Braves Field, featuring 402-foot foul lines and an unreachable 550-foot center field barrier, was billed as "the largest baseball park in the world," an assessment endorsed by pitchers who were further aided by Boston's notorious East wind. "One thing is sure," Ty Cobb declared at first glance. "Nobody is ever going to hit a ball over those fences."

Cobb wasn't far off. Of the 38 home runs hit at Braves Field in 1921, 34 stayed inside the park. The Giants hit four in one game. It wasn't until 1925, the park's 11th season, that a ball hit by Giants catcher Frank Snyder finally cleared the cement left field wall.

Because of those cavernous dimensions and expansive foul territory, Braves Field never enjoyed the sense of intimacy you found in other ballparks of that era. But it wasn't without subtle charms.

A view over the left field fence revealed the Charles River, sometimes filled with the shells of Harvard racing crews, and a railroad yard that gave the park its distinctive smell. Visitors to Braves Field could arrive on the Commonwealth Avenue trolley, which would swing inside the park's main facade and drop them off right at

their gate. But the park's signature feature was the "Jury Box," a fair-territory bleacher section that seated about 2,000 and formed the outer right field boundary.

At first, the right field foul pole connected to the Jury Box and its front wall was the target for lefthanded home run hitters. But later renovations, which came fast and furious after the 1927 season, shifted the foul line away from the Jury Box and cut into a right field pavilion, part of which went from foul territory to fair.

The park was actually divided into four sections—a roofed, single-deck grandstand that curved behind the plate and extended down the lines well past first and third base, two uncovered sections that extended to the foul poles, and the Jury Box. The first scoreboard was ground level on the left field fence. Later versions were elevated atop the wall.

The 40,000-seat ballpark was far less ornate than many of its contemporaries, although a distinctive stucco facade housed the team's business offices and featured arched gateways through which fans could pass into the facility. After 1927, they never knew what they might find.

That was the season management broke down and added bleacher sections in front of the left and center field walls, reducing home run distance by about 70 feet. But opponents feasted on the new dimensions and the bleachers were gone by late season. From that point on, the park underwent almost annual (some claimed daily) renovation before settling on its final look in 1947—337 feet down the left field line, 390 to center and 319 to right with a 25-foot wooden inner left field fence that was covered by double-decked rows of advertising. A right field inner fence was 4-foot high with a 6-foot screen. The 10-foot outer wall remained as an unnecessary backdrop.

BRAVES FIELD (1915-1952)

Before they were the Braves, they were the Red Stockings, the Beaneaters, the Doves (named for George and John Dovey, brothers who owned the team from 1907-1910) and the Rustlers (for former owner William Hepburn Russell). And before they played in Braves Field, they played in South End Grounds and Congress Street Grounds.

In 1912, that all changed. James Gaffney, who had connections to New York's Tammany Hall politicians, acquired the team. Tammany Hall politicians were often called "braves" because its named is derived from an Indian chief named Tamanen.

Hence, the Braves—and Braves Field—were born. Ironically, two of the three World Series played in the facility did not involve the Braves. The 1914 Braves played their World Series "home games" at Fenway Park because Braves Field was under construction. So when the Red Sox won A.L. pennants in 1915 and '16, they used bigger Braves Field as their Series home base.

Boston University purchased the field in the 1950s and built Nickerson Field, the school's football facility, on the grounds. A plaque commemorating Braves Field stands at the Gaffney Street entrance.

First game: August 18, 1915. Hall of Famer Rabbit Maranville drove in the field's first run and the Braves downed the Cardinals, 3-1.

Final game: September 21, 1952. Brooklyn clinched a tie for the N.L. pennant by beating the Braves, 8-2, in a game no one knew would be the Braves' last in Boston. It wasn't until the spring of '53 that the team announced its immediate relocation to Milwaukee.

■ Site of three World Series (1915, '16 and '48)
■ Site of one All-Star Game (1936)

One thing that never changed was Boston's inability to field competitive teams. After second and third-place finishes in 1915 and '16, the Braves forged losing records in 27 of the next 36 seasons with only one pennant—1948—to ease their frustration. Life at Braves Field, despite such capable players as Wally Berger, Tommy Holmes, Rabbit Maranville, Warren Spahn, Johnny Sain and Shanty Hogan, sometimes resembled a comedy act directed by such ringmasters as Judge Emil Fuchs, who doubled one memorable season as the team's owner and manager, and Casey Stengel. The Braves even changed their name to "Bees" from 1936-41, but camouflage tactics proved ineffective.

It all added up to sagging attendance and the shocking 1953 announcement that Braves Field, final home park of the immortal Ruth (1935), would lose its team to Milwaukee. In retrospect, it's not insignificant that of the eight World Series games contested at Braves Field, five were played by the 1915 and '16 Red Sox.

The 'Jury Box' bleacher section in right field (above) seated about 2,000 fans, many of whom would stand in line outside the main entrance (below) for tickets.

Ebbets Field

Two four-homer games: Dodgers' Gil Hodges (left) in 1950, Braves' Joe Adcock in 1954

Where Phillies' Dick Sisler hit his pennant-winning three-run homer on final day of 1950

Babe Herman (above), Dazzy Vance and Chick Fewster all end up on third base after Herman's double, resulting in a double play for Braves, Aug. 15, 1926

Dem Bums won 9 pennants, 6 in 10-year stretch from 1947-56, but only 1 World Series—1955 vs. hated Yankees

Dodgers collect 10 hits, 15 runs in first-inning rampage vs. Reds, May 21, 1952

I t was, in the truest sense, a ballpark—a cozy, friendly little place where you could forget your troubles, inhale a few hot dogs and peanuts and cheer on your beloved Dodgers— boisterously and with passion, like hard-living Brooklyn fans attacked everything in life.

It was a gaudy, colorful, wonderfully-misshapen arena where everything seemed out of sync, balls bounced out of control and you not only learned to expect the unexpected, you counted on it.

It was a shrine in the Borough of Churches, where you could go to

JACKIE ROBINSON:
Second baseman broke baseball's color barrier in 1947, ignited Dodgers' offense over next decade en route to Hall of Fame

Home of three-time MVP catcher Roy Campanella (right), 1951, '53, '55; inaugural Cy Young winner Don Newcombe, 1956

Dazzy Vance:
28 wins,
2.16 ERA, 30
complete games,
262 strikeouts
in 1924

Cardinals' Jim
Bottomley hits two
homers, drives in
single-game-record
12 runs vs. Dodgers,
Sept. 16, 1924

Center
fielder Duke
Snider hit
40-homer
plateau in
five straight
seasons,
1953-57

Uncle Robbie
(Wilbert Robinson)
was master of
Dodgers universe for
18 seasons, 1914-31

Where Cookie Lavagetto's game-winning
double bounced off the concave right field
wall in Game 4 of 1947 World Series, ruining
no-hit bid by Yankee Bill Bevens

Dodgers and Reds
play 19-inning
scoreless tie,
Sept. 11, 1946

Abe Stark's
'Win a Suit' sign

Where Yankee second baseman Billy
Martin made World Series-saving
catch of Jackie Robinson popup in
seventh inning of 1952 Game 7 classic

Cincinnati lefty Johnny
Vander Meer posts
unprecedented second
straight no-hitter in first
Brooklyn night game,
June 15, 1938

Where bird
flew out of
Casey Stengel's
cap in 1918

Where catcher Mickey
Owen missed connections
with third strike in Game
4 of 1941 World Series,
setting stage for Yankees'
winning rally

Cardinals pitchers
Dizzy and Paul Dean
post double-shutout
doubleheader win—
Dizzy a 3-hitter,
Paul a no-hitter,
Sept. 21, 1934

Clem Labine
outduels Bob Turley
in 10-inning thriller,
keeps Dodgers alive
in Game 6 of 1956
World Series

PEE WEE REESE:
Clutch-hitting
shortstop was heart
of Dodgers pennant-
winning teams
in 1940s and '50s

Shorty's Sym-Phony band was part of the fun and flavor at Ebbets Field.

chastised the "Gints", an alien force from somewhere across the East River. "Ya bum, ya" was a daily admonition, not necessarily restricted to Dodgers opponents.

"All I knew about Brooklyn was that it was some strange, outer world. When they told me I'd been traded to Brooklyn (in 1939), I didn't know what on God's great earth to expect," recalled outfielder Dixie Walker, who went on to lasting Brooklyn fame as "The People's Cherce."

The fans were only part of the zany atmosphere of a ballpark that stretches the imagination of anybody unfortunate enough not to have attended a game there. There were critics who called Ebbets Field a ratty architectural disaster, but history cherishes it as an aesthetic treasure. It was non-conformist in every sense, with nuances and physical oddities that affected the way the game was played. It was a stadium overflowing with personality.

Part of it came from the close proximity of the seats to the field, especially around dugouts that seemed to blend into the stands. You could almost reach out and touch some-

worship players named Leo, Newk, Dazzy, Dixie, Babe, Campy, Jackie, Pee Wee and the Duke. It was where Hilda Chester clanged her cowbell and Shorty's Sym-Phony Band stayed out of tune for two decades.

Ebbets Field was charming and charismatic—equal parts madhouse and magic kingdom, a rickety baseball palace where pennants were won, dreams were shattered and your emotions were stretched to the limits of ecstasy and disappointment.

The charm of Ebbets started and ended with its fans—the most raucous, colorful, knowledgeable zealots ever to unite their passions in a common cause. You couldn't empower the Dodgers without talking the talk—a distinctive dialect in which you "moidered dem bums," cheered for "Boit" Shotton and

one in uniform—a closeness that created a special bond with the Dodgers and an irritating dialogue with opponents. "You were so close to the field, sitting anywhere in that old park, that you could hear the players talking to each other," said Red Patterson, a former Dodgers vice president.

The personality started with an ornate rotunda inside the main entrance and extended to the field itself, which must have been constructed by somebody with a sense of humor. The right field wall was a concave nightmare, mastered by Walker and Carl Furillo but a confusing puzzle to most opposing outfielders. Shots off the wall, which sloped inward from the top and bottom, bounced around the field like a billiard ball coming off a cushion. The wall was an inviting 297 feet down the line, but it was topped by a 20-foot fence that protected the

The front entrance of Ebbets Field was a busy place before a game in July 1949.

Big, gaudy, colorful advertisements played a part in creating the sometimes-crazy atmosphere at Ebbets Field.

The Schaefer Beer and Abe Stark signs were scoreboard staples (below) and familiar sights to regulars sitting in double-deck stands behind home plate.

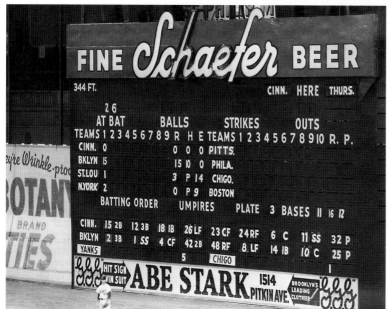

windows of businesses along Bedford Avenue.

The right field wall was divided by a giant scoreboard that jutted onto the playing field—another nightmare for outfielders. And the left field wall, backed by a double-decked grandstand occupied by the rowdiest bleacherites in baseball, made two angled cuts away from the plate before meeting the concave wall in deepest right-center field.

At first glance, Ebbets was a shock to your nervous system. You could become mesmerized by the colorful and gaudy signs that added character to a park that already had more than its fair share. The most prominent signs were on the scoreboard—a full-length strip across the bottom sponsored by Abe Stark, who challenged players to "Hit Sign, Win Suit," and a Schaefer Beer sign in which the "h" and "e" in the word Schaefer could be illuminated to designate a hit or error.

It was easy to become overwhelmed by the personality of Ebbets Field, where several legendary fans gained as much renown as the players they rooted for. The cowbell-toting Hilda was a noisy fixture for years in the left-center field bleachers and the five-piece Sym-Phony band seemed to be everywhere, irritating the opposition with their musical antics while saluting their Dodgers heroes. Hilda, who could bellow an "eatcha heart out, ya bum" put-down that could be heard throughout the park, was an intimidating obstacle for Giants fans who might venture into enemy territory.

Charles Ebbets might have suspected life would be different at Ebbets Field when his Dodgers played their first game at the new park in 1913, but not before bleacher ticketholders were kept waiting outside the gate because someone had forgotten the key, and the dedication march to the center field flagpole was delayed because somebody had forgotten the flag.

Things would only get wilder and crazier. What more perfect setting for Casey Stengel's tip-of-the-hat gesture to heckling Dodger fans, releasing a live bird that flew away to freedom? Where else could the Daffiness Boys of Wilbert Robinson have received such loving affection in the 1920s? Where else could you find a singing newsboy who would regale you with Dodger tales, the tone of his melodies reflecting the team's successes and failures?

Babe Herman, who made it perfectly clear to anybody who would listen that he never was hit on the head by a fly ball, did slide into third once, only to find teammates Dazzy Vance and Chick Fewster already there. Herman's bases-loaded double turned into a double play. Umpire George Magerkurth became a famous Brooklyn figure only because he was floored by an irate fan, who held him down and pummeled away near home plate. Hungry fans, upset at not being able to purchase tickets for a critical game against the Giants in 1924, used a dismantled telephone pole to batter in the gate and flowed into the already-packed stadium.

This was the proper setting for yellow baseballs, a milkman/batting practice pitcher and a dropped third strike that cost the Dodgers an important World Series victory. Where else could Johnny Vander Meer have mustered the strength to pitch his second straight no-hitter—in the first night game ever played at Ebbets Field? What park, with its incredible melting pot of patrons, was more fitting for the great sociological experiment—Jackie Robinson's 1947 breaking of baseball's color barrier? Cookie Lavagetto's 1947 double off the right field wall still bounces through the soul of Brooklyn, a vivid, happy memory of one of baseball's greatest World Series moments.

There were plenty of World Series moments in the 1940s and '50s, when Brooklyn fans watched their Dodgers win seven pennants—but only one

Ebbets Field (1913-1957)

Baseball in Brooklyn was played in a variety of places by teams bearing a variety of names before the Dodgers settled into Ebbets Field. The Wonders, Bridegrooms and Superbas played their games in Washington Park, Eastern Park and Washington Park II. It was at Eastern Park that the team became known as "Dodgers," a shortening of "Trolley Dodgers" referring to fans who had to dodge trolleys to get to the park.

In 1912, Brooklyn owner Charles Ebbets secured the final parcel of a 4½-acre tract in Brooklyn's Flatbush neighborhood. In 1913, on the blighted tract bordered by Bedford Avenue, Sullivan Street, Franklin Avenue and Montgomery Street, Ebbets Field opened.

Sportswriters are credited with encouraging the naming of the park in Ebbets' honor. Over the next 45 years, it was home for nine pennant-winning teams and one World Series champion.

The Dodgers played there through the 1957 season and Ebbets Field stood until 1960. The Ebbets Field Apartments now mark the ballpark's former location.

First game: April 9, 1913. Philadelphia Phillies righthander Tom Seaton made a first-inning run hold up in a 1-0 victory over the Dodgers.

Final game: September 24, 1957. Before 6,702 fans, most of them stunned by the team's announced departure for Los Angeles, the Dodgers shut out Pittsburgh, 2-0.

■ Site of nine World Series (1916, '20, '41, '47, '49, '52, '53, '55 and '56)
■ Site of one All-Star Game (1949)

championship. Twenty-eight World Series games were played at Ebbets, 14 victories and 14 defeats. But, thanks primarily to the talented Yankees, "next year" didn't arrive until 1955, two years before Ebbets Field played host to its final major league game.

All the color, 45 years worth of fascinating memories, all the special ties between players and fans—the heart and soul of Brooklyn baseball—were tainted in 1957 by the Dodgers' announcement they would move to Los Angeles for the 1958 season. It was like a stake in the heart of a city that had invested more than it could afford in a relationship gone bad.

The divorce became official on February 23, 1960, when a demolition crew began dismantling Ebbets Field, effectively removing the last vestige of a special team in a special place at a special time.

Ebbets Field, tucked snugly in the heart of Brooklyn (left), offered an interesting view from beyond its right-center field fence across Bedford Avenue (below bottom). The park's visitor's bullpen, located down the left field line (below top), was a frequent October work area for the cross-town New York Yankees.

Superfan Hilda Chester (above) kept things rocking at Ebbets with her ever-present cowbell. A worker (right) climbs over the right field wall to get a ball that stuck in the screen. This ground-rule double, hit by St Louis star Stan Musial, typified the craziness that happened a lot at Ebbets.

Comiskey Park

Charles A. Comiskey: The Noblest Roman

Park where "Black Sox" lost three times to Reds during infamous 1919 World Series

Eddie Collins, Shoeless Joe Jackson and Happy Felsch get three hits apiece in 8-5 Game 5 win that sets stage for 1917 World Series championship

NELLIE FOX played in record 798 straight games at second base during 14 seasons with Sox

Left fielder Al Smith gets famous beer shower following Dodger homer by Charlie Neal in Game 2 of '59 World Series

Cubs used Comiskey as their "home park" during 1918 World Series loss to Red Sox

Where seven-time stolen base champion Luis Aparicio performed defensive magic and served as catalyst for Go-Go Sox from 1956-62

The first thing you noticed about old Comiskey Park was its imposing brick facade, an all-white, weather-beaten, decaying mirror that reflected the tough South Side neighborhoods surrounding it. It was hard to imagine this worn-down, street-wise structure as the former "Baseball Palace of the World," but neither could you escape the Comiskey spell—a powerful sense of baseball history that drew you around its perimeter like an awestruck tourist.

Bill Veeck: Master showman and king of exploding scoreboards

Site of Bill Veeck's "Disco Demolition" promotion, which causes near riot and results in forfeit to Tigers, July 12, 1979

Fred Lynn hits first grand slam in All-Star Game history as A.L. rolls in classic's 50th anniversary contest, July 6, 1983

Harold Baines ends 8-hour, 25-inning battle vs. Brewers with home run, May 9, 1984

The first All-Star Game was played here, July 6, 1933 . . . Red Schoendienst decides 1950 All-Star classic with home run in 14th inning

Ted Kluszewski muscles up for two homers during 11-0 Game 1 win in '59 Series . . . Dodger Chuck Essegian sets record with second pinch-hit homer in Game 6

1990, final season at old Comiskey: Carlton Fisk (left) sets record for career homers by catcher and Bobby Thigpen posts record 57 saves

Yankee pitcher Andy Hawkins pitches no-hitter—loses to White Sox 4-0, July 1, 1990

LUKE APPLING: White Sox career leader in games, runs, hits, doubles, total bases and RBIs

Bewildered Orioles end season-opening-record 21-game losing streak with 9-0 win, April 29, 1988

Where Mike Squires made brief appearances as the first big-league lefty catcher in 22 years, May 4, 7, 1980

Cleveland's Larry Doby breaks A.L. racial barrier as pinch hitter, July 5, 1947 . . . Minnie Minoso breaks White Sox racial barrier and hits home run in first plate appearance, May 1, 1951

Comiskey Park and the White Sox were drawing fans in the early 1940s, thanks to improving transportation and players like Luke Appling and Ted Lyons.

This was the creation of Charles Comiskey, the Old Roman who opened his modern-day Colosseum in 1910. This was "Home of the White Sox" for 81 years, the stomping ground of Big Ed Walsh, Ted Lyons, Eddie Collins, Nellie Fox, Luke Appling, Luis Aparicio, Minnie Minoso, Carlton Fisk and, of course, Shoeless Joe Jackson. This was where working-class Chicago, blue-collar Chicago, came to watch serious baseball, not the cuddly Cubbies version played on the city's North Side. This was a social melting pot of macho, burly, rowdy fans who could set aside differences and unite in a common cause for a few hours on a Sunday afternoon.

A first visit to the baseball fortress at 35th Street and Shields Avenue was sure to provide instant gratification. Comiskey from the outside, with 12 distinctive ticket booths forming a semi-circular shield at the main

entrance, was imposing. But the feeling inside was personal and inviting. The green seats formed a bond with the grass field below, the grandstand roof hovered overhead like a protective mother and the scoreboard, Comiskey's "Monster," dominated the center field view, ready to explode at a moment's notice.

It was hard to take your eyes off that huge, wonderfully colorful scoreboard—the most distinctive of Comiskey's features for three decades. Baseball's first exploding scoreboard, introduced by former owner Bill Veeck in 1960, released a strange cacophony of sounds ranging from foghorns and a cavalry-charge bugle to crashing trains and a circus calliope when celebrating a White Sox home run. The board, which filled the open center field area above the bleachers (the only area not enclosed

COMISKEY PARK (1910-1990)

Although it was a stately predecessor of Wrigley Field, Tiger Stadium, Fenway Park and Yankee Stadium, Comiskey Park never shared the respect those parks commanded in the late 20th century. It was ahead of its time, both as the showcase ballpark of the American League when it was built and an aging dinosaur in need of retirement over its final years.

Charles Comiskey built it as a replacement for Southside Park, home of the White Sox from 1901-10. It was a park of convenience and comfort, a showcase for fans, a safer place for players and, with steel instead of wood construction, a more fire-resistant structure.

Its enduring features were the upper-deck grandstand that enclosed all but a small center field section of the park, an electronic scoreboard that debuted in 1951 and light-shedding portals in the lower left field grandstands. This was the home of baseball's first All-Star Game in 1933 and a host for four World Series—including a 1918 classic that allowed the crosstown Cubs a larger seating capacity. But years of neglect eventually doomed the park.

Today, new Comiskey sits adjacent to the old ballpark site, which is now covered by a parking lot. All that remains of old Comiskey is an outline of its basepaths.

First game: July 1, 1910. Big Ed Walsh and the White Sox lost to the St. Louis Browns, 2-0.

Final game: September 30, 1990. The White Sox recorded their 3,024th regular-season win (vs. 2,926 losses) at Comiskey—a 2-1 victory over Seattle.

■ Site of four World Series (1917, '18, '19 and '59)
■ Site of three All-Star Games (1933, '50 and '83)

One of Comiskey Park's signature features was its grandstand roof, which was imposing whether you viewed it from above or below.

by the grandstand roof), changed size, shape and color over the years, but its "Disneyland" theatrics never failed to delight fans and draw the wrath of opposing players and coaches.

Once you pried your eyes away from the scoreboard, Comiskey became a menagerie of sights, sounds and baseball memories. The view from behind home plate was dramatic, even if the left field roof did block out a spectacular downtown Chicago skyline. Portals in the lower left field grandstands let in light and diminished the feeling of enclosure. A catwalk allowed fans to pass to and from the upper left and right field grandstands behind the scoreboard and retired numbers of special White Sox players

were featured on the right field wall. A ground-level picnic area in left field provided a marvelous view of batting practice—and a respite from the biting north wind off Lake Michigan that sometimes turned Comiskey into a spring or summer icebox.

How could anyone possibly hit a ball over the double-decked roof, in either right or left? Well, it happened 44 times, including shots by Babe Ruth, Lou Gehrig, Jimmie Foxx and Ted Williams that were temporarily immortalized by signs across the face of the upper deck. Foxx and Hank Greenberg were among the magnificent seven to reach the original center field bleachers, before the White Sox put up a distance-shortening center field fence in the 1980s.

Home runs, no matter how long, were always of interest in Comiskey,

From its early days right on through the Bill Veeck era, Comiskey has always been known for its scoreboards. The early board (far left) had its Longines clock and Veeck's later versions had pyrotechnic displays (above) and a sound system to match.

Promotions were a Bill Veeck specialty, including this 1959 surprise in which little spacemen showed up to capture Luis Aparicio and Nellie Fox.

one of baseball's biggest ballparks over the years. When the stadium was opened with a grandstand roof that wrapped behind home plate from first base to third, the lines measured 362 feet and it was 420 to dead center. When the grandstands were extended in 1927, the lines shortened to 352 but center field moved back to 440—a distance that an inner fence cut to 402 from 1986 through Comiskey's final 1990 season.

"It was a great park, big, a fair park," Appling recalled before Comiskey closed its gates for the final time. "There were no gimmes in right field or left field with a short fence, and center field was so big you could put in another field."

In the quirky, oddly-shaped world of early-century baseball, Charles Comiskey emerged as a champion of symmetry, a principle that was never sacrificed through the park's many renovations. Neither was Comiskey's place in history, which was not always achieved through conventional methods.

The park was the home of one championship team and the site of four World Series, one of which was played there by the Cubs, not the White Sox, in 1918 and another that turned into the most infamous scandal in baseball history—Cincinnati's 1919 win over the "Black Sox." Only the Go-Go Sox of Aparicio and Fox in 1959 reached a World Series over the park's last seven decades.

Comiskey's "palace of baseball" reputation was underscored in 1933 when it was chosen to play host to the first All-Star Game, an honor punctuated by Ruth's game-deciding home run. It was the site of the only opening day no-hitter in history, the debut of the American League's first black player and numerous Negro League World Series. This is where Veeck kept everybody on edge with his crazy promotions and the 1983 White Sox "won ugly" and captured a West Division title.

Comiskey Park entered the 1990 season as the oldest major league park still in use, two years older than Tiger Stadium and Fenway Park. Still stately and regal despite a crumbling, creaky facade, the park passed on its legacy—and the White Sox—to new Comiskey Park, a state-of-the-art facility built right across the street. The new pride of Chicago's South Side.

Old Comiskey Park lasted through the 1990 season before giving way to new Comiskey, which was built right across the street (right).

Crosley Field

Also known as Redland Field (1912-1934)

Dodgers' Leo Durocher circles bases on bunt in wild 1938 All-Star Game

Johnny Vander Meer overpowers Boston Bees, the first of his record two straight no-hitters, June 11, 1938

Reds' Jim Maloney, Astros' Don Wilson fire no-hitters on consecutive days, April 30, May 1, 1969

Where Grady Hatton's pop fly fell among three Braves, robbing Johnny Sain of perfect game, July 12, 1946

Where Dutch Ruether (right), Slim Sallee won first two games of 1919 World Series, with a little help from scheming White Sox

TED KLUSZEWSKI: Big Klu topped 100 RBIs four straight seasons (1953-56)

Mel Ott's ninth-inning homer helps Giants' Carl Hubbell win record 24th straight game, May 27, 1937

Bucky Walters fires shutout, hits homer in key Game 6 win over Tigers in 1940 World Series

Where Ernie Lombardi "snoozed" in Game 4 of 1939 World Series

Where 15-year-old Joe Nuxhall made big-league debut, June 10, 1944

I t was an oasis in the middle of a brick and smokestack-filled desert, a bright green carpet covering a small piece of Cincinnati's drab, deteriorating West End. Crosley Field was a colorful Mecca in a sometimes-gray world, a place of renewal and rejuvenation. Life was simple there—the baseball was entertaining, the heroes were friendly and everybody had fun, no bad times permitted.

It was hard not to love the simplicity and intimacy that oozed from every nook and cranny of this odd-shaped structure. Crosley was cozy, tightly carved into the

Giants hit five home runs in 12-run ninth inning, beat Reds 14-0, Aug. 23, 1961

Mill Creek flood buries Crosley Field in 1937

Slight incline in front of wall makes life interesting for left fielders

MVP Central from 1938-40: Ernie Lombardi (above), Bucky Walters, Frank McCormick

Ewell "The Whip" Blackwell (right), two outs short of second straight no-hitter, surrenders ninth-inning single to Brooklyn's Eddie Stanky, June 22, 1947

Former site of the old laundry, an inviting target for righthanded power hitters

Site of Larry MacPhail's great experiment: The first major league night game, May 24, 1935

47-year-old Satchel Paige becomes oldest pitcher in All-Star Game history, July 14, 1953

Giants 1, Reds 0 in 21 innings—Bob Lee walks home winning run, Sept. 1, 1967

Jim Maloney throws 10-inning no-hitter vs. Mets, loses in 11th on Johnny Lewis' home run, June 14, 1965

Key parts for Big Red Machine (Rose, Bench, Perez) were assembled in final years at Crosley

1961 MVP FRANK ROBINSON hit 324 of his 586 career homers in a Reds uniform

Hank Aaron singles for 3,000th hit, May 17, 1970

framework of the angled streets that surrounded it, and you quickly learned to make visual associations with the landmarks that gave it a special personality.

A laundry, the Superior Towel & Linen Service, covered much of the left field wall on York Street, providing an inviting target for righthanded power hitters until the area was cleared after the 1960 season to make room for parking. Buildings marked "Merchants Paper" and "Lackner Neon Signs" stood sentry over the center and right-center field walls on Western Avenue. Billboards dotted the right-center field skyline, hawking attractions and products like Coney Island, Hudepohl Beer ("Get moody with Hudy"), Shillito's department stores, Young & Bertke sheet metal company, Coca-Cola and Petri wine.

You did not go to Crosley Field to watch baseball. You went to experience it. It was about smells, sights and sounds—peanuts, bratwurst, red hots and beer or lemonade; the buzz that filtered through the park at the sight of players trekking to and from their clubhouse, right through the third base stands; pregame activities and promotions with fans, alongside players, on the field; superfan Harry Thobe, dressed in customary white suit with red tie, doing a victory jig; Smitty's Band, Ronnie Dale's organ music, public-address announcer Paul Sommerkamp's voice; and, of course, park idiosyncrasies like the terrace, the Sun Deck and Goat Run.

The white line and explanation served as a center field ground rule during the late 1940s at Crosley Field. It was made necessary because of the unusual way in which the wire right field bleacher fence connected to the center field wall.

Old-timers still like to tell about Babe Ruth's first experience with the terrace, an incline that started 20 feet in front of the left field fence and gradually sloped upward until it reached a four-foot grade at the wall. The aging Ruth, playing left field in 1935 for the Boston Braves, fell on his face while chasing a fly ball on the terrace, got up and grimly walked off the field, refusing to return. Ruth wasn't alone. Even Reds players, familiar with the incline, hated the deformity, which was caused by an underground stream.

The Sun Deck was a colorful name for the right field bleachers that were

Crosley was in all of its cozy glory and dressed to the hilt for the 1953 All-Star Game (left). Trolley lines marked Crosley's corner at Findlay Street and Western Avenue (right).

backed by the intersection of Western Avenue and Findlay Street. The bleachers intersected at a point with the center field fence, necessitating a white line to the right of which a hand-painted ground rule pronounced, "Batted Ball Hitting Concrete Wall on Fly to Right of White Line—Home Run."

Big Ted Kluszewski tested the line more than once. So did Vada Pinson and righthanded power hitters like Ernie Lombardi, Frank McCormick, Gus Bell, Wally Post and Frank Robinson. But the righthanders were more likely to take aim at the laundry and a small sign, perched above the roof in left-center field, which challenged hitters to "Hit this sign and get a Siebler suit free." Post was the unofficial suit champion with 11 hits.

To be a Reds fan required patience and an ability to accept change. Between its 1912 christening as Redland Field and its 1970 farewell as Crosley, no park underwent more renovations—most of them after Powel Crosley purchased the team in 1934. Its roofed double-decked grandstand was extended from two-thirds of the way down both lines to the left and right field corners, portable seats were installed, removed, re-installed and removed in various areas of the park, home plate was relocated twice, a right field screen went up and down several times and a state-of-the-art scoreboard, with a 7-foot, 10-inch Longines clock perched on top, replaced the old ground-level board in 1957.

Through the constant makeovers, Crosley retained its irregular dimensions.

After 1938, the left field foul pole measured 328 feet, center was a friendly 383 and the right field line was a whopping 366, except for two periods when seats were installed in front of the Sun Deck bleachers, cutting the distance to 342. The so-called "Goat Run" was expected to aid the muscular, sleeveless Kluszewski, but his booming line drives seldom took advantage of the fly ball-friendly seats.

CROSLEY FIELD 1912-1970

Also known as Redland Field (1912-1934)

Its original name was Redland Field, a last-minute decision made by team president Garry Herrmann, who apparently had been leaning toward calling the field League Park. The Redland name recognized the traditional color of Cincinnati baseball teams and the corner of Findlay and Western had been the home of Redland's predecessors, Redland Field I (1884-1901) and Palace of the Fans (1902-11).

In 1934, the name was changed to Crosley Field in honor of new owner Powel Crosley Jr., a Cincinnati businessman who made his money from home appliances and a radio empire.

Today, a number of businesses occupy the Findlay and Western site, about a mile and a half from Great American Ball Park. There is, however, a "New Crosley Field" for those who want to experience the old ballpark. The re-creation, complete with actual artifacts from old Crosley, is located in Blue Ash, a town northeast of downtown Cincinnati.

First game: April 11, 1912. After spotting the Cubs a 5-0 lead, the Reds rallied for six runs in the fourth inning and eventually won, 10-6.

Final game: June 24, 1970. Lee May and Johnny Bench hit back-to-back homers in the eighth as the Reds rallied to beat the Giants, 5-4. A Bobby Bonds groundout closed the doors at Crosley after 4,543 games.

■ Site of four World Series (1919, '39, '40 and '61)
■ Site of two All-Star Games (1938 and 1953)

The great Mill Creek flood of 1937 turned Crosley into a giant swimming pool (far left). Superfan Harry Thobe, dressed in customary white with umbrella and megaphone (left), was a Crosley Field fixture for many years.

Two Crosley trademarks (left): the left field incline and the laundry beyond the left field fence. The overview (above) shows a packed Crosley with temporary seats in front of the outfield walls on opening day in 1937.

Over its 58-year run, Crosley was the home of four pennant-winning teams and two World Series champions—the last in 1940 under Bill McKechnie. It also was the factory where Reds management began piecing together the Big Red Machine that would grind opponents into submission in the 1970s—after the team's move to new Riverfront Stadium.

But Crosley might be better remembered for the zaniness and innovations that created indelible memories. This was the park where the first acts of World Series scandal unfolded, courtesy of the 1919 Chicago White Sox. This is where Larry MacPhail staged the first night game in major league history, Johnny Vander Meer pitched the first of his consecutive no-hitters and The Whip, Ewell Blackwell, barely missed duplicating Vander Meer's feat nine years later. A woman once batted in a major league game here and a 15-year-old lefthander threw his first big-league pitch from Crosley's mound. The magic of Crosley Field was never demonstrated more emphatically than in 1937, when it disappeared —beneath the flood waters of nearby Mill Creek.

When Crosley Field disappeared for good from the major leagues on June 24, 1970, a near-capacity crowd of 28,027 turned out to bid a final, sometimes-tearful farewell. They left with the pleasant memory of consecutive Johnny Bench and Lee May home runs that produced a 5-4 victory over the Giants.

Riverfront
Stadium

Renamed Cinergy Field (1996-2002)

Bench hits final career homer (No. 389) on "Johnny Bench Night" vs. Houston, Sept. 17, 1983

Hank Aaron hits record-tying 714th home run off Jack Billingham, April 4, 1974

Reds score 14 runs on 16 hits in first inning of 18-2 win over Astros, Aug. 3, 1989

Where A's catcher Gene Tenace hit balls in first two at-bats in 1972 World Series

Shortstops Dave Concepcion and Barry Larkin (left) anchored Reds' infield for three decades

Catcher JOHNNY BENCH: N.L. MVP in '70 and '72, was anchor for Cincinnati's Big Red Machine

Reds lefty Tom Browning joins the "perfect club" when he retires all 27 Dodgers in 1-0 win, Sept. 16, 1988

Where Boston catcher Carlton Fisk collided with Ed Armbrister, helping Reds claim controversial victory in Game 3 of 1975 World Series

Inside, it was a mirror image of its cookie-cutter brethren in Philadelphia and Pittsburgh. Outside, it was one of the most endearing venues in the major leagues, protected on one side by the mighty Ohio River and caressed on the other by Cincinnati's inviting downtown skyline. Riverfront Stadium was exactly what its name implied. And its legacy will always be tied to a Big Red Machine that methodically perpetrated baseball mayhem there.

Riverfront was not given to exaggeration or window dressing. What you saw is what you got, a

Sparky Anderson's Big Red Machine produced pennants in '70, '72, '75 and '76

Reds lose 4-3 to Phillies in final game at 'Cinergy Field,' Sept. 22, 2002

Bench's dramatic ninth-inning homer vs. Pirates ties Game 5 of 1972 NLCS . . . Reds secure pennant later in inning when George Foster scores on wild pitch by Bob Moose

Mets' Al Leiter stops Reds on two hits in one-game playoff to decide wild-card playoff berth, Oct. 4, 1999

St. Louis' Mark Whiten ties two long-standing records with four homers, 12 RBIs in second game of doubleheader vs. Reds, Sept. 7, 1993

Rose's 3,000th career hit (May 5, 1978) is merely an appetizer for the big one—record-breaker 4,192 off San Diego's Eric Show on Sept. 11, 1985

1990 World Series champs— unlikely hero Billy Hatcher gets seven straight hits in Games 1 and 2

Second baseman Joe Morgan wins consecutive MVP awards in '75, '76

PETE ROSE: Charlie Hustle was baseball's all-time hits king

Where Tom Seaver pitched only no-hitter of his career, vs. St. Louis, June 16, 1978

Ron Robinson, one out away from perfect game, surrenders single, homer before Reds finally beat Expos 3-2, May 2, 1988

Where Rose bowled over Ray Fosse, giving N.L. a 12-inning win in 1970 All-Star Game

Phillies pitcher Rick Wise makes history when he fires no-hitter and hits two home runs, June 23, 1971

Cincinnati fact of life from its June 1970 grand opening to its 2002 final game. The multi-purpose stadium was a state-of-the-art wonder when it opened, the first to feature an all-artificial turf field with mound and base cutouts, and the only thing to change was public perception—yesterday's marvelous and high-tech is today's sterile and antiseptic.

That certainly was not the case outside, where the circular, concrete structure sat like a flying saucer ready to take off at the first sign of trouble. Riverfront's unimaginative architecture was well camouflaged by serene, almost-quaint surroundings that lulled you into a sense of how baseball is experienced in a picturesque Midwest community.

You could approach the stadium from downtown Cincinnati, over a skywalk that traversed a major expressway. A little shopping or dinner before baseball? The stadium's outside ramps offered a perfect excuse for

Riverfront Stadium stood in the shadow of the Cincinnati skyline (left, right), connected to Kentucky by an old suspension bridge and the mighty Ohio River. Fans were in a lingering mood in 1990 (above) as they waited for the gates to open for a World Series game against the Oakland A's.

lingering with your thoughts—a serenade of horns from old-fashioned riverboats paddling up and down the Ohio, a mesmerizing stream of cars crossing an ancient suspension bridge that connected Kentucky and Ohio. The Cincinnati skyline, brightly lighted at night, cradled Riverfront like a spoiled child.

You could feel the electricity of baseball on the streets when the Reds were playing well. When they' were not, the fans still basked in the aura of Sparky Anderson-style baseball, which literally dripped off the rafter-like overhang that circled the rim of the stadium. A quarter century later, the Big Red Machine was still running roughshod through everybody's mind.

The park was a model of symmetrical (330 down both lines) precision. But who needs quirks, crannies or architectural personality when you've got Johnny Bench, Joe Morgan, Pete Rose, Tony Perez, Dave Concepcion, George Foster, Eric Davis, Barry Larkin and five National League pennants? Before Riverfront was even a year old, it had played host to an All-Star

High-rising Riverfront Stadium formed a scenic backdrop in 1998 for Cardinals slugger Mark McGwire, the newly crowned single-season home run king of baseball.

Game, an NLCS game and two World Series contests. Before it was 7, the Big Red Machine had hammered its way to four pennants and back-to-back championships.

You entered Riverfront on the plaza level—a stadium without bowels—and immediately were greeted by the green, artificial field. Plastic chairs rose around you steeply in color-coordinated schemes and your gaze quickly settled on the expansive fourth-level upper-deck red seats, where only a few sluggers ventured with their mightiest home run swings. High on the stadium rim over center field, was a long, skinny, horizontal scoreboard that stretched into left- and right-center field with myriad forms of information and advertising inducements.

There was nothing really wrong with Riverfront—it was a typical baseball/football facility devoid of the quirky physical characteristics baseball fans now demand from their ballparks. This was a stadium that expected you to focus squarely on the game without the frills and distractions of younger major league parks. It was comfortable, modern, attractive and obsessively clean. It was baseball without a ballpark atmosphere, strange bounces or unusual ground rules.

But that's not to say Riverfront was without distinctions. After the 1966 All-Star Game at St. Louis, Casey Stengel commented that Busch Stadium sure held its heat well. So did Riverfront. On a hot August afternoon, the humidity descended over the field, forced to hang like a blanket over turf that could only reflect, not absorb, its heat.

For a decade and a half, the Riverfront atmosphere included colorful

owner Marge Schott, her dog Schottzie on a leash, parading around the field, chatting with players and surveying her kingdom. Schott, a sixth-generation Cincinnatian, also was visible during games in her "Blue 108" seat—an owner having fun with the fans instead of tucked away in a stuffy corporate box.

In what other city could you park below the stadium? Riverfront was one of few parks with a rimmed lighting system rather than towering standards. Replicas of the team's five retired uniforms hung from the facade above the left field fence, distances were painted metrically on the outfield walls and bullpens were located in foul territory down both lines.

Baseball at Riverfront, which offered some of the lowest ticket prices in baseball, was only occasionally an ear-shattering experience. Cincinnatians are high-standard fans who can't resist the temptation to create a good wave, but otherwise reserve their emotion for just the proper moment. There were a few of those at Riverfront.

This was, after all, where Hank Aaron tied baseball's all-time home run record in 1974 and hometown hero Rose broke the game's all-time hits record 11 years later. Where Cardinals outfielder Mark Whiten rocked the Reds with an incredible four-homer, 12-RBI explosion and the 1990 Reds rocked baseball by pulling off one of the most shocking World Series upsets in history.

Where a well-oiled Big Red Machine once pounded its way to the pinnacle of baseball and, in the process, lifted a city and its cookie-cutter stadium to glory beyond anybody's wildest dreams.

RIVERFRONT STADIUM (1970-2002)

Renamed Cinergy Field (1996-2002)

For most of the 1960s, it was the subject of dreams and discussions, delays and debates. Riverfront Stadium was both an aberration and a state-of-the-art reality when it finally opened its gates in 1970, just in time for the rise of the Big Red Machine and the crush of fans who piled into the 52,953-seat facility to see it in action.

Built on the edge of the Ohio River, "Riverfront" was a logical name although other suggestions included Queen City Stadium, Red/Bengal Stadium and variations of names honoring former President Dwight Eisenhower, former Reds owner Powel Crosley and astronaut Neil Armstrong. Riverfront was the eventual winner.

That changed in 1996, when stadium naming rights were sold and the official name was changed to Cinergy Field.

First game: June 30, 1970. The Braves' Hank Aaron, who would tie Babe Ruth's all-time home run record of 714 at Riverfront in 1974, homered in an 8-2 Braves victory.

Final game: September 22, 2002. The Reds and Jose Rijo lost 4-3 to Philadelphia in the not-so-grand finale at Riverfront.

- Site of five World Series (1970, '72, '75, '76 and '90)
- Site of two All-Star Games (1970 and '88)

League Park

Also known as Dunn Field (1920-1927)

Highlanders' Tom Hughes loses no-hitter with one out in 10th, drops 5-0 decision in 11, Aug. 30, 1910

Johnny Burnett gets nine of Cleveland's record 33 hits in 18-inning 18-17 loss to A's, July 10, 1932

A's slugger Jimmie Foxx hit three homers here in famous 18-17 game

Player-manager Lou Boudreau's office was here from 1942-46

NAPOLEON LAJOIE: Indians were called "Cleveland Naps" from 1903-14 because of popular second baseman Nap Lajoie, a .338 career hitter

Area blanketed by third basemen Bill Bradley, Larry Gardner, Willie Kamm and Ken Keltner from 1901-46

Lajoie gets 3,000th career hit vs. Yankees, Sept. 27, 1914

Senators steal eight bases in first inning of July 19, 1915 game

Tris Speaker gets 3,000th hit off Washington's Tom Zachary, May 17, 1925

It was an oddly-shaped, funny-looking little relic, squeezed tightly into a working-class neighborhood near downtown Cleveland. League Park was a delightful sports playground that tried hard to be cozy and quaint. But it also was a house of insanity, a place where baseball was contorted to fit into the most illogical dimensions ever conceived.

"Wall Ball" is what they called it in Cleveland. And, indeed, most of League Park's mystique emanated from a 40-foot combination concrete-and-wire

From 1932-46, League Park shared the Indians
with massive Cleveland Stadium

Ossie Vitt's Crybabies finish one game
behind Tigers in 1940 pennant race

Ted Williams belted a monster shot here;
Babe Ruth hit a 460-foot shot here

Third baseman Joe
Sewell: 4 strikeouts
in 578 official at-
bats in 1929
Pitcher Jim Bagby:
31-12, 2.89 ERA in
1920

Home of Bill Wambsganss, who
pulled off unassisted triple play
in Game 5 of 1920 World Series,
and pitcher Elmer Smith, who
hit first World Series grand slam
in same contest

Where Yankee great Babe Ruth hit
his 500th career homer, Aug. 11, 1929

Where Addie Joss pitched his
perfect game, outdueling Chicago
ace Ed Walsh, Oct. 2, 1908

Stan Coveleski nails down
only League Park World
Series crown with 3-0
Game 7 win over
Brooklyn, Oct. 12, 1920

17-year-old
rookie Bob
Feller strikes
out 17 A's in
two-hit victory,
Sept. 13, 1936

TRIS SPEAKER:
The Grey Eagle patroled center
field with Hall of Fame grace
from 1916-26

Cozy dugouts put players
shoulder-to-shoulder with
opinionated fans

Fans witnessed the game at League Park, or National League Park, as early as 1891. In 1910, it was rebuilt from a wooden structure to a steel-and-concrete facility.

right field barrier that stood an inviting 290 feet from home plate, a distance mandated by the natural boundary of Lexington Avenue. With the left field line measuring 375 feet and straightaway center a whopping 460 (later 420), the playing field had a peculiar rectangular shape unmatched by any other park.

Babe Ruth, Lou Gehrig and other lefthanded American League sluggers were delighted to see their fly balls turn into 300-foot home runs, but line drives were another matter. The 20-foot concrete right field wall was topped by a 20-foot screen from the corner to the center field scoreboard. The chicken-wire screen was supported by a series of vertical steel beams that created their own special problems.

Line drives hitting the lower wall bounded like a shot past outfielders. Balls hitting the screen could do one of three things: drop straight down; get stuck in the wiring, a ground-rule double; or hit a beam and shoot in any direction, depending on the angle. You never knew what to expect. Balls could deflect all the way to left field—or back to the infield. The fence, much like the Green Monster at Boston's Fenway Park, also turned potential extra-base hits into outs at second—or long singles.

Everything at League Park revolved around the wall. Lefties drooled, righthanders changed their batting stroke, every fielder kept a wary eye on balls hit to right and fans screamed with delight at the strange occurrences they would witness. But the biggest beneficiaries were the kids—packs who, unable to afford a ticket, would position themselves on Lexington Avenue, hoping to pick off a batting-practice ball or home run they could turn in for a free pass.

It was that way from 1910, when the original League Park, which had stood at East 66th Street and Lexington since 1891, was remodeled from a wood-based field into a steel-and-concrete ballpark. Eventually, the field would feature a roofed, double-decked grandstand from the right field foul pole to just short of the left field pole, where a section of single-deck stands wrapped into left and met a narrow section of bleachers fronted by a 10-foot barrier—3 feet of concrete, 7 feet of screen. The big green scoreboard, which was updated by kids hanging numbers on nails, was not flush with the ground, allowing balls to occasionally disappear underneath.

One of League Park's stranger quirks was the positioning of bullpens, which

LEAGUE PARK (1910-1946)

Also known as Dunn Field (1920-1927)

Built at Lexington and East 66th because of that site's proximity to streetcar lines, League Park—its official name was National League Park—was nestled into a neighborhood that had served as home for the National League's Cleveland Spiders as far back as 1891.

In 1910, League Park was rebuilt from a wood-based park into a steel-and-concrete structure. It was known for most of the 1920s as Dunn Field in honor of team owner James Dunn and it shared Indians games from 1932-46 with larger Municipal Stadium.

Standing on the site today, about three miles east of Jacobs Field, is a city playground.

First game: April 21, 1910. Detroit shut out the Indians, 5-0.

Final game: September 21, 1946. The same Tigers defeated the Indians, 5-3.

■ Site of one World Series (1920)
■ Site of no All-Star Games

were crammed into the corners and hidden from view to many spectators by special stands that angled in an arc from the pavilions just behind third base until they almost touched the foul lines. When fair balls rolled into the left field bullpen, outfielders would have to throw over the stands to get the ball to the infield.

Summer afternoons at League Park (Dunn Field from 1920-27) were fun and relaxing—gates open at noon, batting practice, the smell of hot dogs on the grill, smiling players interacting with kids and anticipation of a 3:30 game, after which kids would be allowed to run the bases. Conversely, the pace around the brick-based exterior was furious, kids jockeying for position to chase balls, fighting for knothole spots and battling for wildcat vantage points from the Dunham School fire escape or the roof of the Andrews Storage Company, a dangerous climb.

No matter where you were positioned, you felt like part of the action—mesmerized by the sweet swing of Shoeless Joe Jackson, caught up in the passion of Stan Coveleski and Jim Bagby, looking over Earl Averill's shoulder, shuddering at the crack of a Bob Feller fastball. You had to love Joe Sewell's appreciation for foul balls into the stands and the 1920 World Series-champion Indians. You had to mourn the premature demise of Addie Joss and Ray Chapman. But most of all, you had to admire the incredible ability of Tris Speaker, positioned almost on the edge of the infield, to cover all 460 feet of center field.

League Park played host to Indians baseball for 36 wonderful years, the final 14 as co-host with new, larger Cleveland Municipal Stadium—Sunday, holiday and night games (League never had lights) at Municipal, the rest of the schedule at League Park, which never had a permanent seating capacity over 22,000. Owner Bill Veeck moved the team permanently to Municipal Stadium in 1947.

The overview shows an almost-rectangular field with covered grandstands and a right field fence topped by a screen with steel support posts.

Municipal
Stadium

Also known as Cleveland Stadium
and Cleveland Municipal Stadium

Carlos Baerga homers from both sides of plate in same inning—a baseball first—vs. Yankees, April 8, 1993

Joe DiMaggio's 56-game hitting streak ends, thanks in part to two fine defensive plays by third baseman Ken Keltner, July 17, 1941

Frank Robinson, making debut as Indians player/manager, homers in first at-bat, April 8, 1975

30-year-old Tigers rookie Floyd Giebell shuts out Feller, Indians to clinch A.L. pennant, Sept. 27, 1940

Tigers shortstop Cesar Gutierrez goes 7-for-7 in 12-inning win over Indians, June 21, 1970

Indians hit four consecutive homers off Angels' Paul Foytack, July 31, 1963 (Woodie Held, Pedro Ramos, Tito Francona, Larry Brown)

Beer Night promotion goes awry and Indians forfeit game to Rangers, June 4, 1974

**LOU BOUDREAU
A.L. MVP Lou Boudreau led Indians to 1948 World Series championship**

Y ou have to admire its perseverance, a tired, old concrete-and-steel edifice that stood up to a depression, a burning river, economic turmoil, bad baseball and the ill winds that blow relentlessly off Lake Erie. Cleveland Municipal Stadium was a tough old bird, massive, imposing and scarred from years of neglect and abuse. It also was a proud remnant of a bygone era, when ballparks were measured as much by size and function as by charm and charisma.

Imposing had given way to clunky and awkward by 1993, when the stadium finally closed its gates to baseball after more than six decades. But through most of its existence,

Where Bill Veeck (center, holding hat) literally "buried the pennant" after Indians fell out of 1949 title chase

Pitchers (from left) Bob Lemon, Early Wynn, Mike Garcia and Feller help Indians post 111 wins, capture 1954 A.L. pennant

Boston lefty Matt Young pitches no-hitter, but Indians ruin his day by posting 2-1 victory, April 12, 1992

Where Red Sox slugger Ted Williams hit his 500th career home run off Wynn Hawkins, June 17, 1960

Len Barker pitches a perfect game on a blustery night vs. Blue Jays, May 15, 1981

Senators reliever Dean Stone won '54 All-Star Game, an 11-9 A.L. victory, without retiring a batter when he caught Red Schoendienst trying to steal home

Where Senators shortstop Ron Hansen turned eighth unassisted triple play in major league history, July 30, 1968

Where Negro Leagues legend Satchel Paige took the mound in Game 5 of the 1948 World Series, breaking baseball's postseason color barrier

Montreal catcher Gary Carter homers twice in N.L.'s 1981 All-Star Game win before record crowd of 72,086

Where Herb Score was hit in the eye by Gil McDougald's line drive, May 7, 1957

Luis Tiant strikes out 19 in 10-inning game, July 3, 1968

BOB FELLER
Rapid Robert struck out 348 in 1946, led A.L. in strikeouts seven times and won 20 games six times

Where Vic Power stole home twice in a game vs. Tigers, Aug. 14, 1958

CLEVELAND MUNICIPAL STADIUM (1932-1993)

Also known as Cleveland Stadium and Municipal Stadium

Built in an attempt to attract the 1932 Olympic Games, Cleveland Municipal Stadium was a huge, intimidating concrete structure that seated 74,483 and was more conducive to football than baseball. The hulking, charmless facility was lacking in distinctive features and looked almost desolate when its seats were less than half filled.

Municipal Stadium was a pitcher's park with center field bleachers that measured 470 feet and were never reached by a home run ball. It shared Indians games with tiny League Park from 1932-46 and served as the Indians permanent home from 1947 until its closing in 1993.

The stadium, which was demolished in 1996, was located on the shore of Lake Erie—a site now occupied by Cleveland Browns Stadium, home of the NFL's Browns.

First game: July 31, 1932. In a game that spotlighted six future Hall of Famers— Connie Mack, Lefty Grove, Mickey Cochrane, Jimmie Foxx, Al Simmons and Earl Averill—the Philadelphia A's beat the Indians, 1-0.

Final game: October 3, 1993. The Chicago White Sox defeated the Indians, 4-0.

■ Site of two World Series (1948, '54)
■ Site of four All-Star Games (1935, '54, '63 and '81)

The smile was misguided. The inside concourses were dingy, damp, concrete walkways and corridors that circled and branched endlessly to points unknown. Bathrooms were tiny, concession stands were small and boxes were stacked in corners like the remainders of a past life stored in someone's attic. The first sense of a grand stadium with a historic aura did not come until you reached the field area.

It was hard to get past that first, overwhelming feeling of huge. A double-decked, roofed grandstand filled with small, wooden seats rose up around you like a protective shield, giving you a sense of enclosure. But any claustrophobic fears were quickly relieved by the open center field, through which upper-deck fans on the right field side could get an angled view of the lake.

At this open end were a big scoreboard and some of the most famous bleacher seats in sports—the infamous Dawg Pound section that tormented football opponents of the Cleveland Browns. For baseball, these bleachers were in dead center field, 470 feet from home plate, a target no batted ball ever reached. The seats in the back row of the bleachers were farther away from home plate than any other seats in baseball and the scoreboard, more than 500 feet from fans behind the plate, was hard to see and a very basic blend of information and scores.

Municipal Stadium was big and tough, a monument to old-style, iron-belt baseball.

it had been a perfect match for a tough, no-frills, factory-dominated city in the middle of America's iron belt. It was huge, unpretentious and lacking in the physical quirks and nuances that gave other early-era ballparks personality. It was, in the truest sense, a stadium—a downtown sports arena that survived 62 years of erratic lakefront weather without a lot of love or tender care.

You noticed quickly that Cleveland Stadium had not been pampered like Fenway Park or showered with Wrigley Field-like affection. This was a hulking, horseshoe-shaped fortress with a nondescript sandstone facade and protruding buildings that served as business and ticket offices. On a clear summer afternoon, with the sun glistening off Lake Erie, it looked like a big, beached white whale. The first sign of baseball life was an elevated welcome sign featuring a smiling, toothy Chief Wahoo, bat cocked and ready to smack a long one into the unpaved parking lot.

To really appreciate Cleveland Stadium, you have to recognize it as a child of the Great Depression. Baseball's first municipally-owned park was built as an attempt to attract the 1932 Olympic Games, but that failed and Cleveland was left with an 80,000-seat multi-sports facility that was more conducive to football than baseball. When the Indians played their first game there in 1932, 76,979 fans—more than had ever witnessed a major league game—filed through the gates and everybody marveled at the incredible structure.

"The stadium is perfect," said commissioner Kenesaw Mountain Landis. "It is the only baseball park I know where the spectator can see clearly from any seat. This is perfection."

Landis apparently did not tour the higher altitudes of Cleveland Stadium, where steel girders obstructed the view of many fans. Nor did he anticipate the hollow, empty feeling of a stadium with only 12,000 seats filled. The Indians quickly grasped that problem and spent the next decade and a half jockeying games between Cleveland Stadium and tiny League Park—Sunday, holiday and night games in the larger, more-expensive-to-operate facility.

The original dimensions of the symmetrical field were imposing—470 feet to center, 463 in the power alleys and 322 down both lines. But owner Bill Veeck installed a foul line-to-foul line inner fence in 1947 that cut the center field distance to 410 and the power alleys to 385. The distances were tailored over the years to Indians talent and the area between the fence and the bleachers was used for standing-room, a garden and eventually a family picnic grounds.

An easy first impression was that this building was much more fit for football, a perception perpetuated by Cleveland's long love affair with the Browns. Football games, often played in blizzard-like conditions with a nasty wind whipping off Lake Erie, were always packed. Baseball games, particularly through the lean 1960s, '70s and '80s, were not. The 12,000 or so vocal baseball fans were like lost souls, free to roam from section to section in search of the perfect seat.

It wasn't that way during the 1940s and '50s, when the Indians claimed the stadium's only two pennants and one World Series championship (1948). But economic hard times and weak teams hurt the Indians and lack of upkeep and renovation doomed the stadium, which was sarcastically dubbed "The Mistake by the Lake."

For many years, a smiling Chief Wahoo (right) greeted visitors at Gate A. In later years, a bat-swinging Wahoo was perched on the other side of the stadium.

In retrospect, that's harsh. While the stadium might have been lacking in physically distinctive features, it was easy to get lost in its history—the distinctive Bob Feller windup, the ghosts of Early Wynn, Mike Garcia, Bob Lemon and Feller, who pitched the Indians to an incredible 111 wins in 1954. Names like Doby, Rosen, Colavito, Easter, Averill, Wertz, Trosky, Thornton and, of course, Boudreau assaulted the brain like the rhythmic pounding of superfan John Adams' excited drumbeats. Football memories of Graham, Groza, Lavelli, Brown, Kelly, Sipe and Kosar dangled chillingly from imaginary rafters. Joe DiMaggio, it was said, was still looking in 1993 for that hit to extend his record streak to 57 games.

There's no denying Cleveland Stadium lived most of its life as a haggard, worn-down super-structure from the 1930s—a charmless albatross to disbelieving visitors. But it's also hard to deny Cleveland fans their special moments. There is, after all, no place like home.

A standing-room crowd of 78,431 jammed Cleveland Stadium (left) in May 1948 and eager fans lined up later that year (below) for World Series tickets. Five years later, a new scoreboard (right) divided the center field bleachers and the Cleveland Symphony Orchestra entertained in relative obscurity.

Tiger Stadium

Also known as Navin Field (1912-1937); Briggs Stadium (1938-1960)

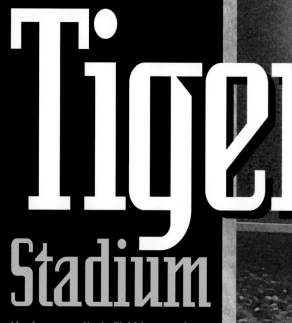

Senators' Frank Howard hits ball over left field roof—his 10th home run in six-game span, May 18, 1968

Cecil Fielder becomes first Tiger to hit ball over left field roof, Aug. 25, 1990 . . . second to hit 50 homers in season, 51 in 1990

Lefty closer Willie Hernandez: MVP, Cy Young double in 1984

Where irate fans showered Cardinal Joe Medwick with garbage in Game 7 of 1934 World Series

AL KALINE, a 10-time Gold Glove-winning right fielder, collected 11 hits while leading Tigers to 1968 World Series title

Pitcher Tommy Bridges pulls off Houdini-like escape after surrendering leadoff ninth-inning triple to Chicago's Stan Hack in Game 6 of 1935 World Series . . . Mickey Cochrane scores winning run in bottom of inning

Tigers (Frank Tanana) outduel Blue Jays (Jimmy Key) 1-0 to complete season-ending sweep and win East Division title, Oct. 4, 1987

Home of Charley Gehringer (left) and Hank Greenberg . . . Big Hank made 1938 run at baseball history with 58 homers

Y ou felt that tingle, a sense of anticipation and incredible history, well before you reached The Corner, the intersection of time, space and baseball at Michigan and Trumbull. It was a good feeling, a response to the sweet Siren's song emanating from inside the great white castle that stood majestically on Detroit's own little corner of the world. This was Tiger Stadium, the house of Cobb and Crawford, Gehringer and Greenberg, Kaline and Kell, Trammell and Whitaker—and all the other friendly ghosts of baseball past.

At first glance, Tiger Stadium was

Denny McLain becomes first 30-game winner since 1934 when Tigers rally to beat A's in ninth, Sept. 14, 1968

Kirk Gibson hits two Game 5 homers, Tigers close out Padres in 1984 World Series.

Where Babe Ruth crushed "626-foot" homer in 1926, a ball that rolled all the way to Brookyn Street before upper-deck grandstand was added

Tigers were 3,764-3,090-19 over 88 memorable seasons here with 6 A.L. pennants, 4 World Series titles

Boston's Ted Williams wins 1941 All-Star Game with three-run, ninth-inning home run

Reggie Jackson's titanic blast spices up 1971 All-Star Game

Where Yankee Lou Gehrig ended his iron man streak at 2,130 games, May 2, 1939

Where Johnny Neun turned unassisted triple play vs. Indians, May 31, 1927

Where Mark "The Bird" Fidrych talked to ball and groomed mound in a captivating 1976 season

Home of longest-running keystone combination in baseball history—shortstop Alan Trammell, second baseman Lou Whitaker, 1977-95

TY COBB: The Georgia Peach compiled an all-time best .367 average, won record 12 batting titles and amassed 4,191 hits

Roger Clemens matches his single-game record in 20-strikeout effort vs. Tigers, Sept. 18, 1996

The 'No Visitors' sign was a laughing matter for many years, but Tiger Stadium's cramped clubhouse facilities were not.

a shock to the system, an explosion of white in an otherwise dark and dingy working-class neighborhood. It was a jewel, guarded by vulture-like light standards that seemed ready to pounce from their rooftop perch and polished by the distinctive sounds of baseball, especially the buzz of milling fans and the pleas of enthusiastic vendors. Its secrets were well hidden, with only specks of peeling paint and other hard-to-spot blemishes revealing a hint of the truth.

There were no secrets inside this aging fortress. From the hard streets of Detroit you stepped into an old-fashioned, throwback ballpark, not all that different from how it looked—and smelled—a half century earlier. Bodies packed into extremely narrow concourses of yellow tile; layers of peeling paint, exposed wires and pipes; old telephone booths, tiny concession stands; a century's worth of hot dog, sausage, beer and peanut fumes literally dripping from the walls and melting your memory. A postcard from the past.

"Walking from the old train station, I thought the park looked like an impressive battleship," said Hall of

Fame right fielder Al Kaline, recalling his first sighting of Tiger Stadium as an 18-year-old rookie. "But then inside, walking through the aisles and seeing the green, green grass and the thousands of seats around, and more than anything feeling the peacefulness, it seemed almost magical. On that day I was awestruck. Today, 46 years later, I find myself still humbled and over-whelmed."

Such was the almost-mystical power of Tiger Stadium, which opened in 1912 in Detroit's historic haymarket district amid news the Titanic had sunk. The steel-and-concrete facility, known then as Navin Field in honor of owner Frank Navin, continued the baseball tradition that had existed at Michigan and Trumbull since 1896 (Bennett Park) and began an 88-year run of its own that would "humble and overwhelm" players and fans through

TIGER STADIUM (1912-1999)

Also known as Navin Field (1912-1937), Briggs Stadium (1938-1960)

Tracing the history of baseball in Detroit has always been easy—just head for the corner of Michigan and Trumbull.

Built in Detroit's historic haymarket district, the playing field was called Bennett Park from 1896 to 1911, marking the city's 1901 debut in the new American League. A 1912 expansion and reconfiguration of the playing field—home plate was moved from right field—also brought a new name, Navin Field, beginning an 88-year stretch in which baseball would be played in the quirky confines of a ballpark later called Briggs Stadium (1938-60) and Tiger Stadium (1961-99).

While no longer home of the Tigers, the still-standing stadium attracts visitors to Michigan and Trumbull, about a mile west of Detroit's new stadium, Comerica Park.

First game: April 20, 1912. Ty Cobb stole home in a 6-5, 11-inning win over Cleveland.

Final game: September 27, 1999. In an emotional farewell, an 8-2 win over the Royals was highlighted by a mammoth eighth-inning grand slam by Rob Fick.

■ Site of six World Series (1934, '35, '40, '45, '68 and '84)
■ Site of three All-Star Games (1941, '51 and '71)

Saturday night fireworks displays were a regular feature of Tiger Stadium's final major league baseball season.

Tiger Stadium, known as Briggs Stadium from 1938-60, was within hailing distance of the Detroit skyline (right).

Bennett Park (above), also located at Michigan and Trumbull, was Tiger Stadium's predecessor.

Baseball was always front and center at Tiger Stadium, but bleacher fans could always find time for a cotton candy break (below).

its emotional final game in 1999.

The real beauty of Tiger Stadium might have been its resistance to change. After a 1938 renovation in which new owner Walter Briggs installed an upper grandstand that completely enclosed the park and a grandstand roof that enclosed everything except straightaway center field, the park remained structurally unaltered for more than six decades. It was during a 1930s renovation that the right field fence was moved in 42 feet and the upper deck was widened 10 feet at both its top and bottom, creating the stadium's signature feature and the most famous overhang in baseball history.

Everything about the inside of Tiger Stadium was quirky, starting with the sense of intimacy and coziness that literally slapped you in the face. Part of it was the enclosed roof overhead that gave the field a bandbox feel; part of it were seats so close to the field that you yearned to reach out and touch someone. When seated behind the plate, every popup, every ball hit toward right looked like a challenge for the inviting upper-deck porch that could suck harmless fly balls into home run heaven.

The right field line was only 325 feet away, 15 feet shorter than a left field line that also looked closer than it really was. Pitchers who could get hitters to drive balls toward the center field bleachers enjoyed a 440-foot margin of error. The center field fence was fronted by a 125-foot flagpole, the tallest fair-territory obstacle in any stadium, and the open bleachers were topped by a huge scoreboard for many years, video and replay boards in their waning seasons.

The best seats in baseball could be found at Tiger Stadium. So could the worst seats, thanks to obstructed views created by support pillars. But you always had

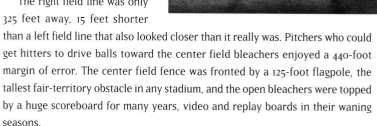

The park's signature feature was an overhang that suspended fans over the right fielder.

a sense of involvement, whether suspended over the right fielder in the front row of the overhang, seated within conversation distance of the players in the dugout or catching a few sun rays in the center field bleachers. Tiger Stadium's seats were cramped and uncomfortable and the narrow aisles were not conducive to between-innings traffic, but it was hard not to like the view they afforded.

That wasn't true for the players, who were confined to the smallest dugouts and bullpens in the major leagues. Dugout ceilings were low and seats were angled awkwardly, forcing players to jump up quickly when balls hit to left disappeared from view. Bam! Instant headache! Relief pitchers were even more limited visually, relegated to life in sunken, caged bullpens (the Submarines) in foul territory down both lines.

But Tiger Stadium was as much about tradition as it was sights and sounds. There, high on the roof in right-center field, was the light standard transformer that Reggie Jackson hit with his prolific 1971 All-Star Game blast. There, perched high on the facade just below the right field roof, were the four Tigers retired numbers (Kaline, Greenberg, Gehringer, Hal Newhouser), four World Series championship banners (1935, '45, '68, '84) and the No. 42 logo honoring Jackie Robinson. There, on the same facade in foul territory, were the names of 12 Tigers Hall of Famers.

Tiger Stadium was charm and character, stark white uniforms with the olde English "D" on the breast, Ernie Harwell at the mike, Mickey Cochrane diving into the dugout after a foul pop, the best dirt in baseball, Kaline playing a corner carom, Willie Horton glaring at the pitcher, foul balls out of the stadium, opening day snowstorms, home runs over the roof and dark green seats that, unfortunately, were changed to orange and blue during a sprucing-up craze. Twenty-nine home runs cleared the right field roof, but only four cleared the roof in left—Harmon Killebrew in 1962, Frank Howard in 1968, Cecil Fielder in 1990 and Mark McGwire in 1997.

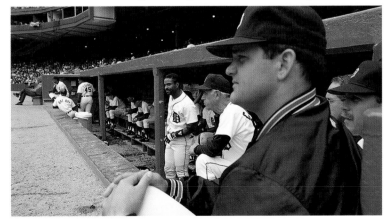

Tiger Stadium was not perfect, as fans and players would attest. Support beams obstructed views and low dugout ceilings (below) resulted in many headaches.

Right up to the end, fans of varying shapes and sizes (right) enjoyed the wonders of Tiger Stadium. So did longtime radio voice Ernie Harwell (above left).

Old timers might remember leather-lunged Patsy O'Toole and his memorable chant of "Boy, oh boy, oh boy!" More recent fans might recall Herbie (the Hoofer) Redmond, the boogieing groundskeeper, or Mark (the Bird) Fidrych, the groundskeeping pitcher. For years, players and team officials chuckled over a sign on the visiting clubhouse door that proclaimed, "Visitors Club House"—"Positively No Visitors Allowed"—"By Order of Joe Cronin, Pres."

Over the decades, Tiger Stadium survived the fiery rampages of Ty Cobb, two World Wars, a depression, some bad baseball, a fire, three name changes (Navin Field to Briggs Stadium in 1938 to Tiger Stadium in 1961), 37 years as home of the NFL's Lions, two World Series losses, 17 seasons with Sparky Anderson and years of premature talk about the Tigers moving to a new facility. That finally came to pass as the millennium came to a close and the curtain dropped on one of baseball's two oldest stadiums—a distinction Tiger Stadium shared with Fenway Park.

Harwell best captured the sense of loss, the feeling of regret, with this reflection that appeared in Detroit's 1999 media guide:

"For almost 40 years, I've spent as much time at the corner of Michigan and Trumbull as I have at home. I've been elated, dejected, thrilled and disappointed. I've sweltered through the summer heat and I've frozen in the spring and fall. Yet, in sickness or in health, it has been my home, my refuge.

"Tiger Stadium was a dear friend. I mourn its passing."

The Astrodome

Judge Roy Hofheinz created "Eighth Wonder of the World", complete with $2 million exploding scoreboard, air-conditioning and baseball's first artificial turf

Phillies' Mike Schmidt hits ball off speaker, turning sure homer into one of longest singles ever hit, June 10, 1974

Mets lefty Jesse Orosco strikes out Kevin Bass to end 16-inning NLCS Game 6 classic, Oct. 15, 1986

M illions of visitors marveled at her grandeur and millions more were mesmerized by tales of her majesty and mystique. During her prime, Houston's Astrodome was the grandest lady in all of sports, the queen of a universe beyond anyone's imagination. During her twilight years, she served as a stately reminder of what can be achieved when vision and dreams are stretched beyond the boundaries.

You never lost that sense of elegance and vision over the Astrodome's 35-year reign as home of the Houston Astros. Whether

First indoor and AstroTurf All-Star Game: Willie Mays scores only run for N.L. win in 1968 classic

Where Nolan Ryan recorded fifth career no-hitter, Sept. 26, 1981 . . . 4,000th career strikeout, July 11, 1985

JEFF BAGWELL: The brawn behind Astros' Killer B's (Biggio, Derek Bell)

Toy Cannon Jimmy Wynn hit 223 homers here . . . Second baseman Joe Morgan began Hall of Fame career here

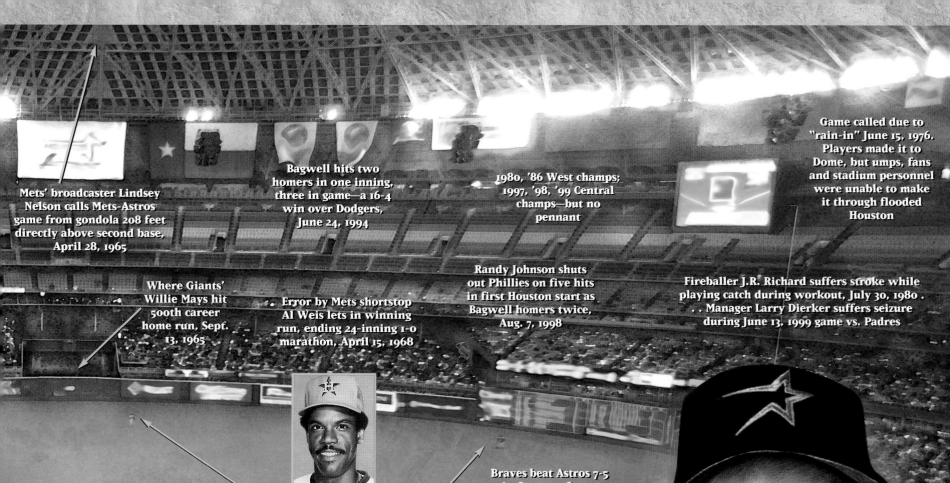

Mets' broadcaster Lindsey Nelson calls Mets-Astros game from gondola 208 feet directly above second base, April 28, 1965

Bagwell hits two homers in one inning, three in game—a 16-4 win over Dodgers, June 24, 1994

1980, '86 West champs; 1997, '98, '99 Central champs—but no pennant

Game called due to "rain-in" June 15, 1976. Players made it to Dome, but umps, fans and stadium personnel were unable to make it through flooded Houston

Where Giants' Willie Mays hit 500th career home run, Sept. 13, 1965

Error by Mets shortstop Al Weis lets in winning run, ending 24-inning 1-0 marathon, April 15, 1968

Randy Johnson shuts out Phillies on five hits in first Houston start as Bagwell homers twice, Aug. 7, 1998

Fireballer J.R. Richard suffers stroke while playing catch during workout, July 30, 1980 . . Manager Larry Dierker suffers seizure during June 13, 1999 game vs. Padres

Cesar Cedeno (above) performed defensive magic here for 12 seasons. . . Jose Cruz did the same for 13

Braves beat Astros 7-5 in Game 4 of 1999 Division Series—final game at Astrodome

Houston native Roger Clemens claims MVP honors in 3-2 A.L. All-Star win, July 15, 1986

Where Phillies' Pete Rose bowled over catcher Bruce Bochy and scored winning run in 10th inning of Game 4 in 1980 NLCS

Mike Scott pitches no-hitter vs. Giants as Astros clinch West Division title in spectacular fashion, Sept. 25, 1986

Second baseman
CRAIG BIGGIO
jump starts the offense

stepping into this futuristic wonderland in 1965 or paying your last respects in 1999, you always came away with a feeling of immensity and history—the sense that this huge, overwhelming, multi-purpose structure was the first of its kind and that the innovations that sprang from it would continue to have an impact on the sports world long after playing host to its final event.

The Astrodome was never about charm, charisma or beauty, characteristics long associated with America's ballparks. It was about that Texas-like appetite for big, powerful and extravagant. Conceived, pushed and coddled to completion by Astros owner Judge Roy Hofheinz in 1965 as an antidote to the oppressive Texas heat, the structure became the most incredible sports facility ever constructed—the so-called Eighth Wonder of the World.

Indeed, the Astrodome will forever be credited as the inspiration for the new craze of sports arenas that gripped the country in the 1970s and '80s. It provided undeniable proof that baseball could be played indoors, it introduced AstroTurf,

a synthetic playing surface that changed the way the game was played, it showed the viability of multi-purpose facilities in today's economic world and it gave credence to the idea that comfort, luxury and other extravagances could be part of the ballpark experience.

Extravagance was the name of the game when the Astrodome was unveiled in 1965 as the world's first covered stadium. It seemed to glow, like a crown jewel, set all by itself in the open fields of south Houston, surrounded only by an expansive parking lot—a 9 1/2-acre fantasy island. The structure was immense, a feeling that really struck home when you stepped inside.

The dome literally exploded overhead, like a cascading fireworks display. The dome's panels were held in place by steel-framed supports that worked their way skyward toward the 208-foot apex—a dynamic, intricately-patterned puzzle for the eye. It was an architectural marvel that never escaped attention, no matter how many times you attended games there.

Animated video characters (top), extravagant suites (center) and vacuuming astronauts were part of the experience when the Astrodome (right) was unveiled in 1965.

In the late 1960s, visitors from all over the world flocked to Houston to get a first-hand look at baseball's Eighth Wonder of the World.

Neither could you escape the eye-blinking vividness of the multi-colored seats, spread over six decks, and a 474-foot scoreboard that wrapped around much of the perimeter above the outfield. The board displayed information as well as animated cartoons, the most amazing of which celebrated an Astros home run with snorting bulls and a six-gun battle between two cowboys over the length of the board. The scoreboard remained an Astrodome landmark until it

The incredible ceiling, speakers dangling from above, waves of seats circling the AstroTurf field: This upper-deck view shows the Astrodome in all of its glory.

was dismantled after the 1988 season and replaced by more state-of-the-art video boards.

"All the comforts of home," as advertised, was not an Astrodome illusion. Cushioned seats looked down on a carpeted field that was designed for baseball. The facility was air-conditioned, escalators transported fans, skylights and floodlights simulated the brightness of a clear, sunny afternoon and there was enough plumbing in place for 40,000 fans to wash their hands simultaneously. The only suffering here was during an Astros' loss.

Hofheinz's vision of a "spectator's paradise", free from the heat, cold, wind, rain and mosquitoes that affect games and comfort levels at other major league parks, was a critical success—an architectural breakthrough that soon would be copied by other cities, but never with the classy vision that went into the Astrodome. It also was Hofheinz's vision to use real grass, but the transparent ceiling panels created such a horrible glare during afternoon games that the panels had to be covered by a translucent acrylic coating. With the sun blocked out, the grass died, thus creating a necessity for AstroTurf.

Over the years, the Astrodome was a good place to watch baseball, even with a few quirky ground rules dictated by the oddities of indoor baseball. Incredulous fans during a 1974 game watched Philadelphia third baseman Mike Schmidt hit what appeared to be a prodigious home run, only to see the ball carom off a speaker and drop into short left-center field for a single. There was even a rule that declared pigeons in play, just in case one might be struck by a batted ball.

The Astros, a 3-year-old expansion team when the Astrodome was built, shared the facility with the National Football League's Oilers for 29 seasons, but no team was more closely associated with a stadium. Early Houston clubs, playing in one of baseball's most difficult home run parks, were turf teams that relied

The Astrodome was less than three weeks old when Lindsey Nelson and producer Joel Nixon broadcast a game for the Mets from the gondola (above) suspended from the apex of the dome over second base.

on speed, defense and pitching. It wasn't until 1980 that a team led by Jose Cruz, Cesar Cedeno, Phil Niekro and J.R. Richard won the Astros' first division title and sustained success did not arrive until the Jeff Bagwell, Craig Biggio-led teams of the late 1990s.

Astrodome patrons have never witnessed a World Series, but the facility has drawn other major events like a magnet. Billy Graham crusaded there and Judy Garland, the Supremes, Elvis Presley and the Rolling Stones made people dance. This is where Muhammad Ali introduced his Ali Shuffle, Billie Jean King overwhelmed Bobby Riggs and Elvin Hayes outdueled UCLA and Lew Alcindor. Movie scenes have been filmed at the Astrodome, as have scenes from a Final Four and a Republican National Convention.

It seemed only fitting that the Astros' final game of the millennium and the final baseball game at the Astrodome would come in postseason play. The Braves' 7-5 Division Series win on October 9, 1999, dropped the curtain on the most heralded, most talked about and most innovative sports arena ever to grace the earth.

THE ASTRODOME (1965-1999)

It officially was named the Harris County Domed Stadium, but to fans who attended sports events there, it will forever be the Astrodome—the inspiration for a new craze of multi-purpose arenas that mixed such novel concepts as domes and artificial turf with luxury and comfort.

The Astrodome, a creation of Judge Roy Hofheinz, opened in 1965, after his expansion Astros had spent three seasons playing in tiny Colt Stadium as the Colt .45s. It was a vision of the future with its incredible dome, air-conditioned interior, synthetic playing field and creature comforts never before associated with sports viewing. It also was a big ballpark that forced the Astros to build around pitching and speed.

The Astrodome remains standing today, a landmark on the city's outskirts and site for various events. Standing adjacent to the Astrodome is Reliant Stadium, home of the NFL's Texans.

First game: April 12, 1965. The Astrodome was officially christened with a 2-0 Phillies victory, three days after the Astros and Yankees had introduced the new stadium with an exhibition game attended by President Lyndon B. Johnson. Mickey Mantle hit the Astrodome's first home run.

Final game: October 9, 1999. The Astros' bid to bring a World Series to the Astrodome was stymied as the Braves beat Houston, 7-5, in a Division Series game.

■ Site of no World Series
■ Site of two All-Star Games (1968 and '86)

County Stadium

Brewers score seven runs in ninth, one in 10th on Jose Hernandez homer in 10-9 win over Astros, May 22, 2000

Two-time homer champ Gorman Thomas (right) patroled center field for Brewers from 1973-83 . . . second baseman Jim Gantner anchored infield from 1976-92

Stan Musial homers in 12th inning to win 1955 All-Star Game

Brewers have unprecedented distinction of competing here as member of both A.L. and N.L.

Giants' slugger Willie Mays ties record with four homers vs. Braves, April 30, 1961

Cleveland rookie John Farrell stops Paul Molitor's hitting streak at 39 games, Aug. 26, 1987

Where Phillies beat Braves to end modern-record losing streak of 23 games, Aug. 20, 1961

Final game at County Stadium: Reds 8, Brewers 1, Sept. 28, 2000

Lefty WARREN SPAHN, 1957 Braves Cy Young winner recorded nine 20-win seasons and won 300th game here, Aug. 11, 1961

Rollie Fingers (right), Brewers' 1981 MVP and Cy Young winner; Pete Vuckovich, '82 Cy Young

Baseball, Milwaukee-style, begins in the parking lot, where lazy summer nights and afternoons have all the feel of aromatic, nobody's-a-stranger family reunions. It happens like clockwork before every game. Baseball's most accomplished tailgaters arrive early, set up their grills and tap kegs, quickly transforming a gray, working-class area into a friendly, vibrant playground.

It's all about fun, a social obsession Milwaukee fans can't seem to resist. The smell of their bratwurst and burgers embrace you, the sounds of their laughter and happy voices give you a sense of what to expect the rest of the night, win or lose. The casual visitor can be overwhelmed by the

Pirates' Harvey Haddix pitches
12 perfect innings, only to lose
1-0 in 13th, May 26, 1959

Where Hank Aaron started his career, 1954-65 with
Braves . . . and ended his career, 1975-76 with Brewers

St. Louis' Mark McGwire hits homers 64 and 65,
Sept. 18, 20, 1998 . . . No. 66 is disallowed by
umpire's controversial ruling

Cardinals rookie center fielder Willie McGee kills
Brewers in Game 3 of 1982 World Series with two
homers, four RBIs and two sensational catches

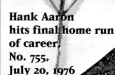

Hank Aaron
hits final home run
of career,
No. 755,
July 20, 1976

Hank Aaron's 11th-inning
homer wins pennant for
Braves, Sept. 23, 1957

Where Eddie Mathews hit
his 10th-inning homer to
beat Yankees in Game 4 of
1957 World Series

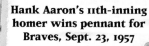

Chicago's Sammy Sosa hits
homers 64 and 65 . . . Cubs left
fielder Brant Brown drops bases-
loaded fly ball in ninth, giving
Brewers three runs and 8-7 win,
Sept. 23, 1998

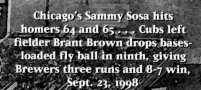

Robin Yount singles for career
hit No. 3,000, Sept. 9, 1992

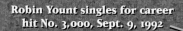

Where Chicago White Sox played
20 "home games" in 1968, '69

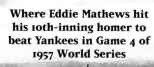

ROBIN YOUNT:
Two-time MVP and leader of
Harvey's Wallbangers, the 1982 A.L.
pennant-winning team

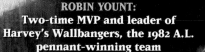

Cecil Cooper (left) and Don Money (right)
hit grand slams in same inning, April 12, 1980

Where Nolan Ryan beat Brewers for
milestone 300th win, July 31, 1990

COUNTY STADIUM (1953-2000)

Milwaukee Braves	Milwaukee Brewers
(1953-1965)	(1970-2000)

Built as a facility for the Brewers, the Boston Braves' top farm team at the time, County Stadium was completed in March of 1953. Three days after opening the park to the public, the Braves announced the team would relocate to Milwaukee and a month later the stadium played host to its first major league game.

Hailed as the first major league ballpark built with lights and entirely with public funds, County Stadium was home to two National League teams— the Braves through '65; the Brewers from 1998-2000—and one American League club— the Brewers from 1970-97. The Chicago White Sox played 20 "home games" there in 1968 and '69.

First game: April 14, 1953. Billy Bruton hit a 10th-inning home run to give the Braves a 3-2 victory over the Cardinals.

Final game: September 28, 2000. On a festive day that reunited former baseball and football greats who once called County Stadium home, the Brewers dropped an 8-1 decision to the Cincinnati Reds.

■ Site of three World Series (1957, '58 and '82)
■ Site of two All-Star Games (1955 and 1975)

contagious enthusiasm and a party atmosphere usually associated only with football.

Big, gray and commanding, County Stadium served as a backdrop for these pregame festivities for 48 years. You knew this would be a special experience the moment you drove into the parking lot and heard an attendant say, "Welcome to County Stadium"—a greeting he really seemed to mean. You quickly got caught up in the tailgating, which was so ingrained in the ballpark experience that the Brewers installed restroom facilities outside the gates.

Soon everything reversed. The enthusiasm, like the mouth-watering smell of ballpark delicacies on the grill, wafted into the park and became the backdrop for baseball, which has been played in much this same context since 1953—when the Braves moved to Milwaukee from Boston. The city's love affair with major league baseball still exists almost a half century later, although the Braves have been replaced by the Brewers, winning baseball has been replaced by mediocrity and a grand old stadium has been replaced by a modern, high-tech facility that was built a line drive away in the same parking lot.

There never was anything high-tech about County Stadium, and that was one of its endearing qualities. Baseball here was much like the people it entertained— down to earth, no-frills and friendly with an upper-Midwest toughness. This was

County Stadium was host to the 1957 and '58 World Series, prompting long lines at ticket booths (right) and a fan-friendly atmosphere (above). Eddie Mathews (41, below) and Hank Aaron walk the long tunnel to the Braves' clubhouse.

bleacher baseball, reflecting a quintessential blue-collar town filled with factories, breweries and a yearning to have fun.

It was no coincidence that many of the closest seats were in the outfield bleacher sections—one that stretched from straightaway left field to the center field backdrop; another between the backdrop and the massive right-center field scoreboard; and another from the scoreboard to straightaway right field. The bleacher seats were benches without backs, the concourses were dingy and cramped and the scoreboard had a video screen that showed replays in black and white—no complaints.

The single-deck bleachers gave the outfield an open, airy, baseball-only feel,

belying County Stadium's four decades as host for two or three Green Bay Packers games per year. Double-decked, roofed grandstands wrapped from foul pole to foul pole, with lower-deck field boxes sitting right on top of a beautiful, symmetrical grass field and higher-seat sightlines obstructed by support pillars.

County Stadium underwent several expansions over the years, raising its original capacity of 36,011 to its final total of 53,192, and the relationship between players and fans changed. But otherwise, it basically was the same functional park the Braves called home in 1953. Players for the Braves, who stayed there 13 mostly wonderful years, can remember fans who turned out in record numbers, gave them

With new Miller Park looming over the right-center field fence, batting practice before 1999 games at County Stadium had a nostalgic feel (left). Bernie Brewer's chalet and beer mug (above) were stadium fixtures for many years.

success. Fans worshiped Warren Spahn and Hank Aaron, who began and ended his pursuit of Babe Ruth here, and they identified with Johnny Logan and Eddie Mathews, tough-edged players in the Milwaukee mold. Beer-drinking Gorman Thomas was vintage Milwaukee, as was disheveled 1982 Cy Young winner Pete Vuckovich. Robin Yount and Paul Molitor were models of the Midwest work ethic.

Most fans, however, will tell you it was the little things that made the difference at County Stadium. And the Brewers leaned hard on their relationship with the community.

Like when Bernie Brewer, positioned over the center field backdrop, slid from his chalet into a giant mug of beer when the Brewers hit a home run. Or when County Stadium turned into a hypnotic, hand-clapping frenzy during "The Beer Barrel Polka," which was played at the seventh-inning stretch. Nothing brought down the house faster than a good race around the warning track by four daring souls dressed like sausages. And where else could you enjoy the self-deprecating humor of broadcaster Bob Uecker or see relief pitchers delivered to the mound in the side car of a locally-produced Harley Davidson?

Only in Milwaukee, where everybody knows how to have fun—and the Brewers seem to care that they do. The Brewers spoke to their fans for 23 seasons through the gentle voice of public address announcer Bob Betts, whose nightly reminder, "Please drive home safely," will forever echo through County Stadium in Milwaukee's baseball memory.

gifts, brought food and birthday cakes to them at the park and showered them with an affection unlike anything found in most other major league communities.

The Braves rewarded them with two National League pennants, a 1957 World Series championship—and their defection to the greener pastures of Atlanta after the 1965 season. The relationship with the American League Brewers, who relocated to Milwaukee from Seattle in 1970 and from the A.L. to the N.L. in 1998, was not quite so personal, although the Harvey's Wallbangers team of 1982 brought pennant fever to Milwaukee with a close-but-no-cigar World Series run.

But Milwaukee has always been more about players and having a good time than

Metropolitan Stadium

Where seat was painted orange in honor of longest homer in stadium history —Killebrew's 520-footer on June 3, 1967

Orioles sweep Twins in first two ALCS, 1969, '70

Where Eddie Stanky managed Texas Rangers for one game before resigning, June 22, 1977

Where Bob Allison (right) made spectacular tumbling catch to help Jim Kaat (left) win Game 2 of 1965 World Series

Killebrew's 1965 All-Star Game home run landed, appropriately, in "Killer Country"

Killebrew hits 500th career home run vs. Orioles, Aug. 10, 1971

It was a visual shock, a multi-decked baseball arena that rose unexpectedly out of an isolated Bloomington cornfield. You couldn't help but smile when you spotted Metropolitan Stadium, which was anything but "metropolitan" when it opened its gates to major league baseball in 1961. Located on a barren 164-acre tract about 15 miles south of Minneapolis, the Met lured you in with its curious patchwork charm and won you over with its folksy, down-home graciousness.

More than anything, the Met was friendly, a sociable,

HARMON KILLEBREW, alias The Killer, holds team career marks for home runs (559), total bases (4,026) and RBIs (1,540)

Bob Allison and Killebrew become first teammates to hit grand slams in same inning, July 18, 1962

MVP shortstop Zoilo Versalles leads Twins to 1965 pennant

278

Where Ken Landreaux compiled 31-game hitting streak in 1980

Tim Laudner homers in first two major league games, Aug. 28, 29, 1981

Twins pound Athletics with five homers in one inning: Rich Rollins, Zoilo Versalles, Tony Oliva, Don Mincher and Killebrew, June 9, 1966

Mudcat Grant's three-run homer, strong pitching win Game 6 of '65 Series

Where .089-hitting pitcher Mike Cuellar deposited wind-blown grand slam in Game 1 of 1970 ALCS

Where Carew tied record by stealing home for seventh time in season, July 16, 1969

Kansas City's Bert Campaneris becomes second player in baseball history to homer twice in first major league game, July 23, 1964

Where Camilo Pascual (above) and Bert Blyleven threw nasty curves at hitters for the better part of 1960s and '70s

Orioles' Jim Gentile hits grand slams in consecutive innings vs. Twins, May 9, 1961

Cesar Tovar plays all nine positions in one game, Sept. 22, 1968

Tony Oliva bats .323, becomes first rookie to win batting championship, 1964

ROD CAREW captured seven A.L. batting titles in 10 years, challenged magic .400 with .388 mark in 1977

A triple-deck grandstand gave way to single-deck bleachers in left field (above). The Met was dressed to kill (left) for the 1965 All-Star Game.

unpretentious ballpark not unlike the personality of Twins teams that called it home for 21 special seasons. It was a hitter's paradise, a home run haven without an attitude. This was the place to go for summer-long fireworks and instant gratification, the perfect spot for baseball with an explosive edge.

At first glance, you had to wonder exactly what the Met's architects had in mind. The park looked like a giant Erector set with a crazy combination of single, double and triple decks that appeared to be squeezed together in a design-as-you-go floor plan. The configuration, while odd, seemed to complement a strange blend of colored brick panels and corrugated metal that gave the exterior a look falling somewhere between charming and tacky.

The stands that wrapped around home plate and the infield were triple-decked and those that continued down the right field line to the foul pole were double-decked, as were the expansive (many claimed ugly) fair-territory stands that stretched from the foul pole to center field. Nestled between the triple-decked grandstand and the left field pole were unusual foul-territory bleachers, single-decked but sectioned with blue chair seats in the lower area and wooden planks in the upper. Fans could enjoy a smaller fair-territory bleacher area in right.

None of the stands was covered, giving the park an open-air feel unlike any other in baseball. On beautiful summer afternoons and evenings, that was a blessing. But when it rained or a gusting wind chilled the Minnesota night air, you might feel differently. Another ballpark oddity was the up-and-down ramps outside the stadium, connected to the back of the grandstands like giant leeches.

This was a between-eras ballpark without the quirky charms of an Ebbets

Field or the natural beauty of a Kauffman Stadium. It was built in 1955 with the hopes of luring a major league team to Minneapolis and it was designed with expansion in mind, an unusual concept at that time. The triple-decked grandstand was in place when the American Association's Minneapolis Millers began play there in 1956, but the second decks were added for the 1961 baseball and football seasons when Calvin Griffith relocated his Washington Senators to Minneapolis and the city was awarded an NFL expansion franchise—the Vikings—raising capacity to 45,919.

No baseball park has been more closely tied to the physical makeup of its teams. And few players have more single-handedly influenced the personality of a stadium than a gentle giant with the unlikely nickname of "Killer." Harmon Killebrew, who packed 210 pounds of muscle into his stocky 6-foot frame, quickly discovered the Met's friendly disposition toward home runs and spent the next 14 years carving his name into baseball's all-time power charts.

It wasn't that Metropolitan Stadium offered short home run distances; balls just shot out of the park, often aided by friendly breezes. The park was a symmetrical 330-412-330 when it opened, an asymmetrical 343-402-330 when it closed after the 1981 season. Distance didn't matter to Killebrew, a Washington holdover who became the centerpiece for an offensive machine and the most popular player in Twins history—a popularity that has not diminished more than a quarter century after his retirement.

The 1961-70 Twins literally powered their way to one A.L. pennant (1965) and two division titles (1969, '70) behind the booming bats of Killebrew, Bob Allison, Jim Lemon, Tony Oliva, Jimmie Hall, Earl Battey, Don Mincher and Rod Carew. No seat in the outfield stands was safe, including the left field second deck that Killebrew once reached with a shot estimated at 520 feet. The power display (the Twins hit 446 homers in 1963 and '64 combined) was so impressive, the Met scoreboard in right-center field began posting home run distances—a baseball first.

That scoreboard was a Metropolitan Stadium staple through most of its existence. The basic, no-frills board, with advertisements across the top and a Longines clock perched above, posted lineups, basic information and out-of-town scores. A rectangular backdrop, centered by a towering flagpole, sat next to the scoreboard in an otherwise open center field area. For many years, bullpens were located in front of the scoreboard.

Layout and intimacy were among the Met's special quirks—as well as the ability to move freely around the park and enjoy an interesting variety of views. You could start in an underground concourse, suddenly find yourself in an open bleacher, cross through a tunnel here, over a runway there. There were so many ways of getting places—in and out, over and around. A chain-link fence formed the 8-foot left field barrier for many years and fans could pass under the elevated stands, stop and get a great field-level view of the action.

By the mid-1970s, the Twins had dropped in the standings and their stadium, poorly maintained, had fallen into disrepair. The Met survived through the 1981 season, after which both the Twins and Vikings moved into Minnesota's new Metrodome—a state-of-the-art facility that could offer comfort and amenities, but never rival its predecessor in intimacy and personality.

METROPOLITAN STADIUM (1961-1981)

Pre-dating Metropolitan Stadium and major league baseball in the Twin Cities were two minor league teams: the Millers, who played in Nicollet Park in Minneapolis, and the Saints, who played in Lexington Park in St. Paul.

The Millers opened Metropolitan Stadium in 1956, despite a February fire that had destroyed part of the stands, and the Saints moved into new Midway Stadium a year later. It wasn't until 1961, when the Washington Senators relocated to Minnesota and were renamed the Twins, that major league baseball made its debut at the Met.

Built in a once remote cornfield, the site now is the center of suburban sprawl. The Mall of America, bound on one side by Killebrew Drive, marks the one-time site of Metropolitan Stadium, which was torn down in 1985.

First game: April 21, 1961. The expansion Washington Senators beat the "old Senators," who had relocated to Minnesota as the Twins, 5-3.

Final game: September 30, 1981. Only 15,900 attended the closer, a 5-2 loss to the Royals.

■ Site of one World Series (1965)
■ Site of one All-Star Game (1965)

Polo Grounds

Rube Marquard beats Brooklyn 2-1 for record 19th straight victory, July 3, 1912

Braves end Giants' record 26-game winning streak, Sept. 30, 1916

Landing spot for Bobby Thomson's 1951 Shot Heard 'Round the World

Visitor's bullpen

Rawlings-to-Kelly-to Frisch double play (4-3-5) brings stunning Game 8 conclusion to Giants' 1921 World Series win over Yankees in the first Battle of New York

Where Heinie Zimmerman chased Eddie Collins across plate in Game 6 of 1917 World Series—the play that gave White Sox championship

CARL HUBBELL: Five-time 20-game winner used nasty screwball to strike out Ruth, Gehrig, Foxx, Simmons and Cronin consecutively in 1934 All-Star Game

Batter's box where Indians shortstop Ray Chapman was struck by fatal pitch from Carl Mays, Aug. 16, 1920

A t first glance, the Polo Grounds was a baseball illusion—an elongated, horseshoe-shaped arena with a compressed field squeezed into its unorthodox contours. It was awkward, clumsy and disjointed, a 19th century relic with a 20th century soul. It was an ugly house of pain for visitors, a stately cathedral for New York baseball worshipers. You had to look deep to see the soul, but you couldn't miss a powerful aura that cloaked one of the great sports venues in history.

The aura was built around a legacy of success and some of the game's most rabid fans. The Polo Grounds, home for three major league teams over its 73-year history, played host to 14 World Series and five champions

Giants pennants in 1904, '05, '11, '12, '13, '17, '21, '22, 23', '24, '33, '36, '37, '51, '54
Yankees pennants in 1921, '22

Park where Casey Stengel and Amazin' Mets lost 120 games in 1962

Ott hits 500th career home run, Aug. 1, 1945

Cubs' Mordecai Brown outduels Christy Mathewson 4-2 in one-game pennant-deciding playoff forced by Merkle's boner, Oct. 8, 1908

Where Joe DiMaggio made final putout of 1936 World Series Game 2 and ran up the clubhouse steps

483 feet to clubhouse facade behind Eddie Grant memorial statue

Spot where Dusty Rhodes' 260-foot game-ending home run landed in opener of 1954 World Series

Spot where Willie Mays pulled in Vic Wertz smash during Game 1 of 1954 World Series

Three players reached center field bleachers with home runs— Joe Adcock in 1953, Lou Brock and Hank Aaron in 1962

New York bullpen

Fred Merkle failed to touch second during 1908 game vs. Cubs, costing Giants a pennant

Where Hubbell shut out Cardinals 1-0 in 18-inning thriller, July 2, 1933

The great John McGraw (left) managed Giants to 10 pennants, 3 championships in 30 years

Christy Mathewson (right) shuts out A's for third time in six days, closes out 1905 World Series with 2-0 Game 5 win

MEL OTT: 511 career home runs, six N.L. homer titles over 22-year Giants career

The horseshoe-shaped Polo Grounds and its bathtub-like field configuration stood as a New York baseball landmark through the 1963 season. Yankee Stadium, which was opened in 1923, was located a few fly balls away, on the other side of the Harlem River.

while providing a Hall of Fame arena for Christy Mathewson, Ross Youngs, Fred Lindstrom, Mel Ott, Travis Jackson, Bill Terry, Carl Hubbell and a young Willie Mays, who learned to Say Hey in its expansive center field. Babe Ruth won two home run titles here before building his own house across the Harlem River.

This was the stage where John McGraw choreographed Giants victories for more than three decades and Casey Stengel choreographed Mets losses for two seasons. Three of the most memorable moments in baseball history occurred on these hallowed grounds—Fred Merkle's boner cost the Giants a pennant in 1908, Bobby Thomson's homer won them a pennant in 1951 and Mays' catch helped them reach championship heights in 1954.

To fully appreciate the modern-era Polo Grounds, you must envision a huge bathtub with a baseball diamond crammed inside. The result was an outlandish field with peculiar dimensions and quirks unlike any other in baseball. The double-deck grandstands circled deep behind home plate (one end of the tub) and rounded off, continuing straight along the entire lengths of the structure before making slight curves at the opposite end. With home plate centered against the two curved ends, half of the side grandstands were in foul territory, the other half in fair.

As a result, lefthanded hitters could pull a fly ball down the right field line and watch it drop into the lower-deck grandstands for a 257-foot home run. Righthanders could line a ball over the 17-foot wall 279 feet down the left field line, or they could drop a fly into an upper-deck overhang that reduced the distance closer to 250. But woe to any slugger who failed to pull the ball. As the grandstands continued, they angled deeper away from the batter, reaching 455 feet at the curve in left-center and 449 in right-center.

Both grandstands made the turn and stopped, leaving an opening in dead center field. They were divided by two bleacher sections that in turn were divided by a 60-foot building housing both teams' clubhouses and administrative offices. The clubhouse, decorated in later years by a Chesterfield cigarette sign and topped by a Longines clock and flagpole, was indented from the field, 483 feet from home plate, and twin staircases on both sides led players to and from their dressing quarters.

Teams without a speedy center fielder were in trouble at the Polo Grounds, where balls eluding an outfielder could roll all the way to Yankee Stadium after striking the angled left and right field walls. Adding to the quirky nature of the park were inconsistent fences—17 feet at the left field pole, rising to 18 in left-

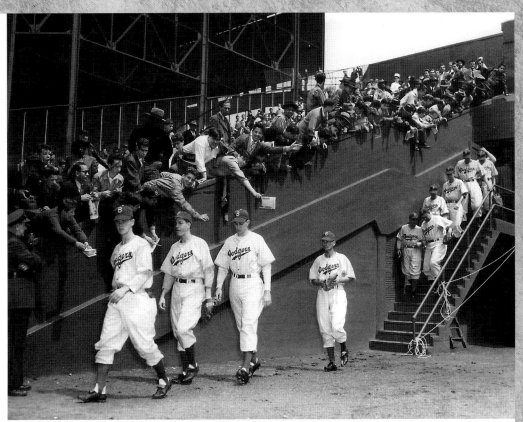

The right-center field grandstand (above) was a long way from home plate, as was the park's signature feature, a center field clubhouse that attracted autograph seekers (above right), especially before games vs. the Dodgers. The clubhouse indent only complicated life for outfielders (below right).

center and sloping to 12 where the grandstand met the bleachers—and sunken outfields that allowed managers standing in their dugouts to see only the top half of their fielders.

Standing in front of the clubhouse, in fair territory, was a 5-foot memorial statue of Captain Eddie Grant, a former Giants infielder killed during World War I, and plaques honoring Mathewson, McGraw and Youngs hung on the clubhouse facade. The bleacher seats were fronted by an 8-foot wall (4-foot wall, 4-foot screen) and two dark-green canvas backdrops (20 feet-by-17 feet) topped the corners of the bleachers, 460 feet from the plate. The bullpens, topped by a slanting roof, were located on each of the off-center field curves—the only fair-territory bullpens in baseball.

Nothing could prepare you properly for a game at the Polo Grounds. Seeing was believing and all you could do was shake your head at the extremes to which the park would take you. Pop flies would turn into home runs if placed accurately down one of the lines. A monumental smash to center could wind up in somebody's glove, a long, unfortunate out.

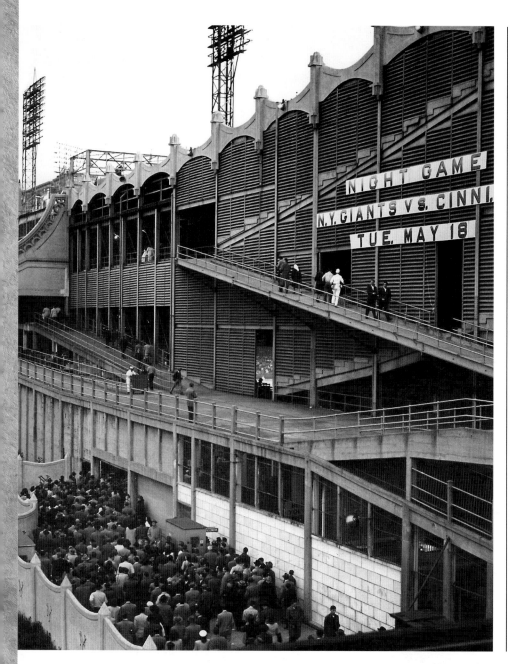

The Polo Grounds, a myriad of ramps and entryways (left), provided a scenic view from Coogan's Bluff (right). The upper-deck facing at the old Polo Grounds (above) was ornately decorated with the coats of arms of all N.L. teams.

Giants reliever Don Liddle understood the park in 1954 when he served up a Game 1 World Series pitch that Cleveland's Vic Wertz drove 460 feet toward the right-center field backdrop, only to see Mays pull it in with an amazing over-the-shoulder catch. In the 10th inning of that same contest, Indians starter Bob Lemon let Dusty Rhodes pull a routine fly ball down the right field line and it dropped into the seats for a 260-foot game-winning home run.

If the cheap home run was a Polo Grounds personality flaw, the center field grand canyon more than compensated. In the ballpark's long history, only three balls reached the distant bleachers—Joe Adcock in 1953 and Lou Brock and Hank Aaron on consecutive days in 1962—and no ball ever struck the clubhouse. The park also was hard on pitchers who had to make the long, ego-deflating walk to the center field clubhouse after being knocked from a game.

The Polo Grounds traces its roots back to 1890, when it was built for a team in the outlaw Players League in the northern half of Coogan's Hollow, a grassy meadow in the shadow of Coogan's Bluff. James J. Coogan, a wealthy landowner and Manhattan borough president, had already leased the southern half of the Hollow to the National League's Giants, where they built Manhattan Field. Broth-

POLO GROUNDS (1891-1957; 1962-63)

It was the third of three parks known as the Polo Grounds. The first—located at 110th and Sixth Avenue on grounds once used for polo matches—lasted from 1883-1888. The second, at 155th and Eighth, lasted from 1889 to 1890.

The third Polo Grounds stood at 157th and Eighth Avenue, the former "Brotherhood Park" built in 1890 for a team in the outlaw Players League. That wooden structure was destroyed by fire in 1911 and Giants owner John T. Brush rebuilt it in the same configuration—but with steel and concrete and an imposing double-deck grandstand.

The Yankees joined the Giants as Polo Grounds co-tenants from 1913-22 before moving into their new park just across the Harlem River. The Polo Grounds' last major renovation took place before the 1923 season, increasing capacity to 55,000.

The Giants moved to San Francisco in 1958 and the expansion Mets played in the Polo Grounds in 1962 and '63—the historic park's final hurrah before Shea Stadium opened in 1964.

First game: April 22, 1891. Boston beat the Giants, 4-3.

Final game: September 18, 1963. Playing before 1,752 fans, the Mets officially closed the historic park with a 5-1 loss to the Phillies. Jim Hickman hit the park's final New York home run.

■ Site of 14 World Series (1905, '11, '12, '13, '17, '21, '22, '23, '24, '33, '36, '37, '51 and '54)
■ Site of two All-Star Games (1934 and '42)

This field-level view shows the Polo Grounds the way it must have appeared to box seat patrons around mid-20th century. Note how close the left and right field foul poles must have seemed to hitters.

erhood Park, the Players League facility, was built in an elongated shape so it could squeeze between Manhattan Field and the bluff.

When the Players League collapsed after the 1890 season, John B. Day acquired the larger Brotherhood Park and moved his Giants into their new home, in the north Harlem section of Manhattan on the west side of Eighth Avenue between 157th and 159th streets. Home plate was directly beneath Coogan's bluff and center field looked out toward the Harlem River.

It was in this wooden ballpark, dubbed the Polo Grounds after a former Giants home, that McGraw built his early championship teams, Mathewson recorded four 30-plus-win seasons and Merkle made his costly boner. Stairs led down from the bluff to the Polo Grounds ticket offices (later replaced by inclined ramps) and the outfield was open, so the gentry could watch action from their horse-drawn carriages parked behind a center field rope.

When the Polo Grounds burned to the ground in a 1911 fire, owner John T. Brush rebuilt it as a steel-and-concrete structure with an imposing double-deck, roofed grandstand that stopped at the foul pole in left and extended well past the pole in right. Coats of arms of all the N.L. teams were displayed on the upper grandstand facade, a feature that eventually was removed. The old Polo Grounds configuration was retained, but now there were single-deck stands circling the rest of the structure.

After the 1922 season, a renovation gave the Polo Grounds a 55,000 seating capacity and the basic look it would retain over its final four decades. The grandstands were extended, the bleachers and clubhouse were added and scoreboards were perched on the second-deck facade at the foul lines. The lower stands behind the plate extended out from the upper deck and circled to a point well down both lines. Lights would not be installed until 1940.

Through much of the Polo Grounds' 73-year existence it was a championship mecca for baseball, pro and college football and boxing. During their 67-year Polo Grounds stay, the Giants set the baseball success standard by which generations of franchises would be measured. The American League Yankees were saucy young wannabes while the Giants were winning pennants and championships in the first quarter of the century and the teams even shared the Polo Grounds from 1913 to 1922—and World Series revenues when all 13 games of the 1921 and '22 classics were played there, both Series wins for the Giants.

That dominance would change. But one thing that wouldn't was the loud, crazy, demanding and cocky fans who viewed McGraw's Giants as superior and liked to rub their success in the noses of Brooklyn fans. The Giants-Dodgers rivalry bordered on hatred and the Polo Grounds was a forum for some of the most intense battles ever staged. The rivalry was epitomized by the incredible 1951 N.L. pennant race that ended in a Dodgers-Giants tie and was settled by Thomson's playoff home run—the Shot Heard 'Round the World.

When the Giants jilted their New York fans for the greener pastures of San Francisco after the 1957 season, baseball cut its ties with the ancient, decaying Polo Grounds for the first time in almost seven decades. The stadium returned to the baseball wars four years later as the temporary home of the expansion New York Mets, but after two Amazin' years (1962 and '63) and 231 losses, the proud old ballpark in the shadow of Coogan's Bluff played host to its final game. It was razed one year later.

The final Giants game at the venerable Polo Grounds in 1957 sent New York fans on a riotous rampage (below). The Giants opened the 1958 campaign in San Francisco.

Shibe Park

Renamed Connie Mack Stadium (1953-1970)

Home of A's $100,000 infield: Home Run Baker, Jack Barry, Eddie Collins, Stuffy McInnis

Jimmie Foxx was first player to clear left field grandstand in 1928 . . . Dick Allen (left) hit longest homer over barrier, a shot estimated at 529 feet in 1965

Shibe, renamed Connie Mack Stadium in 1953, was home of A's 1909-54, Phillies 1938-70

1950 Whiz Kids win first N.L. pennant since 1915, fall to Yankees in World Series sweep . . . 1964 Phillies lose 10 of final 12 games in collapse that costs them pennant

Boston's Jim Tabor hits four homers, two of them grand slams, and drives in 11 runs in 17-7 and 18-12 Red Sox doubleheader sweep, July 4, 1939

In first A.L. night game, Indians defeat A's 8-3, May 16, 1939

Where Bobby Doerr hit three-run homer in 1943 All-Star Game

Down 15-4 after 7 ½ innings, A's rally for 13 runs in eighth and post improbable 17-15 win over stunned Indians, June 15, 1925

ROBIN ROBERTS: Talented righthander recorded six straight 20-win seasons for Phillies, 1950-55

Al Simmons drove in 322 runs over 1929 (165) and '30 (157) campaigns

T o Philadelphia sports fans, it was "the tower." To out-of-town visitors, it was a French Renaissance-style landmark, a dome worthy of any baseball basilica. If you didn't genuflect when you spotted the main entrance of Shibe Park, you at least uttered a little prayer to the timeless spirit and incredible perseverance of the great Connie Mack. This wasn't a church, but it's not hard to understand why most Philadelphians approached it with a sense of veneration and reverence.

Seven American League pennants, one National League pennant and five

Scorecard-waving Connie Mack built and rebuilt teams that won seven A.L. pennants and five championships—1910, '11, '13, '29 and '30—over 50-year managing career

Two Home Run Baker blasts spark A's in 1911 World Series . . . Mule Haas' Game 7 homer helps decide 1929 classic

Eddie Plank (left) fires two-hitter, outduels Christy Mathewson in 1913 Game 5 World Series clincher vs. Giants

Longines clock, 75 feet high

4-3 loss to Giants begins Phillies' major league-record 23-game losing streak, July 29, 1961

Jimmie Foxx's 500th home run, hit fittingly at Shibe, comes in Red Sox uniform, Sept. 24, 1940

Where Hack Wilson lost ball in sun, allowing Mule Haas to circle bases during 10-run seventh-inning explosion that wiped out 8-0 Cubs lead in Game 4 of 1929 World Series

Connie Mack's 34-foot "spite fence" was erected in 1935

Dodgers' Jackie Robinson hits dramatic 14th-inning homer to beat Phillies, set stage for 1951 pennant-deciding playoff vs. Giants

Yankees second baseman Tony Lazzeri powers two grand slams, drives in A.L.-record 11 runs in 25-2 rout of A's, May 24, 1936

Boston's Ted Williams completes .406 1941 season with 6-for-8 doubleheader performance on final day

A's post 24-2 win over team of amateur players recruited by Detroit management to replace striking Tigers, May 18, 1912

Park where Yankee Lou Gehrig (1932) and Chicago's Pat Seerey (1948) enjoyed four-homer games

Where Miracle Braves steamrolled A's in first two games of shocking 1914 World Series sweep

Jimmie Foxx: Two-time MVP pounded 302 of his 534 career homers for Athletics, including 58 in 1932

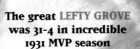

The great LEFTY GROVE was 31-4 in incredible 1931 MVP season

World Series championships were won here. This was where Hall of Famers Eddie Plank, Home Run Baker, Chief Bender, Mickey Cochrane, Jimmie Foxx, Al Simmons, Lefty Grove, Eddie Collins, Robin Roberts, Richie Ashburn and Jim Bunning mastered their craft; where two dynasties were built—and ripped apart. This was a temple and a house divided, a place where fans experienced both winning ecstasy and losing despair while supporting the Athletics for 46 years and the Phillies for 32—16-plus as co-tenants of the North Philadelphia palace at 21st and Lehigh.

To fully appreciate Shibe Park, you first must understand Mack's Philadelphia presence—from 1901 co-founder of the A.L. Athletics franchise with Benjamin Shibe

and eventual owner to 50 years as the team's field boss. From his top-of-the-tower office he ruled the business side of the operation; from his dugout office he dictated lineups and strategy with trademark waves of his ever-present scorecard. No one person more singlehandedly determined the look and personality of a ballpark than the gaunt, grim-faced Mack—baseball's last manager in street clothes.

Shibe Park, like Mack, was always stately, even while its teams ran the gamut from great to awful. Opened in 1909 as baseball's first steel-and-concrete facility, it was hailed as a crown jewel, the prototype by which a whole generation of new ballparks would be measured. Pittsburgh quickly countered with Forbes Field, Chicago with Comiskey Park and Wrigley Field, Boston with Fenway Park and Detroit

SHIBE PARK (1909-1970)

Renamed Connie Mack Stadium (1953-1970)

It opened as home of the Athletics and closed as home of the Phillies. In between, this venerable ballpark lived a full life as a second home for all Philadelphia baseball fans.

Shibe Park, named in honor of Ben Shibe, principal owner of the Athletics, opened in 1909—baseball's first steel-and-concrete stadium. The A's had played their first eight seasons in Columbia Park, just a mile and a half from the eventual Shibe Park site.

While A's fans enjoyed life at the always-classy Shibe, fans of the National League Phillies attended games at Baker Bowl, a bandbox stadium that endured grandstand collapses, fires and well-deserved criticism from 1887-1938. The Phillies, who had been forced to play at Shibe on a temporary basis in 1927, finally moved in as co-tenants in 1938 and shared it with the Athletics until 1954, when the A's bolted for Kansas City. The Phillies continued to play there through the 1970 season.

Shibe was renamed Connie Mack Stadium in 1953, an honor Mack, the renowned Athletics manager and owner, had resisted for years. But in 1952, while Mack was in Florida, the team's board of directors made it official and it remained that way for the remainder of its years.

Connie Mack Stadium was demolished in 1976 and its location at 21st and Lehigh remained vacant until 1990, when a church was built there.

First game: April 12, 1909. Eddie Plank pitched the Athletics to an 8-1 win over the Red Sox before an announced crowd of 30,162—in a stadium that seated 20,000.

Final game: October 1, 1970. Oscar Gamble's 10th-inning single drove home Tim McCarver and the Phillies beat the Expos, 2-1.

■ Site of eight World Series (1910, '11, '13, '14, '29, '30, '31 and '50)
■ Site of two All-Star Games (1943 and '52)

Shibe Park's stately 'tower' (left) stood guard at the intersection of 21st and Lehigh from 1909-70, when the Phillies moved to Veterans Stadium.

with Navin Field. Some could come close, others could match, but none could ever top the energy and dignity Shibe retained throughout its 62-year existence.

"Connie Mack Stadium (its name from 1953-70) had character," Ashburn recalled in a 1975 story for the *Philadelphia Evening Bulletin*. "It looked like a ballpark. It smelled like a ballpark. It had feeling and a heartbeat, a personality that was all baseball. Players could sit in the clubhouse and see and hear the fans, and you could hear the vendors selling hot dogs and programs. It was a total baseball experience."

That character started with the French-style facade that greeted its first visitors in 1909 and extended inside to the innovative folding chairs, sparkling clean corri-

dors, underground garages, below-grandstand tunnels that allowed players private passage from clubhouses to dugouts and even restrooms with attendants and matrons. A double-deck grandstand wrapped behind home plate to the infield edge on both sides and single-deck bleachers extended down both lines to the foul poles.

There was no fair-territory seating, a feature that would change in 1913 with the addition of bleachers that extended from the left field pole to mid-center field, just short of the flagpole. A 1925 renovation added second decks and a roof to all single-deck seats, giving the park a 33,000-seat capacity and the basic look it would retain for the remainder of its years—three-quarters enclosed and roofed, with only right field open to the outside world.

That, too, would change, but not without a battle of wills and much gnashing of teeth among the owners of houses along 20th Street. Early Shibe featured a 12-foot concrete wall in right field, an 8-foot concrete wall topped by a 4-foot wire screen in left. The 20th Street houses offered perfect rooftop perches for fans, hundreds of whom would pay their 25 cents to house owners, climb to makeshift seats and get a suntan as well as a full view of action over the right field wall.

This practice endured from 1909 until 1935, when Mack finally tired of the freebies. He erected a 22-foot wall extension—corrugated sheet iron that brought its height to 34 feet and blocked the view of rooftop squatters. Mack's "spite fence," challenged in court by neighborhood residents, endured through the life of Shibe Park, creating a monstrous challenge for left-handed hitters. "Guys like me just couldn't hit home runs there because of that wall," said former A's outfielder Elmer Valo. "It was just too high."

And unpredictable. The corrugated fence had ripples that resulted in tricky bounces and awkward ricochets, forcing outfielders to keep their distance and surround balls they normally would play aggressively. In the mid-1950s, a 12-foot wooden fence was installed 2 feet in front of the steel wall to protect outfielders from getting hurt. Balls hitting the lower fence traveled 329 feet; balls hitting the upper wall 331. In 1956, a giant electric scoreboard purchased from Yankee Stadium was installed in right-center field, making a big stretch of the wall 50 feet high with a dropoff to 34 on either side. A Longines clock, perched atop the board, was 75 feet above the field.

Activity along 20th Street was always fun, even after the high wall was erected. Kids looking for home run balls that could get them free entrance to a game roamed the street, as did an A's employee who would keep overeager fans from scaling the wall. If a house window was broken by a batted ball, a worker would appear within 15 minutes to install a new one.

Shibe was known as a hitter's park and a showcase for prodigious home runs. The original dimensions of 378 feet to left, 515 to center and 340 to right produced lots of extra-base hits and a 90-foot distance from home plate to backstop turned an agile catcher like Cochrane into a fourth outfielder. But the 1925 renovations reduced left field to 334, center to 468 and right to 331, creating inviting targets for sluggers like Jimmie Foxx, who hit 28 balls over the left field roof; Bill Nicholson and Babe Ruth, who hit shots over the 20th Street rooftops onto Opal Street; Ted Williams, who hit a ball that landed in a back yard on 20th Street; and Dick Allen, who hit the only ball to clear the huge right-center field scoreboard.

Shibe was always an intimate ballpark that put fans close to the action and

From 1925 on, Shibe (above right) was three-quarters enclosed, roofed and open to rooftops in right. The scoreboard, installed in 1956, measured 75 feet to the top of the clock and the mound had a distinctive dirt path to the plate.

encouraged relationships with players. It also was one of the best maintained ballparks in baseball with a crack groundskeeping crew that kept the grass green and manicured to perfection. No team enjoyed a field tailored more to the talents of its players. And sound echoed through Shibe like nowhere else, giving pitchers a psychological edge when their routine fastballs popped the catcher's glove like a 100-mph heater.

Nowhere was success more appreciated, especially during those incredible Mack dynasty years of 1910-14 (four pennants, three Series winners) and 1929-31 (three straight pennants, two Series titles). And nowhere was futility more sustained (four winning records in 21 years from 1934-54, after which the A's were sold and moved from Philadelphia to Kansas City). One of the beauties of Shibe was that you could see a baseball game virtually every day or night there from 1938-54, when the A's shared the facility with the N.L. Phillies, who bought the aging park and continued playing there through 1970.

The Phillies' only run at Shibe Park success came in 1950, when the Whiz Kids captured the team's first pennant since 1915 on Dick Sisler's three-run, 10th-inning, final-day home run that produced a 4-1 victory over Brooklyn. But the Phils were swept by the powerful New York Yankees in the World Series.

The sights, sounds and memories of Shibe Park remain vivid more than three decades after its demise. This was the site of the first American League night game in 1939 and the place where heavy-breathing sportswriters worked from their bird's-eye perch under the roof behind home plate—probably the highest press box in baseball. You could get a brew at Kilroy's Bar, check out the memorabilia in the A's Elephant Room or bite into one of the best hot dogs this side of Coney Island.

But you could not enjoy a ballpark beer until 1961, watch Sunday baseball until 1934 or see advertisements until the 1950s, thanks primarily to city laws. There were, however, plenty of obstructed views to choose from and one of baseball's first loudspeaker systems gave Philly fans such memorable P.A. voices as Dave Zinkoff, Sherry O'Brien and Pete Byron.

Philadelphia fans have long been accepted as the boobird champions of baseball and nobody could match the 1930s heckling artistry of the Kessler brothers, Bull and Eddie, who forced their powerful voices and strong opinions on everyone in the park. The brothers would sit on opposite sides of the field and carry on conversations, directing their comments to a home or visiting player of their disaffection.

There were plenty of colorful characters among the 47 million fans who paraded through the turnstiles to watch players who usually matched their enthusiasm—in spirit if not performance. When Connie Mack Stadium closed after the Phillies' 1970 season, the surrounding neighborhood had deteriorated, cracks were showing in the foundation of baseball's oldest ballpark and layers of paint peeled away its aging secrets.

But nobody ever called it drab. A red interior combined with the still-beautiful green grass to give Philly fans a nostalgic sense of baseball, the way it was played for more than six decades.

Rooftop viewing from across 20th Street was common until Connie Mack put up his spite fence in 1935. This photo was shot during the 1914 World Series.

Forbes Field

No foul ball went unchallenged, thanks to 110-foot distance from home plate to backstop

Bill Mazeroski blanketed second base from 1956-72

Where "Greenberg Gardens" fence was erected in 1947, slicing 30 feet off home run distance for newcomer Hank Greenberg

Where Yankees left fielder Yogi Berra watched Bill Mazeroski's ninth-inning homer sail over the fence, giving Pirates 1960 World Series championship

Big Poison and Little Poison: Brothers Paul (right field) and Lloyd (center field) Waner combined for 5,185 hits as Pirates teammates from 1927-40

RALPH KINER:
Two-time 50-homer man powered his way into hearts of Pirates fans from 1946-53

H onus Wagner marveled at its architectural grandeur. So did the Waner boys, Big Poison and Little Poison, who especially loved its expansive outfield—the better to chase down long fly balls and drop in well-aimed line drives. Pie Traynor scoffed at its rock-hard infield, Ralph Kiner delighted at its inviting "Garden" and Roberto Clemente found peace and harmony with its chummy right field screen.

For 62 years, Forbes Field inspired that kind of affection. This was baseball's second steel-and-concrete stadium, a quirky palace constructed in the affluent Oakland section of

Dale Long hits homer in eighth straight game, May 28, 1956 vs. Dodgers

Phillies' Chuck Klein hits four homers in one game—two on the right field roof, July 10, 1936

Where right fielder Roberto Clemente won four batting championships and 10 of his 12 Gold Gloves

Babe Ruth's final three career home runs—including the first to clear Forbes Field's right field roof—come in a May 25, 1935 game for Braves

Rip Sewell baffles Browns slugger George McQuinn with "ephus pitch" in 1944 All-Star Game

Harold Arlin became baseball's first radio broadcaster when he described a Pirates-Phillies game here over station KDKA

Babe Adams shuts out Tigers in Game 7 of 1909 World Series, gives Pirates first championship

Reliever Roy Face wins 17th straight game of season, 22nd over two years, Aug. 30, 1959

Pirates played Reds in baseball's last tripleheader, Oct. 2, 1920

Where Pirates were overpowered by 1927 Yankees in first two games of World Series

HONUS WAGNER: Bow-legged shortstop, an eight-time batting champion, mesmerized fans with his defensive prowess through 1917

Willie Mays triples home winning run in eighth inning of first 1959 All-Star Game

Where Pirates' Glenn Wright (May 7, 1925) and Cubs' Jimmy Cooney (May 30, 1927) turned unassisted triple plays

Pie Traynor performed defensive magic at third base from 1920-37

Landing point of Kiki Cuyler's double, which decided 1925 World Series

Three's a charm: Chief Wilson hit record 36 triples in 1912

Where 37-year-old Walter Johnson made "last stand" in mud and rain during 9-7 Game 7 loss to Pirates in 1925 Series

Pittsburgh near the beautiful and pastoral Schenley Park. Ornate and magnificent at its 1909 opening, quaint and worn down at its 1970 demise, Forbes Field never lost its rough Pittsburgh edge while retaining its ability to charm even the toughest of baseball souls.

Charm has never come easy in the Steel City, where beauty is measured by hard work and results, sports heroes are judged by grit and determination and "powerful" wins out over "attractive" in sports venues. The main entrance to Forbes Field was pure Pittsburgh—a grand, old, imposing, theater-like edifice with ornate carvings and designs, deep vertical windows and a porch roof covering arched doorways.

Everything around Forbes set an imposing tone. Three miles away, on the main-entrance side, was the skyline of downtown Pittsburgh. The University of Pittsburgh bordered the left field grandstands, its massive Cathedral of Learning towering into

the factory smoke-filled stratosphere. Schenley Park offered an attractive diversion over the left field fence; Carnegie Tech commanded a view over the center field wall. Surrounded by such beauty and culture, Forbes Field had to be special.

At first, it was mostly big. The original outfield distances of 360 feet down the left field line, 462 to center and 376 to right made it a perfect fit for baseball's dead-ball era. This was a park that demanded fleet outfielders and rewarded speedy gap hitters. The distance from home plate to the backstop was a whopping 110 feet (later reduced to 75), turning an agile catcher into the equivalent of a fourth outfielder.

The original double-decked grandstand wrapped behind the plate in a U-shaped arc that created the backstop expanse. A roofed mini-third deck—early skyboxes?—topped the grandstand, which extended just beyond first and third base. The park's only bleacher section was in foul territory down the left field line and the entire out-

Beautiful Schenley Park provided a nice backdrop beyond the left field fence at Forbes Field.

field was open, interrupted only by a ground-level, hand-operated scoreboard that was topped by a Longines clock—hit the clock, win a home run.

Amazingly, the park underwent only two major renovations during its lifetime. The big one in 1925 extended the double-decked grandstand down the right field line, around the corner and into fair territory, covering a significant portion of right field. That reduced the foul-line distance from 376 to 300, prompting the Pirates to compensate with a 28-foot screen that extended out to the 375-foot marker in right-center. The second, in 1938, added the major leagues' first elevator, which took passengers to a covered third deck behind home plate—a bird's-eye cove for broadcasters and reporters that would become known as the "Crow's Nest."

While major renovations were infrequent, Forbes became known for its quirky nuances. Like the caged light-tower bases that appeared in left-center, center and right-center fields in 1940, creating wall projections and erratic bounces during games. And the 12-foot red brick left field wall, covered with ivy, that replaced the wooden fence in 1945, keeping the park in tune with the look and feel of Schenley Park behind it.

After acquiring aging slugger Hank Greenberg in 1947, the Pirates strung up a chicken-wire bullpen enclosure in front of that wall, lopping 30 feet off home run distances, and dubbed the area "Greenberg Gardens." Greenberg struggled through his one Pittsburgh season, but the enclosure survived through 1953, renamed "Kiner's Korner."

Into this odd-shaped, sometimes-illogical setting fit much of the Pirates' history—a story of success that included names like Wagner, Clarke, Carey, Waner, Cuyler, Traynor, Mazeroski, Greenberg, Kiner, Clemente and Stargell; a story of colorful, quirky memories that gave Forbes Field a personality beyond it players and their accomplishments. Four pennants and three world championships (1909, '25, '60) attest to the historic and success-oriented bottom line, but you had to stop, look and listen to get the real flavor of Forbes Field.

In the 1930s, you might have marveled at the powerful (most said annoying) lungs of Bruce "Screech Owl" McAllister, a screaming superfan also known as the "Forbes Field Siren." In the 1940s and '50s, you basked in the colorful descriptions of broadcaster Rosey Rowswell—"doozie marooney" (Pirate extra-base hit); "dipsy doodle" (Pirate strikeout); "oh, my aching back" (a Pirates loss); or his sound effect-aided "Get upstairs Aunt Minnie" home run calls. Green Weenies and Polish babushkas were all the wave of the 1960s.

Physical oddities also spiced up life at 35,000-seat Forbes Field. During World War II, a wooden 32-foot U.S. Marine sergeant stood guard in left field fair territory near the scoreboard. A plaque honoring Forbes Field builder Barney Dreyfuss was a long-

By the 1950s, the main entrance of Forbes Field was a little worn and weatherbeaten, but it still was an imposing baseball masterpiece.

FORBES FIELD (1909-1970)

Before Forbes became baseball's second steel-and-concrete stadium in 1909, the Pirates played in Exposition Park, at the same site near the confluence of the Allegheny, Monongahela and Ohio Rivers as future home Three Rivers Stadium.

After years of playing in small parks under the threat of flooding rivers, owner Barney Dreyfuss announced in 1908 his plan to build a first-class stadium in the affluent Oakland district, on the edge of Schenley Park and the University of Pittsburgh about three miles from downtown.

Forbes Field, named after John Forbes, a British general who captured Fort Duquesne (from which the city of Pittsburgh rose) during the French and Indian War, initially seated 25,000 and was hailed for its architectural beauty and imposing size. It ramained one of the great ballparks in baseball through its final season in 1970.

Remnants of the old Forbes Field site today can be found on an expanded University of Pittsburgh campus. Home plate is encased on the floor of a university building and a section of the brick left field wall still stands on a sidewalk outside the building, conjuring visions of Bill Mazeroski's 1960 World Series-winning home run. It's here that on October 13 of each year, Pirates fans gather to celebrate Maz's heroic shot. For years, another section of the wall was displayed in the Allegheny Club at Three Rivers Stadium.

First game: June 30, 1909. A standing-room crowd of 30,388, many curious to see Dreyfuss' wondrous new park, watched the Pirates drop a 3-2 decision to the Chicago Cubs.

Final game: June 28, 1970. The Pirates sweep the Cubs, 3-2 and 4-1, in an era-closing doubleheader.

■ Site of four World Series (1909, '25, '27 and '60)
■ Site of two All-Star Games (1944 and '59)

The final game at Forbes in 1970 ended with fans attacking the left field scoreboard (right) in search of souvenirs—only a few yards from where Bill Mazeroski's World Series-winning homer left the park in 1960, a spot marked by a plaque (above left) on what is now the University of Pittsburgh campus. Announcers got a bird's-eye view from their perch high above home plate (above).

time decoration on the right-center field fence and an 18-foot Wagner statue monitored Forbes Field proceedings from Schenley Park, just behind the left field wall, from 1955 to the park's 1970 closing. The rock-hard infield (broadcaster Bob Prince's "alabaster plaster") was a Forbes trademark, a quirk that helped decide the seventh game of the 1960 World Series.

An old, decaying Forbes Field finally gave way to new Three Rivers Stadium midway through the 1970 season, leaving Pittsburgh fans to ponder hundreds of priceless memories and several distinctions unmatched by any other six-decade ballpark—no advertisements ever appeared on Forbes Field's outfield walls and nobody ever pitched a no-hitter from its mound.

Three Rivers Stadium

Honus Wagner stood proudly on his Gate C pedestal, watching as another line drive sailed toward the distant Pittsburgh skyline. Gate A was manned by Roberto Clemente, off and running after his vicious shot over the mighty Ohio River. Outside Gate D, quietly pondering the view of his beloved city, sat Art Rooney, the venerable founder and former owner of the NFL Steelers.

The sea of concrete that surrounded Three Rivers Stadium was nothing if not sentimental. It also was set dramatically into one of the most beautiful baseball backdrops ever conceived. Stationed strategically at the point where the Allegheny River joins the Monongahela River to form the Ohio, Three Rivers was only a fly

Stargell becomes first big-leaguer to hit 11 home runs in April, April 27, 1971

Extra, Extra—a no-hitter. Francisco Cordova (9) and Ricardo Rincon (1) stop Astros in first combined extra-inning no-hitter in baseball history, July 12, 1997

Phil Garner hits grand slams in consecutive games, Sept. 14 and 15, 1978

Phillies star Mike Schmidt makes 500th career homer a dramatic one—a three-run, ninth-inning shot that beats Pirates, April 18, 1987

Pirates lose third and final game of '75 Championship Series, despite John Candelaria's 14 strikeouts

Baseball's first World Series night game: Reliever Bruce Kison Keys Pirates' 4-3 win over Orioles in Game 4, Oct. 13, 1971

"Pops" Stargell, head of Pittsburgh's 1979 "Family", led the Bucs to World Series win over Baltimore

After allowing leadoff single vs. Braves, Jim Bibby retires next 27 batters, May 19, 1981

1978 N.L. MVP Dave Parker was right field fixture from 1975-83

Where Phillies second baseman Mickey Morandini turned the first unassisted triple play by N.L. player since 1927, Sept. 20, 1992

Bob Walk fires Game 5 three-hitter vs. Braves and keeps Pirates' flickering hopes alive in 1992 NLCS

WILLIE STARGELL belted four upper-deck home runs, all of which are marked by stars on the seats where they hit

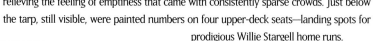

The Clemente statue (right), scenic views from the Ohio River side of Pittsburgh's Golden Triangle (opposite page) and fan participation (left) were part of the Three Rivers experience.

ball or two away from picture-postcard ecstasy.

You never got that sense from close-up photographs that revealed a round, gray, concrete mass, similar to the cookie-cutter multi-purpose facilities in Philadelphia and Cincinnati. Aside from the statues, there was little in sight to suggest character or charm. But when you put Three Rivers in the context of its surroundings, you saw an almost stately structure that tried hard to fit in with an aggressive downtown skyline.

Three Rivers at night could be spectacular. Lights from downtown buildings reflected off the Allegheny, providing a laser-like escort for tugs and other boats chugging along the water. The outlines of bridges added color, as did the lights from houses atop the hills on the distant Ohio bank. Activity on the Duquesne Incline, with a tram delivering patrons to a nightlife strip on the top of Mount Washington, provided an alternative sidelight on the opposite banks of the three-river confluence, slightly upriver from Pittsburgh's Golden Triangle.

If nothing else, the scenery put you in a receptive mood. That's good because what you got inside was a symmetrical expanse of artificial turf with base and home plate cutouts and a bowl-like feeling of enclosure. Like Riverfront Stadium (Cinergy Field) in Cincinnati and Veterans Stadium in Philadelphia, this was a facility designed for football with little to offer by way of distinctive features.

One thing it did have was color—a kaleidoscope of reds, yellows, blues and greens that exploded from each of the five seating levels and the playing surface. A tarp with decorative championship logos covered most of the outfield upper deck, relieving the feeling of emptiness that came with consistently sparse crowds. Just below the tarp, still visible, were painted numbers on four upper-deck seats—landing spots for prodigious Willie Stargell home runs.

For predominantly blue-collar Pittsburgh fans, Three Rivers Stadium, devoid of the frills and trappings that fans in other cities have come to expect, was a satisfactory 47,972-seat ballpark. This was the Steel City, home of the rugged Steelers and one of the most successful baseball franchises in history. Names like Clemente, Stargell, Dave Parker, Bill Madlock, Al Oliver, John Candelaria, Kent Tekulve, Barry Bonds and Doug Drabek passed through, leaving a three-decade legacy of nine East Division titles, two pennants and two World Series victories. Combined with the Steelers' stunning Super Bowl success in the 1970s, Three Rivers was a well-honored championship venue.

In July 1970, it was simply a glittering, state-of-the-art baseball wannabe, a major departure from the old-style Forbes Field

THREE RIVERS STADIUM (1970-2000)

It sat on the same site as Exposition Park, where baseball was played as far back as the 1880s, but Three Rivers was a far cry from Exposition and its immediate predecessor, Forbes Field. The multi-purpose facility with artificial turf and a sterile, symmetrical interior served as home of the Pirates for 30-plus seasons and witnessed two baseball championships.

The aging Forbes fell victim to the stadium-building craze of the 1960s, after the NFL's Steelers had moved to Pitt Stadium. When the University of Pittsburgh purchased the ballpark with the idea of expansion, Forbes Field's days were numbered.

Ground was broken for Three Rivers in April of 1968 with the intention of opening the stadium for the 1969 season. Delays, however, pushed the stadium's debut to the middle of the '70 campaign and the Pirates won a World Series a year later..

Three Rivers also fell victim to a ballpark-building craze, playing host to its last major league game at the end of the 2000 season. Its replacement, PNC Park, combined the best of both worlds—Three Rivers' location and Forbes Field's intimate baseball charm.

First game: July 16, 1970. In a stellar pitching matchup of the Reds' Gary Nolan and the Pirates' Dock Ellis, Cincinnati beat Pittsburgh, 3-2. Coincidentally, it was the same score as Forbes Field's debut game in 1909, a 3-2 Chicago victory.

Final game: October 1, 2000. Local boy John Wehner hit a two-run homer, but the Pirates' bullpen faltered and Chicago scored a 10-9 victory in the farewell to Three Rivers Stadium.

■ Site of two World Series (1971 and 1979)
■ Site of two All-Star Games (1974 and 1994)

atmosphere that Pirates fans had absorbed since 1909. Three Rivers' only connection with the past was its location (the former site of Exposition Park, the team's home before Forbes Field), the Wagner statue that had stood behind Forbes' left field wall and artifacts from Forbes that were placed in the Allegheny Club—an 8-by-12-foot section of the brick outfield wall, 12 Romanesque window frames and a Babe Ruth plaque marking his 714th home run.

In 1971, the Pirates' first full season at Three Rivers, Clemente led them to the franchise's fourth Series championship. Before the '70s were complete, the Pirates had secured four more division titles and another championship—the 1979 "We Are Family" charge sparked by Pops Stargell. Three Rivers, only 10 years old, already had witnessed more postseason excitement than many stadiums do in a lifetime.

Not much changed cosmetically over the years. The original scoreboard, a narrow horizontal strip that stretched from left-center field to right-center, not far above the 10-foot inner fence, was removed and a new board was installed just below the stadium's upper rim in straightaway center—a binoculars view for fans behind home plate. Two hard-to-ignore giant billboards sat on top of the rim in the park's latter years—between light standards and above the scoreboard.

Three Rivers was short on quirks, but it did have fenced-off bullpens down the lines and dugout-view seats behind the plate. It also had a few amenities that might interest even the most baseball-intense fans. The Bullpen Cafe allowed diners to watch game action from just over the left field fence, the Allegheny Club offered a nice blend of refreshment and nostalgia from its third- and fourth-level perch in foul territory down the first base line and a Three Rivers Stadium Hall of Fame kept patrons aware of Pittsburgh's rich sports heritage.

But the stadium's greatest asset was the beautiful, progressive city it served with quiet competence from its riverside perch along Roberto Clemente Memorial Park—the ground upon which George Washington-led troops once fought for Fort Duquesne in the French and Indian War. Three Rivers Stadium was a modern-day battleground—with a view.

Candlestick Park

Renamed 3Com Park at
Candlestick Point (1996-1999)

The 'Stick: Wind, fog, cold
and 40 years of memories

Diminutive reliever Stu Miller gets
blown off the mound in windy 1961
All-Star Game

Bay Area World Series featuring
Giants and A's is interrupted by major
earthquake, which causes death and
destruction moments before the start
of Game 3, Oct. 17, 1989

Astros' Eddie Mathews
hits 500th career homer,
July 14, 1967

Joe Morgan's dramatic final-day,
three-run homer wrecks the
pennant hopes of hated Dodgers,
Oct. 3, 1982

Where Jack Sanford won
his 16th straight game,
Sept. 11, 1962

They called it "the Hawk," a reverent tribute to the mean-spirited wind that soared over, into, around and through Candlestick Park for four decades, bewildering and frustrating the men who tried to play baseball there. The Hawk was an invisible ghost, a howling, swirling, darting and dancing demon that tortured San Francisco fans, made life miserable for players and stretched the boundaries of everyone's endurance and imagination.

Back-to-back no hitters . . .
Sept. 17-18, 1968; Giants'
Gaylord Perry (left) on 17th
(1-0), Cardinals' Ray
Washburn on 18th (2-0)

WILLIE MCCOVEY:
Giants first baseman
1959-73, 1977-80;
521 career homers,
1,555 RBIs.

All in the family:
Bobby Bonds (right) topped 30 homers
three times for Giants; son Barry has
three 40-plus homer seasons

Mays hit N.L.-record-breaking 512th homer on May 4, 1966 and joined 3,000-hit club on July 18, 1970

Barry Bonds becomes second member of baseball's 40-40 club, 1996

Where Juan Marichal pitched a one-hitter in big-league debut, July 19, 1960, and beat Warren Spahn, 1-0, in a 16-inning game decided by a Mays homer, July 2, 1963

Braves pitcher Tony Cloninger becomes first N.L. player to hit two grand slams in same game, July 3, 1966

Where Dodgers manager Tommy Lasorda stopped to blow kisses to heckling crowds on his long treks from visiting clubhouse near right field corner to the third base dugout

Where Bobby Richardson caught McCovey's line drive, ending 1962 World Series

Cancer victim Dave Dravecky posts inspirational 4-3 win over Reds in comeback bid, Aug. 10, 1989

Where Houston's Bob Watson scored baseball's 1-millionth run, May 4, 1975

WILLIE MAYS
.302 career average, 660 homers, 3,283 hits, 1,903 RBIs

Where Juan Marichal attacked Dodgers catcher John Roseboro with a bat, Aug. 22, 1965

Wind and fog (below left) were consistent problems at Candlestick Park, but there was nothing wrong with the stadium's picturesque setting on Candlestick Point (left).

No natural or man-made phenomenon has consistently affected baseball games more than the ill winds of Candlestick—the gusts that blow off the Pacific Ocean and collide with Bay View Hill before fragmenting into swirling, gale-force mini-cyclones that turned pop flies into home runs, foul balls into unexpected outs and competent defenders into bumbling fools. No ballpark in baseball history was more vilified, more joked about, more cursed and more universally hated, even by the people who called it home.

"My fondest memory of that stadium is the day they tear it down," said former Los Angeles Dodgers outfielder Rick Monday. "When you go there you don't walk inside to see a ballpark, you go inside to see an arena. You expect gladiators to come out; the last one standing is the victor, and the last one standing is always the wind."

But the reality of Candlestick was not just the wind and the bone-jarring cold of a July or August night. It also was a Willie Mays catch, a Juan Marichal leg kick, an Orlando Cepeda gapper, a Gaylord Perry spitter, a Barry Bonds moonshot or the courageous effort of Dave Dravecky. It was Willie McCovey's line drive right at Yankees second baseman Bobby Richardson in Game 7 of the 1962 World Series. It was Tommy Lasorda blowing kisses to the maddening crowd as he made the long death march from the visitor's clubhouse in the right field corner to the third base dugout. It was the sound of a foghorn proclaiming a home run, a cable

car bell—one clang for every run.

When the 'Stick opened in 1960 as the permanent home for the transplanted New York Giants, it was anticipated as a baseball showcase and hailed as the "Taj Mahal of games." And at first glance, Candlestick was not so far removed from those expectations when it kicked off a stadium building boom that changed the look of baseball in the 1960s and '70s. It was the first ballpark to be built entirely with reinforced concrete, the first with unobstructed sightlines and the first with radiant heating—a novel idea that, unfortunately, never worked. It also had the biggest, most modern scoreboard in the major leagues.

And throughout its 40-year tenure, you would have been hard-pressed to visit Candlestick and not come away with a sense of personality you'd never find in the cookie-cutter stadiums of Pittsburgh, Cincinnati, Philadelphia and St. Louis. It started with the location.

The 'Stick sat on Candlestick Point, which jutted into the San Francisco Bay and commanded a magnificent view of the harbor and rolling water that, under a warm, clear sky, would be filled with diving birds, white sails and colorful sports boats. You could stand outside the stadium and look down Cardiac Hill to the filling parking lot or to the harbor where yachts and other vessels delivered their passengers to a game.

Inside, Candlestick was a ballpark, not the horrid snake pit of an arena so often portrayed by the national media. You might not feel the tradition of a Yankee Stadium, the charm of a Crosley Field or the personality of a Fenway Park, but you did get the character that was missing from so many parks of its era and a friendly openness that was not lost when Candlestick's open end was enclosed during a 1972 renovation that accommodated the NFL's 49ers and raised baseball seating capacity to

58,000. Life was good when you could sit back and enjoy the anticipation of a game against the hated Dodgers on a beautiful sun-drenched afternoon, complete with a grass-covered field, the smell of the ocean and, of course, a world-class Polish sausage.

And then came the Hawk. The wind whipped up at midafternoon and funneled into Candlestick, turning the field into a dust storm and shooting hot dog wrappers through the air like giant snowflakes. Wind currents swirled and whirled unpredictably throughout the stadium, often with an average velocity of 16 mph and occasional gusts up to 60. Balls hit to left and left-center field were knocked down, balls aimed toward right often were lifted right over the fence. Anything in the air became a potential nightmare, including thrown and pitched balls.

Diminutive reliever Stu Miller could attest to the wind currents that literally blew him sideways during mid-delivery in the 1961 All-Star Game, resulting in a balk. Ken Boyer's throw to first during the same contest was blown sideways, result-

Bay View Hill, as seen during the 1961 All-Star Game (left), overlooked the park. No discussion of Candlestick would be complete without the names (left to right) Mays, McCovey and Cepeda.

ing in an error. Former infielder Duane Kuiper tells of a foul pop that catcher Milt May chased to the backstop, gave up on and as he was walking back to the plate, the ball hit him on top of his head. The one-time symmetrical park even changed shape because of the wind as management shortened the left and left-center field fences to help beleaguered right-handed hitters.

The wind usually subsided by 4 or 5 p.m., at which time the fog rolled in and, acting like an air-conditioner, dropped temperatures 10 or more degrees. It wasn't unusual to start a game on a picturesque 75-degree afternoon, suddenly feel the wrath of the wind and then finish in a 55-degree chill. Life at Candlestick was erratic.

The wind problems diminished when the stadium was enclosed, but Candlestick never escaped its ignominious ties to the weather. Games were occasionally delayed by fog, fans bundled themselves in parkas for summer contests and a packed stadium was even rocked and damaged by a major earthquake just moments before Game 3 of the 1989 World Series—one of Candlestick's two fall classics.

But structural damage was repaired, the Giants went on to lose the Bay Area Series to Oakland and the stadium survived for another decade. Candlestick finally closed her gates to baseball after the 1999 season, to the cheers of many and the tears of those who knew her best.

CANDLESTICK PARK (1960-1999)

Renamed 3Com Park at Candlestick Point (1996-1999)

After two seasons as temporary tenants of Seals Stadium, the relocated Giants (from New York to San Francisco) opened Candlestick for the 1960 season. Its name, determined by fan balloting, referred to the park's location on Candlestick Point, overlooking San Francisco Bay.

Most fans remember Candlestick Park for its game-affecting winds and chilling midsummer night temperatures. But the facility actually was praised as a pioneer in stadium design when it opened. It was the first to be built in a suburban setting, the first to be constructed exclusively with reinforced concrete, the first to be built without view-obstructing pillars and the first to be built with radiant heat—a novel idea that, unfortunately, did not work.

Candlestick opened with a natural grass field and a center field view. The grass was replaced by artificial turf in 1971 (it remained until 1979) and the outfield was enclosed during a 1972 renovation to increase seating for the NFL's 49ers.

Through wind, rain, fog and the chill of night, Candlestick-style baseball survived for four decades, an accepted inconvenience for Giants fans and a shocking reality for unprepared visitors.

First game: April 12, 1960. Vice President Richard Nixon witnessed the Giants' 3-1 victory over the St. Louis Cardinals.

Final game: September 30, 1999. The Giants lost, 9-4, appropriately, to the rival Dodgers—under inappropriately warm, balmy, ideal weather conditions.

- Site of two World Series (1962 and '89)
- Site of two All-Star Games (1961 and '84)

A powerful earthquake brought a temporary end to the 1989 World Series and sent A's players scrambling to find their families (above). The Series continued 12 days later, after repairs were made to the 'Stick (below).

The Kingdome

It was ugly, a stark, gray, dingy circle of cement. Players, coaches, fans, broadcasters—everybody agreed the Kingdome was no work of art. It was a giant mushroom growing in an industrial area just south of downtown Seattle, a wart on the city's otherwise beautiful landscape. Criticized, ridiculed and abhorred, baseball's second domed stadium kept a stiff upper lip near the shore of Puget Sound for 23 sometimes-difficult seasons.

Visually, the Kingdome deserved the abuse. But the essence of the white, wavy-topped facility goes much deeper than appearance. The reality of the Kingdome is that it put Seattle on the major league sports map, served as a launching pad for the careers of Ken Griffey Jr. and Alex

DH Edgar Martinez becomes first A.L. righthanded hitter in half century to win more than one batting title—.343 in '92, .356 in '95

Gaylord Perry beats Yankees 7-3 for 300th career victory, May 6, 1982

Willie Horton's high drive hits speaker, costing him his 300th career homer, June 5, 1979

Where Griffeys, 20-year-old Ken Jr. and 40-year-old Ken Sr., took field as first father-son duo to play together in major league game, Aug. 31, 1990

Mariners beat Angels in one-game playoff, claim first division title in team's 19-year history, Oct. 2, 1995

ALEX RODRIGUEZ: Baseball's first 40-40 shortstop and its first shortstop with back-to-back 40-homer seasons ('98, '99)

Where Dave Parker throws cut down Jim Rice and Brian Downing, saving day for N.L. in 1979 All-Star Game

Alvin Davis, Mark Langston finish 1-2 in A.L. Rookie of the Year voting, 1984

Mike Blowers becomes 13th player to hit grand slams in consecutive games, May 16, 17, 1993

Catcher Dan Wilson chugs home with inside-the-park grand slam, May 3, 1998

Randy Johnson strikes out 19 White Sox, becomes first to reach that plateau twice in one season, Aug. 8, 1997

After retiring first 26 Oakland batters, Brian Holman loses perfect game when Ken Phelps hits home run in eventual 6-1 Mariners win, April 20, 1990

Mike Parrott ends 18-game losing streak, beating Brewers in Rene Lachemann's first game as manager, May 6, 1981

Randy Johnson: 18-2, 2.48 ERA, Cy Young in 1995

Griffey Jr. ties major league record with homer vs. Minnesota—his eighth straight game with home run, July 28, 1993

Second baseman Harold Reynolds anchored infield for 10 seasons, 1983-92

Griffey Jr. ties record with fifth homer in a postseason series and Mariners bring down Yankees in Game 5 Division Series thriller, Oct. 8, 1995

Where Lenny Randle illegally blew ground ball foul, May 27, 1981

Griffey Jr. slams three-run homer and Mariners thrill sellout crowd with Kingdome-closing 5-2 win over Texas, June 27, 1999

Griffey Jr.: First Mariner with back-to-back 50-homer seasons (1997, '98), three straight 140-plus RBI campaigns (1996, '97, '98)

KEN GRIFFEY JR.: Seattle's record book is dominated by Gold Glove center fielder, the A.L.'s 1997 MVP

Four ceiling tiles fall prior to game vs. Orioles, forcing Mariners to play remainder of schedule on road, July 19, 1994

MARINERS

Rodriguez and combined with the towering Space Needle to make the city a Great Northwest tourist attraction. It was the ugly duckling from which a new-millennium swan (Safeco Field) emerged.

"It's been called ugly by a lot of people through the years, but it will always be beautiful to me," said Dave Niehaus, the Mariners' play-by-play broadcaster since their expansion debut in 1977. "It's been a huge part of my life. I'm going to miss it. Aesthetically? No, I won't miss it. I know people are excited to see it go, but remember, we wouldn't have baseball here at all if it wasn't for the Kingdome."

That's an impressive legacy. The Kingdome sprung out of Seattle's need for a major league facility after the city fumbled its first shot at big-league baseball. The expansion Seattle Pilots were whisked away after a difficult 1969 season at tiny Sick's Stadium and it took the promise of a domed, multi-purpose facility to lure professional

THE KINGDOME (1977-1999)

Seattle became a major league baseball city in 1967, when American League owners awarded it an expansion team. By March of 1970, the Pilots had been relocated to Milwaukee after one season—the shortest franchise tenure in modern baseball history.

The plan was for the Pilots to play in Sick's Stadium, a Pacific Coast League facility that had opened in 1938, until a domed stadium could be built. But Pilots officials ran into financial troubles and the team was sold to Milwaukee interests before the 1970 season.

To redeem itself and get back in baseball's good graces, Seattle went ahead with its plans to build a domed stadium. In 1972, after protracted debates over location, the site was selected in King County. In 1977, construction was completed and another expansion team—the Mariners—opened their first season in the Great Northwest.

First game: April 6, 1977. California lefty Frank Tanana shut out the expansion Mariners, 7-0.

Final game: June 27, 1999. Led by Ken Griffey Jr.'s 377th career home run, the Mariners defeated the Rangers, 5-2.

■ Site of no World Series
■ Site of one All-Star Game (1979)

sports back to the city—the expansion Seahawks of the NFL arrived in 1976 and the Mariners opened play a year later. The Kingdome, unlike Houston's Astrodome, was a building of function rather than flash.

The outside was plain, hard and gray, with little around it to draw visitors without a baseball agenda. The view of Puget Sound, with boats chugging to and from port, was enchanting, the distant sight of Mount Rainier on a clear summer day spectacular, the twinkling lights from the Seattle skyline embracing. But no attempts were ever made to present the facility itself as anything more than a lump of concrete with a lonely American flag blowing in the salt-water breezes from its apex.

One of the Kingdome's greatest attributes was accessibility—next to Seattle's King Street railroad station, which made baseball trips convenient from Portland, Spokane and Vancouver; a few blocks from the waterfront, making it easy for boaters; walking distance from downtown and only a few miles from the Space Needle. But its greatest weakness was personality.

The dome (250 feet from field level to apex) sprawled over the turf-covered field like a gigantic umbrella, protecting its patrons from the rain and chills of Seattle's inclement weather. Speakers suspended from the ceiling provided grounds-rule nightmares and the Mariners tried to dress things up with banners, bunting and red, white and blue ceiling streamers, but nothing seemed capable of relieving the cavernous, morgue-like atmosphere that plagued the building through much of its tenure.

The field was an asymmetrical 331 feet to left, 405 to center and 312 to right, and the turf was hard and fast, inviting an offensive playing style. A 23-foot wall made life interesting in right and right-center (a mini-Green Monster nicknamed Walla Walla) and a huge scoreboard dominated the left field view above the third-deck grandstand. An out-of-town board, installed in 1990, flashed scores on the right field wall and a giant tarp covered a portion of the right field upper deck in the early '90s, relieving some of the stadium's normal empty feel.

The 59,856-seat Kingdome did have some distinctive sights and sounds. For several years, outfield dimensions were offered in both feet and fathoms and through most of the 1980s the USS Mariner, a gold ship positioned behind the left-center field fence, would rise up and salute Mariners home runs and victories with a cannon blast. This was the home of Rick Kaminski, one of the best-known peanut vendors in the world, and "Ruuuuuuuupe" —the nickname for popular outfielder Ruppert Jones from 1977-80.

Baseball life in Seattle took its most dramatic turn in 1995 when the Mariners captured their first A.L. West Division championship. That title, which was repeated two years later, ignited a fan fury that transformed the stadium from a tomb into a loud, raucous house of fun, complete with offensive bombers named Griffey, Rodriguez, Jay Buhner and Edgar Martinez and a flame-thrower named Randy Johnson, a k a "The Big Unit."

With that success came some of the personality Mariners officials had always sought. Griffey and A-Rod became national figures. The popular Buhner, alias Bone, attracted his own right field following—a section called the Boneyard. One of the more fascinating Mariners promotions was Buhner Buzz Night, when hundreds of fans would shave their heads (like Buhner) for free admission to the game.

Ironically, the Kingdome was a more fun and happy place when it closed its doors to baseball in mid-1999—a baseball home that was functional, but never really appreciated.

"I really liked it on those days when it was 40 degrees outside and raining," said former first baseman Alvin Davis, who spent eight of his nine major league seasons in Seattle. "For me, the Kingdome is baseball in Seattle. This place is like home to me."

The Kingdome was plain, hard and gray (below), a building of function over flash. It also was a house of pain, a park without a division title until the Mariners broke through in 1995 and 1997 (left).

Sportsman's Park

Also known as Busch Stadium (1953-1966)

I t was home for the Gashouse and Knothole Gangs, a playground for unlikely heroes named Dizzy, Rajah, Pepper, Frankie, Ducky, Enos, Gibby and Stan the Man. This is where the Horse Lady whinnied and a goat was used to trim the outfield grass—some say a little too close for comfort. Sportsman's Park was a sometimes-wacky, always-raucous baseball funhouse—a place of magic where a midget and one-armed outfielder could play with the big boys and the game's most depressed franchise could rise to storybook prominence and win a pennant.

How could you not like Sportsman's Park, where life was never dull and

Cardinals brought 10 pennants, seven championships to Sportsman's Park

Landing point for final-day, ninth-inning grand slam by Hank Greenberg that gave Tigers 6-3 win over Browns and 1945 A.L. pennant

STAN THE MAN MUSIAL: Cardinals' three-time MVP, seven-time batting champ collected 3,630 career hits, fourth all-time

Musial goes crazy: five home runs, nine RBIs in doubleheader vs. Giants, May 2, 1954

Where one-armed outfielder Pete Gray made big-league debut for Browns, April 17, 1945

MVP Ken Boyer led Cardinals to 1964 pennant; Bob Gibson secured World Series championship with Game 7 win over Yankees

Dean brothers, Dizzy and Paul, combined for 49 wins in 1934

Browns' Bobo Holloman fires no-hitter in first major league start, May 6, 1953

— Where Mike Shannon's 1964 World Series homer bounced off scoreboard

Point where Max West's All-Star Game-deciding home run landed in 1940

Point where one of Babe Ruth's three Game 4 home runs cleared bleachers in 1926 World Series, breaking auto dealer's window across Grand Avenue

A 33-foot screen topped fence fronting right field pavilion

Great defensive shortstop Marty Marion wins 1944 MVP, Cardinals defeat Browns in World Series—the only all-St. Louis fall classic

Chet Laabs homers twice, Browns beat Yankees 5-2 and win only A.L. pennant, Oct. 1, 1944

Browns first baseman George Sisler (below) batted .420 and compiled 41-game hitting streak in 1922; six-time Cardinals batting champ Rogers Hornsby hit .424 in 1924

Basepaths where Enos Slaughter made his Mad Dash to win seventh game of 1946 World Series

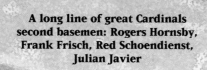
A long line of great Cardinals second basemen: Rogers Hornsby, Frank Frisch, Red Schoendienst, Julian Javier

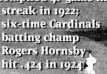
Where Browns' Bob Cain outdueled Indians star Bob Feller 1-0 in double one-hitter, April 23, 1952

DIZZY DEAN: Colorful righthander clinched 1934 pennant on final day by beating Reds 9-0, recording 30th victory

Batter's box where Eddie Gaedel, Bill Veeck's midget, drew walk in surprise appearance vs. Tigers, Aug. 19, 1951

Tigers 38-year-old player-manager Ty Cobb hits 3 homers, double, 2 singles and drives in 5 runs in 14-8 win over Browns, May 5, 1925

Where Horse Lady Mary Ott drove everybody crazy

Fans manage Browns in another Veeck promotional stunt, Aug. 24, 1951

The center field corner of Grand and Sullivan (above) braced for the power onslaught of the Babe Ruth, Lou Gehrig-led Yankees during the 1928 World Series. Six years later, Sportsman's (right) played host to a Cardinals-Tigers World Series.

memories of the people who cheered and competed there remain as vibrant as the colorful Budweiser eagle that flapped its wings atop the massive left field scoreboard for more than a decade, as if threatening to carry the ballpark and everybody in it off to baseball heaven? This was a ballpark of the people, where stars were revered, characters often were bigger than life and popularity was as much a measure of personality as success.

In retrospect, it's hard to imagine how Sportsman's Park thrived for 34 years as a house divided—between the American League Browns and the National League Cardinals from 1920-53, the longest ballpark co-habitation in history. The Browns were owners and the Cardinals paid rent for most of that period, but Sportsman's Park will long be remembered for the Cardinals' successes and the Browns' desperate and creative attempts to simply remain solvent.

SPORTSMAN'S PARK (1902-1966)

Renamed Busch Stadium (1953-1966)

The origin of Sportsman's Park—the name and stadium site—reaches well back into the 1800s. But the modern era of Sportsman's Park really began in 1892 when the Cardinals franchise played its first National League season at the Grand and Dodier facility before moving to a park at the corner of Vandeventer and Natural Bridge—the future Robison Field.

It wasn't until 1902 that Sportsman's Park became a permanent home for major league baseball. The American League Browns were tenants and the Cardinals joined them in 1920, beginning a 34-year association that marked the longest ballpark co-habitation in big-league history.

The Browns, as owners, often played second fiddle to their tenants, who played in 10 World Series. The Browns' 52 years at Sportsman's Park produced only one pennant—in 1944, when they lost to the Cardinals in an all-St. Louis World Series.

In 1953, the Browns relocated their franchise to Baltimore and Anheuser-Busch purchased the Cardinals. Sportsman's Park was renamed Busch Stadium, a name it would retain through its final game in 1966.

When the Cardinals moved into new Busch Stadium, the former park's grounds were donated to a local boys club. The park's stands and infrastructure are gone, but the field's site remains intact.

First game: April 23, 1902. The Browns beat Cleveland, 5-2.

Final game: May 8, 1966. The Cardinals lost to the Giants, 10-5.

■ Site of 10 World Series (1926, '28, '30, '31, '34, '42, '43, '44, '46, and '64)

■ Site of three All-Star Games (1940, '48 and '57)

Sportswriters and broadcasters got a bird's-eye view of game action from their pressbox perch high on the second-deck roof behind home plate.

Located at the intersection of Grand and Dodier, this was the third version of Sportsman's Park at the famous St. Louis corner, which had served the city's baseball needs dating all the way back to 1871. Built for the Browns after the 1908 season — although the Browns played at the site as early as 1902 — while the Cardinals still were playing at tiny Robison Field, the reconstructed steel-and-concrete structure stood as a sports monument into the 1966 season in a thriving area near Gaslight Square, the Fabulous Fox theater and upscale residential neighborhoods.

That 1909 Sportsman's Park featured a roofed double-deck grandstand that wrapped behind home plate from first base to third, a covered single-deck grandstand that extended down the left field line and single-deck bleachers that bordered the entire outfield, with lines that measured 353 feet (left) and 320 (right) and a center field distance of 430. A renovation after the 1925 season nearly doubled the capacity to 34,000 and gave the park what sportswriter Red Smith called "a garish, county fair sort of layout"— a look it would retain over the next four decades.

The covered double-deck grandstand was extended down both lines to the foul poles, the wooden bleachers were replaced by concrete and the right field stands were roofed, creating a pavilion that would become the park's signature feature. Because the right field line was reduced to 310 feet, the 11½-foot fence was topped by a 33-foot screen that extended 156 feet toward center — a Green Monster-like barrier that would stand from mid-1929 through the life of the park, with only a one-year respite in 1955.

"The screen made it much more interesting," said former Cardinals right fielder Stan Musial, who saw many of his potential home runs get sucked back into play by the imposing barrier. "The ball would fly out there and the runner didn't know if it was going to hit the screen, go over it or how it would bounce. It was hard to score (because outfielders played so shallow) on a single to right in that park."

The pavilion, with its screened view, was the last vestige of segregation in major league baseball—the area to which blacks were restricted into the 1944 season. Overall, fans not obstructed by steel support beams were close to the field and interaction was encouraged. The players' clubhouse walkway traveled through the home dugout and an inside corridor that was open to the fans—at first with no restriction, later with only a chain-link fence providing seclusion.

St. Louisans measure their baseball memories by landmarks and Sportsman's Park had its share—Wally Post hit the Longines clock, perched high on a light standard above the right-center field wall; Mike Shannon's 1964 World Series blast smacked the huge left field scoreboard that screened prodigious clouts from reaching Sullivan Avenue; the right field screen and pavilion roof; the shrubs beyond the center field fence; the Griesedieck Beer sign in right; Grand Avenue home runs; and, of course, the scoreboard eagle, which arrived after August A. Busch purchased the facility from Browns owner Bill Veeck in 1953, renovated its badly neglected infrastructure and renamed the park Busch Stadium.

A year later, the Browns moved to Baltimore, leaving the Cardinals to reign for 12 more seasons over the St. Louis kingdom they had technically ruled

since 1926, when they won the first of Sportsman's Park's 10 National League pennants and seven World Series championships. The Browns were gone, but not the memories of George Sisler's .420 season, Pete Gray's one-armed outfield play, Satchel Paige's bullpen rocking chair and all the crazy Veeck promotions, from midget Eddie Gaedel to the Grandstand Managers and Good Old Joe Earley Night.

Cardinals fans take equal delight with their memories—Mary Ott, the renowned 1930s-era Horse Lady who would tug at her ear and release ear-splitting neighs that could reportedly cause stampedes across the state in Kansas City's stockyards; a 1940s striptease club located under the stands in center field; the rock-hard infield, Pepper Martin's Mud-Cat band, Knothole kids in the left field bleachers, the penthouse pressbox, perched on top of the grandstand behind home plate, where Harry Caray delivered his colorful play-by-play, and a shattered window at the Wells Motor Company on Grand Avenue, courtesy of a 1926 Babe Ruth World Series home run.

But the most precious memory belongs to those fans lucky enough to witness the Cardinals' 1944 all-St. Louis "Streetcar World Series" victory—the only fall classic in which the lowly Browns would ever compete. For one glorious postseason, the baseball spotlight fell exclusively on Sportsman's Park—the house that Sisler, Hornsby, Frisch, Medwick, Musial, Slaughter, Schoendienst and Gibson built.

Life inside Sportsman's early manual scoreboard (top photo, right) could be hot and confining; the later scoreboard was topped by a Budweiser eagle that flapped its wings in excitement (above). The park's signature feature was a right field pavilion fronted by a fence with a 33-foot screen (below).

Exhibition Stadium

Where Tony Fernandez performed with Gold Glove efficiency from 1983-90

I t was an impromptu baseball field, a football facility incapable of doing a quality impersonation. Exhibition Stadium's greatest sin was that it never really looked, felt or smelled like a ballpark, a personality flaw that generated unfair criticism, ridicule and contempt ("Excruciation Stadium") over much of its 12-plus-year major league existence. Its greatest qualities were perseverance and grace under fire—as a Canadian interloper to America's national pastime.

In retrospect, Exhibition might have been a perfect fit for the 1977 expansion Blue Jays and baseball's second venture onto foreign soil (the Montreal Expos had started play in 1969). Because of the facility's exaggerated horseshoe shape, the

Minnesota's Randy Bush gets broken-bat single leading off ninth inning, ruining Jim Clancy's bid for perfect game, Sept. 28, 1982

Blue Jays get 24 hits, batter Orioles 24-10, June 26, 1978

DAVE STIEB, Blue Jays career leader with 175 wins

First A.L. game in Canada: Expansion Blue Jays survive cold and snow flurries to beat White Sox 9-5 as Doug Ault hits two home runs, April 7, 1977

Angels slugger Willie Aikens hits grand slams in consecutive 1979 games vs. Blue Jays

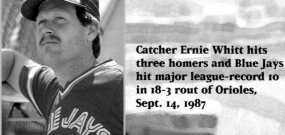

Catcher Ernie Whitt hits three homers and Blue Jays hit major league-record 10 in 18-3 rout of Orioles, Sept. 14, 1987

Where a warmup throw from Yankees center fielder Dave Winfield killed a snoozing seagull, resulting in his postgame arrest, Aug. 4, 1983

Where fly ball by Jim Sundberg struck top of fence—a bases-loaded triple that helped Royals complete comeback from three-games-to-one deficit in 1985 ALCS

Stieb pitches five-hitter and Blue Jays record 6-1 win over Royals—first postseason victory in franchise history, Oct. 8, 1985

Otto Velez becomes fan favorite after crashing four home runs in doubleheader, May 4, 1980

George Bell won A.L. MVP with 47 homers, 134 RBIs in 1987

Yankees veteran Phil Niekro, refusing to use his knuckleball on final day of season, shuts out Blue Jays for career win No. 300, Oct. 6, 1985

Good line of first basemen in Toronto: John Mayberry, Willie Upshaw, Fred McGriff, John Olerud, Carlos Delgado

Blue Jays win 9-0 forfeit when Earl Weaver pulls his Orioles off field because umpires refuse to remove tarp in Blue Jays' bullpen, Sept. 15, 1977

For second time in six days, hard-luck Stieb loses no-hit bid with two out in ninth as Orioles' Jim Traber bloops hit over first base, Sept. 30, 1988

Jerry Garvin picks off 22 runners in 1977

LLOYD MOSEBY: Centerpiece for hard-hitting outfield that included George Bell and Jesse Barfield

EXHIBITION STADIUM (1977-1989)

After enduring temporary homes for more than four decades, Toronto's first "permanent" baseball facility opened in 1926—Maple Leaf Stadium, home of the minor league Leafs. It would remain the centerpiece for Toronto baseball for 42 years, until the Leafs were dissolved.

In the 1950s and '60s, with an eye toward major league baseball, Toronto officials discussed appropriate playing facilities. Numerous proposals were recommended—enlarging the Canadian National Exhibition facility, building a domed stadium—but it took until 1974 for anything to be approved. The expansion of Canadian National Exhibition became a reality.

In 1976, Toronto appeared ready to become a new home for the Giants, who were trying to relocate from San Francisco. That move was shot down by N.L. owners, but Toronto got its team when baseball awarded it an expansion franchise—baseball's second in Canada.

Exhibition Stadium's short major league history began in 1977. And it began in the true spirit of Canada's northern springtime exposure. With snow covering the infield and fans shivering on a frigid afternoon, the Blue Jays opened play at the reconfigured football facility.

Exhibition Stadium served as the Blue Jays' home for 12-plus years and it remained standing 10 years after SkyDome opened in 1989 in downtown Toronto. It was razed in 1999.

First game: April 7, 1977. First baseman Doug Ault christened Exhibition Stadium with two homers and a run-scoring single as the Jays posted a 9-5 comeback victory over the White Sox.

Final game: May 28, 1989. George Bell's walkoff homer in the 10th inning, the stadium's final hit, gave the Blue Jays a 7-5 win over the White Sox.

- Site of no World Series
- Site of no All-Star Games

The mood was festive when the Jays opened the 1988 season vs. the Yankees.

playing field and grandstands were makeshift and unsophisticated, much like the young team that lost 318 games during the franchise's first three years and the enthusiastic fans who struggled to learn the American game. Exhibition Stadium was a first house—no-frills, basic and comfortable as its young Blue Jays matured into a contender; outdated, overmatched and underequipped when they sprouted their championship wings.

The simple fact is major league baseball might never have embraced Toronto without Exhibition Stadium, a pre-1900 facility that expanded over the decades while serving as the showcase for events at the Toronto Fairgrounds. The 350-acre fairgrounds site, a complex of buildings, landscaped gardens, an amusement park, restaurants and concert facilities, still thrives in downtown Toronto as home of the Canadian National Exhibition, an annual three-week fair that attracts millions of world visitors.

The fairgrounds—a stroll through the park, literally—provided a favorable first impression of Exhibition (alias CNE Stadium) while the distant Toronto skyline, CN Tower and nearby Lake Ontario offered a scenic backdrop that few ballparks could match. The clean, landscaped walkways and a modern glass-and-concrete facade suggested life—and baseball—might be good inside. But first you had to get over the shock.

Exhibition Stadium was a long, college football-style facility that was converted for baseball use—much like the Los Angeles Coliseum was transformed into a temporary home for the Dodgers in 1958. The Canadian Football League's Argonauts had played at Exhibition Stadium since 1959 and baseball was an awkward fit, no matter how you tried to twist, turn or manipulate the basic diamond. Facing single-deck stands extended the length of the field, dictating the construction of an elbow that connected one sideline with end zone seats—forming the home plate backstop as well as first and third base stands.

As a result, the main football grandstand, the only covered seats in the stadium, became a left field general admission pavilion. The seats behind the plate and down both lines were really glorified bleachers. A temporary 12-foot chain-link fence (the lower 8 feet padded) formed the perimeter of the outfield, a fence that followed the left field grandstand into deep left-center before curving away and crossing the field at about the football 35-yard line. The symmetrical result (330-400-330) left a large dead area beyond the right field fence and rendered useless the seats that extended beyond the fences to the distant end zone—except for binocular-wielding diehards.

It took several minutes to get a grip on exactly what you were seeing. The playing surface was artificial, seats on the first base side were aluminum benches. There were no multi-decked stands and the only luxury boxes were on top of the left field "bleachers," obviously constructed for football use. One of the strangest sights was the location of the 41-foot-high scoreboard, far away from everything in the opposite end zone.

Once you got past its peculiar appearance, Exhibition Stadium (baseball capacity 43,737) could be a fun place to visit. It was always clean and its bright green and blue coloring lifted spirits. Winds whipping off the lake made for some interesting highlights as well as cold night games, ice and snow were early spring givens and there were always the sea gulls—hundreds and hundreds of scavengers that would wait patiently for games to end and their feast to begin. If you didn't run for the exits when the game ended, you faced the possibility of a scene straight from Alfred Hitchcock's "The Birds."

Unlike many other high-tech parks, baseball was always front and center here and all seats within the playing field area were close to the action. There was always something to appreciate as the Blue Jays grew steadily from a baseball infant into an American League power—a rise fueled by such players as Dave Stieb, George Bell, Fred McGriff, Lloyd Moseby, Jesse Barfield, Jim Clancy, Jimmy Key, Roberto Alomar, Joe Carter and Tony Fernandez.

Exhibition Stadium took on a festive atmosphere in 1985 when the Jays captured their first A.L. East Division title and extended the Royals to the seventh game of the ALCS. A 1989 midseason move to the grand and glorious SkyDome presaged the team's rise to even greater heights—the beginning of another era in a baseball palace that would play host to World Series championships in 1992 and 1993.

Exhibition Stadium, with the CN Tower and Toronto skyline providing a scenic backdrop, was a football field with a baseball diamond fitted inside. Notice the dead area behind the right field fence and the distant scoreboard at the open end of the facility.

Griffith Stadium

Also known as National Park (1903-1920)

Landing point of Mickey Mantle's 565-foot home run off Chuck Stobbs in 1953

Indians' 43-year-old Cy Young wins 500th game, July 19, 1910

Highs and lows: Goose Goslin hit six home runs in the 1924 and '25 World Series . . . Shortstop Roger Peckinpaugh committed Series-record eight errors in 1925

Johnson, pitching his 14th opening day game, defeats Eddie Rommel and A's 1-0 in 15 innings, April 13, 1926

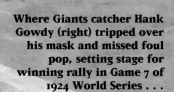

Where Giants catcher Hank Gowdy (right) tripped over his mask and missed foul pop, setting stage for winning rally in Game 7 of 1924 World Series . . .

Where Earl McNeely's (left) 12th-inning grounder bounced high over head of Fred Lindstrom, giving Senators their only championship

BUCKY HARRIS: Boy manager led Senators to only championship as player-manager in 1924; managed team to 1,336 wins overall

Detroit's Walt Dropo gets record-tying 12th straight hit in second game of doubleheader, July 15, 1952

I ts tenants were Senators and the President of the United States was an influential neighbor. Through its gates passed key decision-makers and men of power who shaped the political direction of the nation from their offices only a few blocks away. For the best-connected facility in baseball history, Griffith Stadium sure was a major underachiever—a plain, surprisingly unpretentious and championship-starved ballpark of the people.

To appreciate Griffith Stadium you first have to understand the Washington Senators, a franchise that spent more than half a century living up to the old Vaudeville joke, "First in war, first in peace and last in the

Center field indent provided
backyard space for five duplexes

Babe Ruth hit homer into trees over
center field indent . . . Lou Gehrig hit
ball out of stadium in '37 All-Star Game

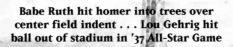

A's slugger Jimmie Foxx hits
58th home run, Sept. 25, 1932

Tigers rookie Schoolboy Rowe drives in
deciding run, gains record-tying 16th
straight win, Aug. 25, 1934

Mel Ott's 10th-inning homer off Fred
Schulte's glove ends Game 5, gives Giants
1933 World Series title

Where Sam Rice
tumbled into temporary
stands while making
sensational Game 3-
saving catch vs. Pirates
in 1925 World Series

Cardinals' Ken Boyer leads N.L. to 1956 All-Star
win with three hits, three defensive gems

Johnson: 36-7, 1.09 ERA, 243 strikeouts,
11 shutouts in remarkable 1913 season

Johnson beats Detroit
for 300th win, May 14, 1920

Where Earl Averill smashed Dizzy Dean's
toe in 1937 All-Star Game

Home of two-time A.L. batting
champion Mickey Vernon

Where President William Howard Taft set
precedent by throwing out first ball in 1910
season opener, then watched Johnson
throw a one-hit shutout

WALTER JOHNSON:
Fireballing Big Train,
won 416 games
and compiled 2.17 career ERA

American League." While the Yankees, Red Sox, Tigers and A's dominated the A.L. standings, the Senators plodded through life, sometimes lovable, only occasionally talented enough to challenge for a pennant. This was a team that fit its ballpark—a patchwork structure built on the fly during baseball's steel-and-concrete era; a park that lacked a championship aura but made up for it with charm and character.

Griffith Stadium was a ballpark where you could hit a home run into a center field tree, bounce a ball off a 30-foot (make that 31) right field wall, watch pitchers warm up in a fair-territory bullpen, ricochet a shot off a right-angle fence, marvel at misconstructed grandstands or see a President throw out a season-opening pitch. It was a misshapen, rickety old pitcher's park, constructed under the direction of a former 237-game winner and in the image of the greatest righthander in baseball history.

Clark Griffith was a fading former pitcher in 1911 when National Park, home of the A.L. Senators since their 1903 relocation from American League Park, burned to the ground while the team was in spring training. Remarkably, enough of the facility was rebuilt (with steel and concrete) over the next three weeks to open the season on time and construction would continue gradually over the next decade, eventually producing a ballpark that would undergo only minor changes from 1920 until its 1961 demise.

As manager (1912-20), president and eventual team owner, Griffith molded the ballpark that would eventually carry his name around a big Kansas farmboy named Walter Johnson—an overpowering righthander who would win 416 games over a 21-year career. It was no coincidence that reconstructed Griffith measured 407 feet down the left field line, 421 to center and 328 down the right field line—with the imposing concrete wall to slap down deep line drives.

The original roofed double-deck grandstand wrapped behind home plate, extended just past the infield and gave way to covered single-deck stands that stretched to the foul poles. The 1920 renovation added second decks to the single-deck stands, but the new roof was about 15 feet higher than the original, giving the park a strange, patchwork look. The higher roof was necessary because the foul pole stands had been graded more steeply than those behind home plate.

GRIFFITH STADIUM (1903-1961)

Also known as National Park (1903-1920)

The history of Griffith Stadium dates back to 1892, when a 6,500-seat ballpark was built at the intersection of Florida Avenue and 7th Street NW for the Washington team in the National League. The location would serve Washington baseball fans for the next 70 years and the stadium, known officially until 1920 as National Park, would eventually be transformed into the bigger and more memorable Griffith Stadium.

From 1903-11, National Park also was referred to informally as League Park and American League Park—a tribute to the new A.L. Senators who played their games there. The ballpark began its steel-and-concrete transformation in 1911, after it was destroyed by fire during spring training and hastily rebuilt for the season opener. Construction and expansion would continue for almost a decade.

In 1920, National Park was renamed Griffith Stadium in honor of Clark Griffith, a former pitcher and manager who became the Senators' principal owner and determined the course of Washington baseball through the 1950s. The aging ballpark served the Twins through the 1960 season, when they relocated to Minnesota, and the expansion Washington Senators as a one-season home in 1961. The stadium was demolished in 1965.

First game: April 22, 1903. The Senators beat the New York Highlanders, 3-1, at then National Park.

Final game: September 21, 1961. Washington's former team—the Minnesota Twins—beat the new Senators, 6-3.

■ Site of three World Series (1924, '25 and '33)
■ Site of two All-Star Games (1937 and '56)

The double-deck grandstands added in 1920 were about 15 feet higher than the original grandstands (above), which wrapped behind home plate. The outside of Griffith Stadium (left) was not ornate or stately, like the facades of its stadium counterparts in Philadelphia and Pittsburgh.

Such oddities were plentiful at Griffith, where the field-level fences seemed to jut, turn and twist without reason as they snaked around the park's perimeter. Right field foul territory was more expansive than left field and the stands were notched behind the plate to form a backstop. The grandstands arced to a point at the foul lines—about 15 feet before reaching the poles. Thus there was a gap between the left field grandstand and long left field bleachers that stretched all the way from the foul pole to the center field indent.

Everybody remembers Griffith for that infamous indent, a spot in center field where the fence detoured around five duplexes (the owner wouldn't sell) and a huge tree, jutting to a point in the field of play and creating right angles on both sides. An American flag rose proudly from the point and a loudspeaker horn was mounted on top of the 30-foot barrier, which connected to the right field wall at the deepest point of the park.

A right-center field scoreboard was the same height as

the wall and for most of the stadium's existence it was topped by advertisements featuring, at different times, National Bohemian Beer, Old Georgetown Beer, Chesterfield cigarettes and Coca-Cola. The National Bohemian sign had a three-dimensional beer bottle that protruded from the top, 56 feet above the ground. For a while, the home bullpen was a boxed-off area connecting the indent and wall in right-center field.

Griffith's color was not limited to physical oddities. This was the home of baseball's original megaphone man, E. Lawrence Phillips, and the site where, in 1910, William Howard Taft began a tradition that would continue throughout the park's Washington history—U.S. Presidents officially opening a season with a ceremonial first pitch from the box next to the first base dugout. This also was the home of the NFL's Redskins and a part-time home for several Negro League teams, including the Homestead Grays and power-hitting catcher Josh Gibson, who reportedly belted two moonshots over the left field bleachers.

When Griffith died in 1955, his nephew and adopted son Calvin took over the team and built an outfield bleacher addition, raising the park's peak capacity to 27,410. He also relocated the bullpen behind a 6-foot fence in the corner, reducing the left field distance to 350 feet and providing an inviting target for sluggers Harmon Killebrew, Bob Allison and Jim Lemon. That configuration remained intact until Calvin relocated his team to Minneapolis in 1960 and the expansion Washington Senators played their only Griffith Stadium season in 1961.

It was during the 1950s renovation that team officials discovered the right field foul line, which had always been marked at 328 feet, was really 320, and that the 30-foot right field wall was really 31 feet high. Such is the crazy mystique of Griffith Stadium,

where the Senators failed to post winning records in 40 of their 58 A.L. seasons. Three of their winning marks did produce A.L. pennants, however, and one, in 1924, gave Washington its only World Series championship.

Early Griffith featured a manual scoreboard perched atop its outer bleacher wall in left field—and topped by that popular Longines clock.